THE CITIZEN ARTIST:
20 YEARS OF ART
IN THE PUBLIC ARENA

The Citizen Artist:
20 Years of Art
in the Public Arena

An Anthology from
High Performance magazine 1978-1998

Edited by
Linda Frye Burnham and Steven Durland

Volume 1

First Edition, Copyright © 1998

Published by *Critical Press*,The publishing arm of the *Gunk Foundation*

PO Box 333

Gardiner, NY 12525

gunk@mhv.net

http://www.gunk.org

The following writers' articles have also appeared in: Robert C. Morgan *Art into Ideas: Essays on Conceptual Art* (Cambridge University Press, 1996); Arlene Raven *Art in the Public Interest* (Da Capo, 1993); Coco Fusco *English is Broken Here* (The New Press, 1995); William Cleveland *Art in Other Places: Artists at Work in America's Community and Social Institutions* (Praeger1992); Susan Perlstein and Jeff Bliss *Generating Community: Intergenerational Partnerships Through the Expressive Arts* (Elders Share the Arts, 1994); Douglas Paterson "Theatre of the Oppressed Workshops," *Webster's World of Cultural Democracy* (World Wide Web), 1995.

Available through D.A.P./Distributed Art Publishers

155 6th Ave, 2nd Floor

NY, NY 10013

Tel: (212) 627-1999   Fax: (212) 627-9484

This book was desktop published using QuarkXpress, and typeset using Gill Sans. Cover design by Bolle Design, interior design by Christine Heun Design. Additional thanks to Ann Rubin.

Printed and bound in the U.S.A. The paper used in this publication meets the minimum requirements of American National Standard for Information Sciences—Permanence of Paper for Printed Library Materials, ANSI Z39.48-1984.

ISBN: 1883831-10-5

Library of Congress Catalog Card Number: 98-70739

Dedicated to

Susanna Bixby Dakin

Thinking Publicly: The New Era of Public Art

The Citizen Artist is the second book of The Gunk Foundation/Critical Press series *Thinking Publicly: The New Era of Public Art*

As public space becomes increasingly saturated by corporate culture, a new generation of artists is emerging. Frustrated by the insulated art world, encouraged by the politicization of art in the '80s, and desirous of the rupture between high and low art, artists are looking into the space of everyday life to find a new canvas. The cement wall, the basketball court, and the bathroom stall have all been recent galleries for these artists. Public art, as it moves away from its traditional association with the bronze-man-on-horse statue, is rethinking some fundamental questions of the postmodern era: What is art? Who is the audience? Who is the artist? What is the message? Most importantly, artists working in the public realm are attempting to challenge corporate leverage on the production of knowledge and to reclaim public space as the site of political, social, and cultural thought.

In attempt to understand this changing realm of art and thought, the book series Thinking Publicly will broach many of the crucial topics relating to this field. How do we define art, the public, the artist, the community? Who should make the decisions about public art and who does? How does the meaning of art change when it is no longer sequestered into the museum/gallery/private home? Thinking Publicly intends to question the current market-dominated system of art production and to understand how the function of art transforms when it is moved out of the market and into the "public realm."

Series Editors:
Nadine Lemmon
Michael Read

Table of Contents

Part II: THE ARTIST AS ACTIVIST

Part III: THE ARTIST AS CITIZEN

List of Illustrations

Acknowledgments

This book would obviously not exist if it were not for the hundreds of innovative and dedicated artists we have met over the last three decades. Many of them never appeared in *High Performance,* and many of those who did, do not appear in this book. But without them our work would not be what it is, and we thank them.

Thanks, of course, to the writers all over the world who worked for less than 25 cents a word to produce all the millions of words we published in 75 issues, especially Guillermo Gómez-Peña and Jacki Apple, who wrote about half of them.

Heartfelt thanks to Richard Newton, who was there at the very beginning of the magazine, provided essential help with every aspect of creating it, buttonholed people at art openings and strongly suggested they subscribe, and thought of the name "High Performance."

Thanks also to art historian Moira Roth, who, when Linda told her in 1977 that she wanted to start a magazine, didn't laugh. And who, for 20 years, has supplied encouragement, writing, tea, sympathy and the wonderful book we were so lucky to publish in 1983, *The Amazing Decade: Women and Performance Art in America 1970-1980.* Thanks, too, to Suzanne Lacy, Lucy Lippard and John Malpede, whose artwork and writing made a difference.

Thanks to those most vital contributors, our staff, who worked long hours for relatively little pay, put up with a difficult working environment in downtown L.A., and understood when we had to downsize for survival—especially Karen McCarthy, Lin Osterhage, Jan (Ventura) Freya, Lewis MacAdams, Francis Shishim, Rebekah Berendt, Jane Leslie, Judith Spiegel, Karla Dakin, Claire Peeps, Sara Wolf, Dylan Tran, Carole Tormollan, Eric Gutierrez and the rest, too numerous to mention. Thanks also to our contributing editors over the years, especially Arlene Raven, from whose book, *Art in the Public Interest,* we took the name of our nonprofit organization. And to the many members of our boards of directors, who helped keep the magazine alive, especially to our current board—Kathie de Nobriga, William Cleveland and Alan Dachman—each of whom is an inspiration in his/her own work with art-in-the-community.

Thanks to the residents of the 18th Street Arts Complex in Santa Monica, California, for their diligent work in creating the inter-cultural community we were part of in the early '90s, especially Tim Miller, who was Linda's partner in creating Highways Performance Space at the Complex. And to the 200+ members of Alternate ROOTS, whose vital work drew us to the Southeast in 1993.

Thanks to all the funders who helped us publish the magazine over the years, especially the National Endowment for the Arts, the states of California, New York and Illinois and the County and City of Los Angeles.

We're grateful to Jan Williamson at the Complex for her help in mining the *High Performance* archives for many of the pictures in this book. And thanks to Nadine Lemmon, Critical Press and the Gunk Foundation for publishing it.

Thanks to our mothers, Margaret Frye and Sheila Durland Fitting, who sent money even when they weren't sure they understood what the hell we were doing, and to Linda's sister, Jan Freya, and her daughter, Jill Burnham, who truly did understand.

And last, but of course not least, all our thanks and blessings to Susanna Bixby Dakin, our partner, patron, spiritual guide and dearest friend, without whose support *High Performance* would have gone the way of all small arts magazines by 1980. Whatever good the magazine has done is due to her faith in us and in our quest to ascertain the place of art in our world.

INTRODUCTION

By Steven Durland

Throughout its 20-year history, *High Performance* magazine has been a journalistic home for new, unrecognized and innovative work in the arts. From its beginnings in performance art to its last few years covering community-based art, the magazine maintained a steady focus on art that was serious in its personal artistic intent and under-appreciated in public perception. If an artist was doing it and some-one else was screaming, "That's not art!" we took that as our cue that *High Performance* should take a look at it.

We were traveling editorially through territories that weren't on the map yet, and when you travel like that, you find your way by talk-ing to the locals. In our case, the "locals" were the artists who were doing the work. From the first issue to the last, *High Performance* has relied heavily on the artist's voice, with interviews, firsthand accounts or artists writing about other artists. We never really considered this a "critical methodology" rather it was the only logical strategy, given that the ideas these artists were working with were so new that there was no critical vocabulary to apply to them.

We considered our editorial approach to be a useful foundation for, and a necessary precursor to, the development of critical discus-sion around the art we covered. And when a form such as perfor-mance art became validated to the point of being part of the critical discourse, it was time for us to look in new directions.

Our editorial journey took us down some roads that later became freeways, and some roads that are now overgrown with weeds. The magazine reflects a wide variety of concerns that devel-oped in the arts during its 20-year history. In considering what we might include in an anthology of writings from the magazine, we real-ized that there was no one anthology that could both reflect the his-tory of the magazine and at the same time exist as a coherent book. So we settled for the fact that this is *an* anthology from *High Perfor-mance,* but it is not *the* anthology from *High Performance.*

What we chose to do in developing this anthology was to look at both where the magazine started and where it ended. Interestingly, the first essay in the first issue was Richard Newton's interview with Suzanne Lacy, and the last essay in the last issue was Aida Mancillas' firstperson essay "Citizen Artist," both of which are included in this book. We realized immediately that not only was there a direct connection between the two stories, but that they gave coherence to one particular thread that ran throughout the magazine's history. That thread was the artists' ongoing concern with art that reached beyond the traditional forms, content and context of the arts to engage itself in the lives of the broader community.

We used the title of Aida Mancillas' essay, "The Citizen Artist," to title the book because we felt it was this impulse by artists to locate themselves in the concerns of the world around them that best characterized this collection of essays. We have divided the essays into three broad areas of more specific concern; "The Art/Life Experiment," "The Artist as Activist" and "The Artist as Citizen."

These three areas of concern also roughly reflect three chronological time periods in the magazine's existence. Certainly this chronology is significant to the magazine and reflects in some ways the development of its editorial concerns. It also reflects the fact that these artistic concerns had a certain prominence when we chose to write about them.

However, it would be overly simplistic to suggest that this was a linear progression of ideas in the manner that is so common to art history. History, as it's defined by events, influences and precedents, is an elusive and cyclical thing. Ideas are constantly being developed and then forgotten, only to be rediscovered by later generations. In fact, it might be said that ideas remain constant through time; there are just moments when they resonate with greater purpose. So while we might, in retrospect, cite numerous precedents to the work presented here, it seems more to the point to suggest, not that these ideas are new, but that for this particular moment they have a resonance and a relevance that makes them worth noting.

Some of the artists presented here represent bodies of work that could easily encompass all three areas of concern, and their inclusion in any one area should not be viewed as limiting. Others have

remained committed over time to a single focus. Some have a scholarly awareness of the precedents to their work, while others have
found themselves serendipitously involved in similar directions.

In addition to our focus on selecting essays that reflected this
particular thread, we also focused on selecting essays that reflected
the artist's voice. The vast majority of essays are either interviews with
artists, often by other artists, or firstperson essays by artists. As a
result, sometimes the analysis one often expects in an anthology is left
up to the reader; in its place is an intimate view of the artist's concerns and motivations. We consider that intimate view to be a valuable addition to the critical and documentary books already in existence (see bibliography).

Setting the Table

In preparing to read these essays, it's useful to consider the cultural and artistic context that existed in the late '70s when *High Performance* was founded.

Formally, the arts had been going through an extended period
of radical experimentation dating back to the 19th century. The post-
World War II period alone had seen such seminal activity as John
Cage's revolutionary concepts of sound and music, and his interdisciplinary collaborations with the likes of dancer Merce Cunningham and
painter Robert Rauschenberg; the theater experiments of Jerzy Grotowski, the Living Theater of Julian Beck and Judith Malina, and others;
Alan Kaprow's Happenings and Joseph Beuys' Social Sculptures; the
postmodern dance experiments that took place at the Judson Church
Theater; and the improvisational poetry of the Beats. This list is far
from complete, but illustrates the fact that by the mid-'70s artists had
essentially established the permission to manifest their art in whatever
form they chose.

Politically, young adults of the '70s had experienced the Civil
Rights and Feminist Movements, Vietnam War protests, worldwide student demonstrations, Black Panthers, multiple assassinations and the
resignation of a President in disgrace. People were empowered to be
outspoken and to "take it to the streets" if necessary. The idea that
the arts could be adjunct to political causes was already firmly estab-

lished in the work of such groups as the Free Southern Theater, Bread and Puppet Theater and the Chicano muralists who supported the United Farm Workers.

Socially, artists were still experiencing the anarchistic freedoms of the '60s, the impact of Eastern philosophies and the more pragmatic self-empowerment movement. New and accessible technologies were blossoming, from video to xerography, synthesizers and cassette tape recorders. Postmodern thought was at work in various enclaves. The U.S. government created the National Endowment for the Arts (NEA) and the Comprehensive Education and Training Act (CETA), both of which channeled all-important money into the hands of artists.

All of these events together created a time so ripe for artistic experimentation that one can hardly imagine it in today's more conservative political, social and artistic climate. It produced both innovation and excess, and it was left to those who succeeded it to sort the wheat from the chaff.

20 Years of Art in the Public Arena

During the '70s there was much discussion among artists about "the public," and lots of the art that was done reflected experiments on the part of artists to circumvent traditional art venues and establish a direct connection to the intended audience. Newly accessible technology was viewed as a means to "democratize" art, and artists armed with portable video units or cassette recorders began creating, presenting and even broadcasting their own experimental media productions. The copy machine was often the tool of choice for producing "unlimited multiples"—correspondence art, artist's books and periodicals—that could be cheaply created and distributed. There were impromptu public performances and temporary site-specific installations. Serving all of these ideas was the development and growth of artist co-ops and artist-run alternative spaces, where artistic experiments could have direct public access.

All of these developments came together in the art/life experiments of the time. Members of the public who dared venture a peek often found themselves bewildered by formal experiments they had no vocabulary to comprehend, or annoyed by confrontations they had no desire to engage with. When these art/life experiments succeeded it was usually through the appropriation of mass-media techniques, which the public could definitely understand, or through a certain imaginative charm that made the effort to understand more palatable for the public.

At the time, southern California was a particular hotbed of artistic experimentation. Exposure to artists like Chris Burden and Paul McCarthy and, in particular, the work coming out of the strong feminist art community inspired Linda Burnham to found *High Performance* in 1978. The magazine was created in response to the need for a journal of record to document these art experiments. Its name derived from the fact that, for better or worse, most of this work was done under the rubric of "performance art."

This self-imposed view of *High Performance* as a performance art magazine worked well for the first three or four years, but it gradually became apparent that such editorial specificity was arbitrarily limiting. The creative impulses that guided that early performance art could be found throughout the creative arts—in dance, theater, music and beyond. And it was these creative impulses, not a commitment to the definition of performance art, that inspired the magazine in the first place. As a result, the magazine started expanding its editorial focus to look at art and its public experiments through a multidisciplinary lens.

Nor could the magazine remain focused on the experiments with form that were so typical of the earliest work it covered. By the mid-'80s, experiments with the formal boundaries of art were on the decline, in part because the alternative spaces had now become institutional homes for experimental art. Perhaps unwittingly, institutionalization brought with it the development of formal parameters, and the resulting staged performances and gallery exhibitions took much the same structure as they might in a traditional venue. It was also true that the best of the work itself was achieving an acceptance that made it accessible to such venues.

A generation earlier, feminist artists had taken advantage of the freedom in the formal experimentation of the time to introduce social and political content into their work. This inspired a broad range of artists to use their art to address such issues as the environment, cultural diversity, homophobia, disarmament and more.

Artists had an overwhelming sense that they no longer had to separate the task of creating art from the social issues that had an impact on the rest of their lives, and for many, a sense that the content was the most important aspect of the art. They were often dealing with such life-and-death or highly charged issues as AIDS, racism, and pollution. The savvy activist artist knew that if your form alienated the public, your message didn't get through. So the form got more conservative as the content got more radical.

This "artist as activist" work sometimes came up short because, in spite of expressed concerns for social good, artists often remained a subculture separate and alien from the public they purported to serve. "Preaching to the converted" was an oft-heard criticism of artists who remained inside the art world structure to present their politicized point of view, and it was not a criticism the artists took lightly.

Both the activist artists and the presenters who supported them got bolder in their efforts to find a public for their messages. In this atmosphere of increased stridency, the arts suddenly found themselves at war with a conservative public in 1989. Regardless of how politicized the content of artists' work was up to that point, the *de facto* content of the work now became "freedom of expression," as critics tried to muzzle controversial artists and presenters, as well as do away with any government agency willing to fund them. It's a war that's still going on as we write this book, with battles won and lost on both sides. But one of the most significant, though less recognized, losses for activist artists has been the co-opting of their content. Too often the focus has been on their right to speak, not on what they say when they're given a voice.

For many, the Culture Wars red-flagged the fact that in spite of the artist's sense of art being important for the public, the public, by and large, did not share that view. And it was further evident that artists were having little impact on that perception by battling with conservatives in the media. Consciously or not, artists had cultivated the perception that they were somehow separate and different from the public, and conservative critics were all too pleased to use that historical bit of arrogance to keep artists alienated and on the defensive.

In this atmosphere in the early '90s we began to notice that more and more socially committed artists were changing the context of their work. Artists who used to regularly appear in the pages of the magazine were dropping out of sight. When we tracked them down we found that they were now doing art with at-risk youth or in prisons or hospices or just in their neighborhoods. They believed that the arbitrary separation of art world and real world had made them less effective as artists, and caused them to call into question their commitment to the public. This new sensibility didn't necessarily reject the art world, but rather viewed it as one of many contexts in which art could exist. It followed that the context of art was just as crucial to its success as the form and content.

These artists have chosen to invest themselves directly in the public in such a way that they are no longer viewing the public from the outside, but rather are an integral part of that public. In such a context, the art that develops is a direct reflection of the particular culture in which it is created. This creates an entirely different relationship between the artist and the public, because where the artist is invested in the public, the public is invested in art. The art need be no less innovative or experimental when the public views the work as developing from a common experience.

The irony, or course, is that this is not really a new context for art at all, but rather one of the oldest—the artist as an integral part of a larger community. It's a traditional context that is still common in many societies and even within isolated subcultures of our own society. But it's in direct contrast to the isolationist view of the artist that has dominated Western culture.

It's the "artist as citizen," a concept that seems so obvious that one can only wonder how it became so alien. Is it a threat to traditional Western art practice? Hardly. Nor should it be. It's to everybody's benefit that the arts have multiple contexts in which to thrive. Socially committed, community-engaged artists add depth to our culture and re-enchant their chosen publics, coming back to the reason why art was ever important in the first place.

Of the People, By the People and For the People: The Field of Community Performance

By Richard Owen Geer

One concern that unites the artists who appear in this book is their fascination with the charged relationship between the artist and the public. Within that broad field there are many levels of artistic intent, and many levels of engagement by the public. In this essay, theater director Richard Owen Geer attempts to define those various levels—in performance, and by extension, in the arts in general. At the time of this essay, Geer was especially focused on community performance, since he was deeply involved in a collaboration with a whole town. Geer, Tennessee writer Jo Carson and the citizens of Colquitt, Georgia, created Swamp Gravy, *a piece that arose from the oral history of Colquitt's people, was performed by them and owned by them. It continued after Geer's return to his home in Chicago, and eventually became the State of Georgia's official "folklife play." Geer's meditation on performance is presented here as a preface to this anthology, in the hope that it will provide some context for the art that follows.   —Eds.*

As the anthropologist listened to the Native American informants his excitement rose. They explained the meaning of the designs embroidered on the sashes of the kachina dancers. He noted a pattern in their responses and began to form an hypothesis about the meaning of the designs. Then one of the Hopis asked an awkward question: "Why are you paying no attention to the most important fact?" Abashed, the anthropologist asked what he had overlooked. "The sash," the Hopi responded incredulously. "Without it the designs would not even exist."

The anthropologist's problem is, I think, a metaphor for theater in our culture. Most American theater misses the fact that its matrix and support is the community. As a consequence, theater is self-absorbed, as if it were a universe unto itself.

Community performance, by contrast, is in service to community as the senses are in service to the body. Community *performance* signals a breadth of practices, and distinguishes it from community *theater*. Community performance is synonymous with community change.

When a community performs its beliefs and traditions it makes meaning. Fuel, oxygen and heat are required to make fire, and a similar relationship exists between the elements in community performance. People are the fuel, their beliefs and traditions the oxygen, and performance is the heat. Metaphorically, fire and performance are similar. Fire makes nutrients available for digestion and provides illumination and warmth. Performance cooks experience into meaning, provides illumination and security. In tribal societies fire and performance occur at the community's center.

Our tribal forbears applied stage rules to ordinary life. Modern performers know that *on stage* everything matters, and our tribal ancestors knew that *in life* everything mattered. The first is called stage performance, the second community performance. Mythologies that teach the sacredness of everything are artifacts of community performance.

Once performative communities stretched from Asia to Europe, Africa and the Americas, but over the span of European history and the conquest of America, community performance attenuated. An important event happened in 1844. That year the telegraph began reporting news *as it happened* from geographically remote locations. Events were not influenced by the distant audience, nor were the observers' lives affected—except emotionally. Faraway dramas pulled people's attention away from the neighborhood. Community performance was doomed as well by America's territorial imperative. Land that is "there for the taking" is not sacred land. Explorers who *claim*, settlers who *grab*, miners who *stake*, mark out the fault lines of a shift in community belief away from Chief Seattle's image of the brotherhood of living things, or Black Elk's vision of an all-sacred creation, a performative world.

Native Americans shaped tribal life through local varieties of community performance and everyone participated in the group task of culture building. By the early 1880s the Oglala Sioux were a depressed people whose culture was being dismembered by America's manifest destiny. Black Elk, a warrior and medicine man, had a dream in which a whole and holy world was *re*-membered. Black Elk taught every being in his village, even the horses, to perform his healing vision; everybody sang and smoked the pipe. Afterwards, he said, even the horses were healthier and happier.

But as factories replaced forests the patterns of performance shifted. Like the telegraph, 19th century European American theater carried no local information. Instead it broadcast a "one size fits all" brand of entertainment created by a cultural elite. This professionalized performance genre used play to cloak its culture-shaping work. Theaters were factories for the production of mass culture. Theaters herded people into stalls and milked them for applause, laughter or tears. Audiences oiled the machine with money and submitted to it in respectful silence as it milled them to the dimensions of consuming commodities.

This specialization, this distillation, cost performance its "central driving place" in culture, said anthropologist Victor Turner. In the good old days before commodification, performance was diffused in the community. It welled up to mark the passage of ordinary people as water does to fill a footprint, and each muddy step reflected a little patch of sky. Community performance didn't create stars—distant individual points of light surrounded by darkness—it had humble and direct uses. It created community autobiography in what anthropologist Barbara Meyerhoff called "definitional ceremonies." It took over from play the job of teaching older children in a mimesis called apprenticeship. In times of high emotion, at the death of a loved one for instance, it allowed people to modulate their feelings. It bound the community in times of crisis, honed skills and effected changes in relationships between people and things. It wasn't all serious. It was dances, celebrations, enacted storytelling, carnivals and cross-dressing. It wasn't always kind. It was mobs, shunnings and mass hysteria as well. But it *was* community life. Through it people gained perspective on themselves, their actions and their group. And when the images were especially bright and clear as with the Horse Dance of Black Elk, a single performance—enacted by everyone—could transform a community.

In 1951 Maryat Lee devised a modern variant on the ancient tradition of tribal performance. Lee, a young white woman with a loathing
for traditional theater, went to Harlem on a dare. There she facilitated
a piece of street theater based on the utterances of gang members
and performed by the youngsters themselves. *Dope!,* in the early '50s,
was a theatrical and social aberration. In spite of its success—a spread
in *Life, Variety* and inclusion in *The Best Short Plays of 1952-53*—no one
wanted to fund further work, nor was anyone in 1951 interested in
fashioning amateur theater from oral history. Lee had to wait until
1975 to create EcoTheater in West Virginia. EcoTheater (the name
means "a place to see one's home") regularly produces oral history-
based scripts and performs them with local nonactors.

Lee's friend, Ossie Davis, labeled this way of working theater *of,
by* and *for* the community. In the '60s artists made protest theater. In
the mid-'70s, with the cessation of the Vietnam War, the temperature
of confrontation dropped and conciliatory performance practices
began to appear. As the political climate became more conservative in
the '80s, liberalizing performance processes like Lee's, designed to
work within conservative communities, appeared.

Performance that defines itself through some kind of relationship
with community comes in a wide range of types, from sensational
dramas that exploit the local culture to original productions engi-
neered by the community to catalyze cultural change. These extremes
are the edges of a poorly defined field of practices. What are they?
What are the advantages/disadvantages of each? Can a given performance process be analyzed? Can one predict outcomes? It is possible
to shed some light on these questions through the use of the terms
of, by and *for?* Singly and in combination they characterize practices
and reveal pitfalls in the terrain of community performance.

Community can be defined in one of three ways, according to
Alternate ROOTS (Regional Organization of Theatres South): by location, spirit or tradition. Communities of location are neighborhoods or
towns. Communities of spirit convene around beliefs or values; far-
flung examples might be Catholics, gays and Trekkies. Communities of
tradition are groups constituted around shared activities and main-

tained over time through these activities; college fraternities and Americans of Armenian origin are examples. I will not count theater-goers as a community. First, because all theater thereby becomes a variety of community performance; second, because theater-goers do not bring community identity with them to the theater. Baz Kershaw, in his valuable book on this subject, *The Politics of Performance,* suggests that for social change —the hallmark of community performance—to result, the audience must be constituted as a community *before* the event. A congenial audience of Chicago theater-goers watching the touring production of *Miss Saigon* are not, therefore, a community; the multi-ethnic residents of Chicago's Howard Street gathering to watch 150 of their neighbors perform a play about the neighborhood *are.* Many groups fit in two categories, and it is a feature of tribes that they comprise all three.

"Of," for the purposes of this discussion, means "about" or concerning; theater that is *of* the community is *about* the community. "By" means through the agency of; theater that is *by* the community is created (storied, written, performed and produced) by the community members themselves. "For" means in the presence of and in support of a previously constituted community. I have added the second phrase, "in support of," to denote social responsibility. Dope dealers, for instance, perform for a community but they do not act in support of it.

Point of view is a critical determinant of the degree of community performance. *My Beloved Blue Coast* by the Yakut Drama Theatre of Siberia may be community performance to its author and cast, but not to the Chicago audiences who saw its tour; therefore I will specify point of view under each category.

The Spectrum of Community Performance

Of, by and for create the following eight categories of performance:

Not Of, By or For: Most professional theater in America fits into this category. Nonlocal events written about by nonlocal playwrights are performed by nonlocal actors for a noncommunity of local theater-goers.

Of: Performance that is about a particular community but that is neither by it nor in support of it. According to Appalachian writer Jo Carson, Robert Schenkkan's *Kentucky Cycle* is about her culture, but its violence, sensationalism and cultural voyeurism code the performance as neither by the community nor for it. The cachet of such a performance is exploitation.

For: Performance directed at a particular community but neither about it nor by it. The performance of Catholicism in black parishes before Vatican II was *for* those communities, but the performance of Catholicism by white priests and nuns employing white images did not reflect black experience. An attribute of such performance is alienation.

By: The Theater Laboratory of Jerzy Grotowski was a center for research into the actor's art. With unlimited time and absolute concentration, the nature of acting could be fully explored. Laboratory productions were based on classic Polish and international texts, but their essence lay in the specific artistry of the group that created them. One cannot imagine another company doing *Akropolis,* nor an actor besides Ryszard Cieslak playing the Constant Prince. Communally created performance whose *tour de force* style overwhelms other aspects is theater by a community. Who watches it (*for*), or what community is revealed in its content (*of*) are relatively unimportant. Though the artistry may be stunning, even overwhelming, as an audience member I remain detached, aware that my presence as spectator contributes almost nothing.

Of & By: Lexington, Kentucky's community performance group Working Class Kitchen performed theater of and by their community at the 1993 Alternate ROOTS Annual Meeting in North Carolina. The Hevehe tribal dancers of New Guinea compete against other tribes for cash prizes at annual government-sponsored tourist jamborees. Whether performance *of* and *by* one community *for* another is sharing or exploitation is dependent on other factors.

Of & For: In the late '70s, Dakota Theatre Caravan created theater for and about the people of rural South Dakota. Their work, based on the oral histories of the region's people and performed by college students on summer vacation, was a huge popular success. In the '60s, white middle-class college students from my undergraduate school created street theater to show farm workers how to resist oppression. In both cases the performances were *of* and *for* previously constituted communities. Following are two polar opinions of the value of this type of performance. Dakota Theatre Caravan's founder Doug Paterson: "[T]o identify with a people," he said, "to be theatermakers who were as much a part of the community as a grocery store clerk, homemaker or gas station attendant, and to root one's work deeply in the people's lives and stories—this was a step toward cultural alliance." Paterson asserts that the cast was part of the community, but a few weeks of sensitive and respectful work doesn't qualify one for community membership. And, though the performance was adapted from the stories of the people, it was created by the collective labor of the young company. Here is Maryat Lee's opinion of such work:

> Street theater died…because…not one of the companies, not *one*, had street people on the stages…[T]hey were well-intentioned theater folks bringing culture to the streets, or they were activists wanting to stir the people up to action 'for their own good.' They were, in fact, deadly and shortsighted…The naïveté of asking theater people to perform the oral histories belonging to the people is mind boggling.

The bright side of this kind of theater is cultural alliance—Theatre Caravan's success probably resulted from it. The other side of theater *of* and *for* can be condescension and appropriation.

By & For: I am not convinced this is a real category, but what it reveals about performance is useful. If a performance is *by* and *for* a community it is almost surely *about* it, though the relationship may be disguised. In performance, texts can be inscribed with community-specific information—Iron Curtain-era East European productions of Shakespeare, for instance. Such codes may be invisible to oppressors even as they broadcast to the oppressed. In the slave South, spirituals imparted information for living the while appearing to speak of the life to come; people in the community where I work remember that "Wade in the Water" was sung to divert the overseer's attention and signal the runaway that it was safe to ford the river to freedom. In another guise, this category is the theatrical equivalent of myth, and speaks to the unconscious through image and metaphor. Performance that is *by* and *for* but not, apparently, *of* employs distance and metaphor to deal with important issues.

Of, By, & For: A community performing its own culture for its own ends is community performance. This type of performance, according to England's John McGrath, can accomplish several things: enrich cultural identity, amplify marginal voices, attack cultural homogeneity, increase community self-determination and challenge the dominant power structure.

Even with these eight categories, I am still left to ask the question: Which of them are community performance? Since pure community performance—of the people, by the people, for the people— probably does not exist outside isolated a-literate societies, it is pointless to set purity as the standard. It is probably not even desirable. On the contrary, optimal community performance may be aided by the Other. Outsiders can bring in a fresh eye. Outsiders, too, are free from obligation, and can enable culturally democratic art.

The boundaries of communities shift with time; exploitation can become advocacy and vice versa. Theater that is *of* and *for* may become of, for and *by* through performers putting down roots in that community. Some performers begin by performing their Otherness, their very lack of community. They start as irritations and end as a pearls, communities solidifying around the spirit that their performances define. Other performance workers teach their skills to members of a community not their own, and assist in creating theater that is (ironically) of, by and for everyone but themselves. All these are community performance. All these link back (in Latin "re-ligio") to the roots of performance in the soil of ordinary life.

True community performance is not an event but a continuous cycle. Through it the community is able to see itself and respond. Generically, we call this cycle "art-imitating-life-imitating-art." It's out of whack in our culture. Instead of community performance that bonds small-scale human groups in networks of mutuality, we are plagued by the global performance of numberless, often destructive, fads (copycat killings, skyjackings, etc.). The major feature of rapid, performative, global social change is its insensitivity to local environments. This alienation defines our existence.

Contrast our system of local indifference and distant involve-ment with a natural ecosystem. In ecosystems, organisms respond to changes in their immediate vicinity. Planetary ecology is nothing more than the network of such locally sensitive ecosystems. The current trend toward community-based solutions acknowledges this eco-truth and strives to put it in practice at the local level. In the task of bringing awareness back home and perspective back to the neighborhood, community performance can fill a vital ecological niche.

Winter 1994

The Art/Life Experiment

By Linda Frye Burnham

High Performance first appeared in the world with a woman on the cover, sitting on a dragster. It was so powerfully automotive an image that many people initially thought *High Performance* was a car magazine.

The drag racer on the cover was a driver all right, the driver of a potent and exciting art scene in downtown Los Angeles: Suzanne Lacy. As we geared up *High Performance,* Lacy's work as an artist and a teacher at the Woman's Building was making news. She was one of the feminist artists who took advantage of the prevailing atmosphere of formal experimentation and firmly stirred social content into the bubbling aesthetic cauldron. The feminist dictum "the personal is political" might as well have been blazoned across her dragster like a corporate slogan. Addressing the burning issue of violence against women, she organized several notorious performance events in Los Angeles during 1977, ranging in scale from the intimate to the massive, and always proceeding from—and operating as—real events in women's lives.

Lacy's *Three Weeks in May* featured two enormous city maps of Los Angeles installed in City Mall Plaza, with the word "RAPE" stamped on them where women had been raped over the three-week period. *She Who Would Fly* was a gallery installation of women's shared memories of sexual assault, including a lamb cadaver with large white wings, suspended as if in flight; four women, nude and stained blood red, crouched like birds, intently watching the audience from a ledge above the space. *In Mourning and In Rage...* was a media event organized by Lacy and Leslie Labowitz and others, conceived as a response to their grief and rage over the incidents of rape-murder in Los Angeles connected with the so-called Hillside Strangler case, and as a demand for self-defense education in the schools. Nine women mourners, dressed in black and towering seven feet tall, emerged from a hearse at the steps of L.A. City Hall where they spoke, one at a time, in memory of the victims of violence wreaked upon women: "I am here for the rage of all women, I am here for women fighting back." Intended to manipulate the media into showing images of women acting powerfully and decisively in unison, as a counter to the images of fearful, terrorized and isolated women current in the media, the event was covered on six television news shows (one national feed) and several talk shows.

The Woman's Building was the intellectual gymnasium of the moment for Suzanne Lacy and her colleagues. At the time of our

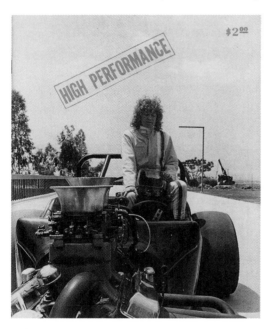

interview Lacy was teaching in the Feminist Studio Workshop graduate art program at the Building, then five years old. *Acting Like Women* by Cheri Gaulke, herself a student, then a teacher/administrator at the Building, precisely described the art/life method by which new art forms were forged there. Performance art, feminist education and consciousness-raising were the tools; the lives of the students were the materials. Only about a mile from the *High Performance* office in downtown L.A., the Building was a true hothouse of activity, and a magnet for women from all over the world. The art strategies, community-building techniques and coalitions created at the Building are models for art schools, women's action groups and community organizations far and wide, outliving the Building itself, which closed its doors in 1991.

So much of early feminist work made previously private realms public. Bonnie Sherk exemplifies the public artist whose material is private space. An environmental performance sculptor, her *Public Parks* were personal landscapes in which the public participated: a dead-end section of a freeway that for one day was covered with live turf and palm trees, and occupied by a cow and Sherk herself, "an oasis in the desert"; a picnic site on two concrete islands under a freeway, with cows, chickens and bales of straw; a downtown street closed for two days and covered with turf, trees and additional animals—sheep, goats, llamas. In her *Sitting Still* series, Sherk inserted herself in existing landscapes, such as a pool of water that had gathered in a disused parking lot, where she sat in an overstuffed chair to create a "frame" for the environment for passersby. When we interviewed her in Fall 1981, she had just completed her most ambitious piece to date, *The Farm*.

The space between two human beings became public art when two artists, Linda Montano and Tehching Hsieh, galvanized the attention of the country by vowing to spend a whole year in New York City tied together at the waist by an eight-foot rope. During this time they agreed not to touch.

Montano's previous work included a variety of performances or actions during the 1970s that tested the boundaries between art and life: She was handcuffed to another artist for three days; she lived for four days with two other artists, calling all they did during that time art; she declared her house a museum, with advertised tours. Tehching Hsieh performed a series of one-year pieces in New York in which his life was labeled as art, with certain prescribed limitations or "frames." He spent one whole year in a cage inside his studio, during which time he spoke to no one and no one spoke to him. The following year he punched a time clock every hour. The year after that he vowed to stay outdoors without ever going inside.

For this interview, we turned to Alex and Allyson Grey, performance artists married to each other. In addition to their own diverse work in painting, they created a number of performances and environments in which they appeared as the embodiment of male and female halves of a whole, addressing stark and arresting questions about love and life and death. They seemed like the perfect couple of couples.

Rachel Rosenthal's eclectic methods of art making and workshop teaching focused openly on personal transformation. Her work speaks directly to the centrality of art and creativity in the life of the individual and the universe. Classically trained in art and theater, and exposed to the inner circles of the art world since her childhood in Paris, Rosenthal never stops growing, inquiring into new schools of thought, and scouring her own psychology for new insights to be used in her work. When we interviewed her in 1984, she was steeping herself in New Age philosophy and new information about the structure and function of the brain, and crafting new works about the well-being of the Earth. There was no telling where making art left off and the "mind/body spa" of The D.B.D. Experience began. People from all walks of life were flocking to her weekend marathon workshops for spiritual cleansing and creative rejuvenation. Nobody left her Los Angeles studio unchanged.

Barbara T. Smith is an artist whose artworks are, as she once wrote, "actual vehicles for personal transformation. They represent current art issues and reflect my inner personal developmental level at the same time." She has laid bare and literally experienced aspects of her life in performance, including *Birthdaze,* an examination of her relationship with men on her 50th birthday. This piece included an extended Tantric ritual with a male friend, for which they fasted for five days. Since the mid-'80s Smith has increasingly studied shamanic practices. Her article, written at the time of the Harmonic Convergence in 1987, discusses the uses of performance as potent community ritual.

Can community ritual actually create change? This has been a lifelong question at the heart of the work of choreographer Anna Halprin. A pioneer and innovator in the universal language of dance, Halprin has often changed our ideas of what dance and art can be. A legendary teacher in northern California, and founder of the San Francisco Dancers' Workshop (1955) and Tamalpa Institute (1978), she is known internationally for her community-specific rituals with large groups around the world. At the time of this interview she was working on *Circle the Earth: A Dance in the Spirit of Peace,* a dance for 100 participants. Here she discusses her deep belief in the power of art to affect essential change in human life on a universal scale.

Mierle Laderman Ukeles brought the "transformation" discourse down to earth, in an exceedingly practical exercise that related private matters to public life. Robert C. Morgan describes her motives in her massive real-time performance work, *Touch Sanitation*. During a pregnancy, Laderman conceived of a public artwork that would examine the caretaker role of women, and then caretaking itself. As part of the piece, she shook hands with more than 8,500 sanitation workers on the job in New York City. Morgan looks at the work both as traditional art and humanistic endeavor, laying down some basic precepts of the Art/Life Experiment.

In 1987 we published an issue on art and the environment, including the essay in this collection about the work of Helen Mayer Harrison and Newton Harrison. The Harrisons are known for their large-scale projects that observe, comment on and alter our ecology. While their choice of subject matter leads to the assumption that they are environmental activists, we have placed them in this section on the Art/Life Experiment because their ultimate concern is the human environment—human well-being, human discourse, human interactivity.

Guillermo Gómez-Peña, in the first of many seminal articles he wrote for *High Performance,* directed our attention south of the border with "The Streets: Where Do They Reach?" We have excerpted sections on street performance from this lengthy report on performance art in Mexico City. Gómez-Peña discusses these prolific happenings as essential in the life of their culture, deftly relating them to the events of their time. An astute cultural commentator in both his essays and his own performance work, Gómez-Peña went on to win a MacArthur Foundation "genius" award and take his work to the most prominent art and theater venues in North America and Europe. His early work is described by critic Emily Hicks in "The Artist as Citizen" in the second section of this book.

These are only a few examples of stories in *High Performance* about the belief of artists that art is central to real life, and vice versa. We are firmly convinced that they laid the groundwork for other artists to attempt to affect real change, as activists and as members of their communities. Read on…

She Who Would Fly:
An Interview with Suzanne Lacy

By Richard Newton

Suzanne Lacy and Richard Newton were both performance artists based in Los Angeles at the time of this interview; both used sexual imagery in a social context. Lacy was making head-lines with her large-scale performances about rape, aging and the status of women in U.S. culture. Newton, an associate editor at High Performance, *was making performances and films con-cerned with "the integration of the male and female personae within us all." This was HP's first cover story.* —Eds.

Suzanne Lacy: I came from Wasco, a town of about 6,000 in the cen-tral part of California. I was exposed to art through the paintings of the Great Masters Series. That's all one really had in Wasco. I went to school in zoology, with two years of graduate work in psychology. During my second year of graduate school in psy-chology, I met Judy Chicago, who was doing the Feminist Art Program at Fresno State College.

I had been involved in the feminist movement and had become increasingly alienated from academic studies because of their representation of women. I found such fulfillment relating to other women through the Feminist Art Program that I changed plans in midstream and went off to California Institute of the Arts, where Judy Chicago and Miriam Schapiro were beginning the Feminist Art Program.

I entered the Design School as a social design major and studied with Allan Kaprow, Judy, Sheila De Bretteville and Arlene Raven. I tried drawing and sculpture, but it would take a long time for me to learn how to draw well enough to put forth ideas accumulated after 26 years of living. I moved toward con-ceptual work because it's a more facile mode to express ideas without the need to learn laborious drawing skills. Plus, I was educated as a social activist. I had been in VISTA (Volunteers in Service to America) for a while and worked in mental hospitals.

There was a strong emphasis on performance in Judy's programs, so I was exposed to it there. The first pieces I did were involved with body identity and used biological imagery. I did things like tying myself and the audience to beef kidneys and bathing in cows blood. It was similar to a lot of people's early work at that time—very visceral.

Richard Newton: What is performance art? Are there parameters?

SL: Performance's definition is rapidly changing. It is in a state of flux right now. Five years ago performance was defined as an offshoot of happenings—the mass environmental activity of happenings was reduced to the actions of one person. It was psychodynamic, about the experience of the artist as he or she performed.

> **What's happening now is that politics are coming back into the framework of art.**

In the last five years it's mushroomed in 100 different directions. People like Yvonne Rainer have begun making movies. People like Lynn Hershman have gone in a whole other direction, one that hasn't yet been defined—a kind of environmental performative activity. Her work comments on culture, is in a public place, and the artist acts as either a director or, if as a performer, as simply one element in the piece.

RN: Do you think performance is an art form or a movement? Is there a time when performance will simply be over?

SL: There has always been a performative form for every art movement. The Surrealists were a small and coherent performance movement. Futurists also had a performance activity— the same people that were performing were also painting. Happenings were a performative form of abstract expressionism. People like Kaprow and Oldenburg who did happenings also did sculpture and painting.

I think performance has become more specialized, so it might be that it has become elaborated and exists as a form in itself. People who perform are becoming specialists in that sense, there's not the same kind of connection with painting any more.

I think painting and sculpture are behind the times. Performance has taken over. Performance, conceptual photography and video work seem to have taken off into areas of concern away from any connection to painting and sculpture.

RN: Do you think art without political content is merely decoration?

SL: (laughs) A loaded question.

RN: I'm just trying to find a place for abstract painters.

SL: No, to say that would be historically imperceptive. I think the development of formal thinking through art has taken more or less political turns throughout the centuries. The Futurists were very political (and very fascist while they were at it). There's been attempts to interpret the Abstract Expressionists as being political…. What's happening now is that politics are coming back into the framework of art. There's allowance for that kind of content, and for content in general, to become manifest in art works. Before, there was a hard emphasis on formalism. Each of these concerns advance the body of information and body of knowledge that is art. I would never put one of them down.

On the other hand, I don't personally find work interesting that is not politically meaningful—and I use the word political broadly, because pictures of me floating in guts wouldn't be interpreted as political by most people. Art that is not personal, not reflective of existing in this culture, not somehow attempting to improve or change the culture—that kind of work bores me. So I don't look at it a lot.

Work that is "immoral"—that is, work that perpetuates very real and serious problems without questioning—I think that is laziness on the part of the artist. For Larry Bell to exhibit flocked pink nudes is plain old laziness. But it's easiest to go along with the images we've always had in our culture, and you get a lot of guys patting you on the back for pink flocked nudes, obviously. When there is no real attempt to deal thoughtfully with the meaning of these images, when you just kinda slide your work into the way everybody thinks, I think it's just lazy and tacky.

I hate Les Krims' *Wheat Cake Murders,* for example. It's a series of black-and-white photos where nude and half-clothed women are lying around in different household scenes. They are poured with Karo syrup that looks like blood in black and white. A woman's head might be stuck in a washing machine and there's a stack of wheat cakes in the photo, the signature of the killer. I think they are really disgusting and immoral. They are immoral because the reality of the world is that many women are murdered and when Krims picks up on those images and does not critique them, he just reinforces that kind of image of what is expected for women and of women.

But Abstract Expressionists—well, they're fine, they don't bother me.

RN: How do you separate a public concern for something like rape from your own artistic ambitions? There's a real immediacy to a problem like rape that doesn't stop, and I can see it absorbing all your energy.

SL: The first three years of my career, when there was an emphasis on organizing, like starting the Woman's Building, I didn't do a lot of art work. The first pieces were slow to come. Now I've pretty much got it under control because I've learned enough about how to make art and I can make it a lot faster. I've done three major pieces in two months. Three years ago, I did three a year. They're becoming much clearer and the energies are much stronger.

I think there is a deeper implication to what that you're saying. It has to do with why I choose to make art and how I survive. I am trying to represent myself to the feminist community as an artist and not as an organizer. I greedily hold on to the ability to make my own images, and make clear-cut distinctions about how much organizing I'm going to be involved with. I start with an incident that I want to react to, that is very painful for me or an image that's very personal. For example, I feel very deeply about violence towards women. With this last piece [*In Mourning and In Rage...*] we had a meeting with all the women's organizations in town that deal with violence, and we said we wanted to do this piece, and we wanted to support them, and we wanted them to support us. Immediately, one of the women from one of the centers jumped up and said we think the way you can support us is that you can help us do a self-defense lecture-demonstration and then you can serve on the hot line and we need help doing that. And we said NO, we're artists, and we have skills in this area and we're going to talk with you about it. There was a struggle because they didn't understand what we were trying to do as artists; they don't trust art. Realistically enough, what's art ever done for them? What's art done for political organizations in the past ten years? So there was a struggle to educate them to what we can do, and about the power of this imagery and what it can do. *After Three Weeks in May*, I left town right away for Las Vegas. I did another piece there, with Leslie Labowitz. I think it was a physical way of cutting myself off from the tendency to continue an involvement on an organizational, rather than artistic level.

RN: How involved are you in the overall visual presentation of your work?

SL: I think that it's very important to me and I'm just realizing that recently. The last few pieces—the old lady pieces, *Three Weeks in May*, the Hillside Strangler piece—when I see them in slide, I realize the visual images are strong for me. I don't think I visualized them in detail before they are made, but I'm compelled by a sense that I've got to have that...whatever it is. I've begun an aesthetic move toward the creation of something, and I don't care what my politics are, I'm going to have that image there. I work to make my politics work with the image. I have faith that whatever comes out of my unconscious is going to be in some way political. *In Mourning and in Rage...* got a wonderful response from the women's political community. People don't necessarily know that the power—and a lot of people were very moved by that power—is not because we [Suzanne and Leslie Labowitz] are good organizers, it's because we know how to make visual images. It's because those images hit you in the stomach. The general public doesn't know that, but artists do.

With the *She Who Would Fly* performance installation, the audience is looking at documentation of sexual assaults on women, and suddenly they become aware that they're being watched, they look up and at that moment they are confronted with these nude women painted blood-red, crouched like vultures. Images from the past—Sirens, Valkyries, mutilated, vengeful women Furies, dislocated spirits—all that opens up to a shock of recognition. It's a piece that is political, but it rests on two very strong visual images—a flying lamb carcass and the at first hidden, red-stained nude woman. I think the visual is very important to me but since I wasn't educated in visual things, it's taken me a while to recognize it.

Spring 1978

Acting Like Women:
Performance Art of the Woman's Building

By Cheri Gaulke

The Woman's Building, on Spring Street near Chinatown, was arguably the first art space to open in downtown Los Angeles. Named after the Woman's Building at the Chicago World's Fair in 1893, it quickly became notorious internationally as a center of women's culture. When it closed its doors in 1991 it was calling itself "the oldest feminist institution in history." Cheri Gaulke, as graduate student and artist, then teacher and administrator, was essential to the development of the Woman's Building. Here she puts her finger on why it was so important a catalyst of change for art and for women: its deliberate fusion of art and life.

—Eds.

When I was growing up I used to make my bed with precision movements, imagining that somehow the boy I wanted to marry was watching my performance and judging it. In the magazines and on television, we see women posing while mopping the kitchen floor, and we too learn to pose—as women. We played house only to grow up to get the starring role. Performance is not a difficult concept to us. We're on stage every moment of our lives. Acting like women. Performance is a declaration of self—who one is—a shamanistic dance by which we spin into other states of awareness, remembering new visions of ourselves. And in performance we found an art form that was young, without the tradition of painting or sculpture. Without the traditions governed by men. The shoe fit, and so, like Cinderella, we ran with it.

•••••••••••

Judy Chicago introduced women to performance in the first feminist art programs at Fresno State, and later at California Institute of the Arts. Consciousness Raising (CR) was the process by which each artist's content was discovered; often, exploring this personal experience was painful. Performance was a way of exposing the raw material, transforming it, and healing oneself. Much of this early work was crude and done within the context of the classroom.

Womanhouse (1972, Los Angeles) was an environmental artwork collaboratively created by women in the CalArts program. It brought women's performance art out of the school environment, into the public sphere, communicating through the media to a national audience. For one month, the artists took over a whole house, filling it with images that ranged from elaborate theatrical fantasy to simple real-time activities (reflecting current mainstream art concerns about the relationship between art and life). The shared intent of these different works was to make public women's private lives within the home. Each evening, packed audiences watched while a woman scrubbed the floor, applied make-up or enacted dramatic characterizations.

As in Consciousness Raising, the first step for these early performances was to make private experience public. In 1972 Judy Chicago, Suzanne Lacy, Sandra Orgel and Aviva Rahmani put together a performance about rape entitled Ablutions. From the personal experience of several women, recounted during the piece, a collective, thus political, reality was portrayed. Ablutions explored both internal and external constrictions on women through rape—how we are prisoners of our fear as well as the social system that supports rape. A woman was bound to the chair and then tied to everything in the room. In the end, the entire set was immobilized and the last line of the audio repeated: "I felt so helpless all I could do was lie there and cry." The piece took place at a time when there was little social information about rape in the culture. The powerful images shocked the art audience, who, like the general population, did not yet understand women's experience of violence. Ablutions, strong as a contemporary performance, as well as in its revelation of women's hidden experience, paired an avant-garde form with feminist political vision, contributing to the beginning of the anti-violence movement.

In 1973 the Woman's Building opened. The organizers, Judy Chicago, Sheila de Bretteville and Arlene Raven, saw it as a physical space that women would occupy and bring alive—a vision conducive to performance. Women performance artists from across the nation came to share their work, many using the supportive atmosphere to try out new ideas. Eleanor Antin did her first performance before an audience at the Woman's Building in 1974. Before her premiere in New York, she presented for the first time her autobiographical work as the Ballerina on her way to the Big Apple. Helen Harrison performed making strawberry jam—from growing to picking to canning—an early performance of the large-scale ecologically concerned work she did with her husband Newton.

The Woman's Building also provided a place where important connections could be made. In 1974, women in the Feminist Studio Workshop (FSW) and performance artists in the community organized a month of performance art that included performances, lectures and the first documentary exhibition of West Coast women's performance art. The following year, the first national conference on women's performance art was held at the Woman's Building. At the conference, Linda Montano spent three days blind, patches on her eyes, and first met composer Pauline Oliveros, who performed sonic meditation for the conference. These meetings provided dialogues and collaborations that enriched the performance community. Others who performed or lectured at the Woman's Building are Bonnie Sherk, Nancy Buchanan, Barbara Smith, Martha Wilson, Yvonne Rainer, Joan Jonas, Rachel Rosenthal, Lynn Hershman, Sharon Shore, Barbara Hammer, Mary Fish, Martha Rosler, Ulrike Rosenbach and Motion, a women's performance collective.

Perhaps the most significant contribution of the Woman's Building to performance is through its educational programs. Out of the Feminist Studio Workshop (FSW), the first independent feminist art-educational institution, a new aesthetic has emerged, informed by the collective experience of the feminist educational process. This aesthetic has moved beyond simple theatricality and incorporates elements of networking, working within a real-life environment, and communicating with a mass audience. Performance content reflects a wide range of topics, such as women's participation in the work force, sexuality, relationships and violence, all recreating our definition of women. With voices intensely personal, as well as broadly political, women performance artists are establishing women's reality as a cultural fact.

This work has affected both women's and men's art, which can be charted through mainstream trends in autobiographical, erotic and social art. Very little writing has been done about this historical movement in art (and what has, has been done mostly by the performance artists themselves). This article and its accompanying exhibition at the Woman's Building are the first attempt at looking at the performance art of the Woman's Building as a body of work.

In the second year of the FSW, performance artist Suzanne Lacy, who had been a student in feminist art programs at Fresno and CalArts, was invited to join the staff. She describes the next three years as a "hothouse." Unlike other art schools where students' work is compared and molded to fit the mainstream, the FSW was a "room of their own," a nonstifling environment where women's work was allowed a maturation period. The staff put much of its creative energy into teaching, nurturing new and distinct forms. Out of that embryonic space came autobiographical images and fantasy characters. Fantasy was a step in taking personal power, and the characters reflected women's images of themselves in the world. Eleanor Antin established characters as a legitimate concern in art with her creation of four characters: the Ballerina, the King, the Black Movie Star and the Nurse. At the Woman's Building, Nancy Angelo created a nun, Sister Angelica Furiosa, as a symbol of her search for order in a community of sisters. I created Cinderella, who runs from male-identification to self-definition in feminist community, and finds herself continually running, in a constant state of transformation.

Ritual performance has figured significantly in the educational programs of the Woman's Building. Ritual takes the audience on a journey of catharsis and self-healing. In 1975 Cheryl Swannack, Marguerite Elliot, and Anne Phillips presented a healing ritual, *From Victim to Victory*. It was the exorcism of an experience of being brutalized by the police. In *Cancer Madness* (1977) Jerri Allyn transformed her studio into a hospital ward and confined herself to bed for a week. Her purpose was to heal herself of her death-wish related to her mother's cancer and grandmother's madness. She created a performance structure that allowed her community to participate in her move toward health, and presented information about health issues. Evening bedside events included a poetry reading, psychic healings and a lecture on the politics of cancer treatment.

Anne Gauldin, who was studying prehistoric goddess worship in the FSW, began doing rituals in her backyard and invited other women to participate. Here ritual became a community exploration and expression of female spirituality—a lost religion once officiated by women. Gauldin's concern with spirituality combined with my own work about the religious repression of female sexuality in a collaboration entitled *The Malta Project.* Gauldin and I traveled thousands of miles to the Mediterranean island of Malta, where they brought together an international group of artists, Maltese people and government officials to participate in a ritual performance in two prehistoric temples of goddess worship.

Consciousness Raising has affected the form and structure of performance art as well as the content of the works. The basic structure of CR is equal time and equal space for each woman to share her experience and define herself. Arlene Raven defined the function of feminist art, "to raise consciousness, invite dialogue, and transform culture." Performance artists have taken the invitation to dialogue literally by creating CR-like "performance structures" in which others could participate.

One way this has been done is by bringing people into the space of the Woman's Building. Barbara Smith brought various older people who frequented a nearby city park into the Grandview Gallery at the Woman's Building, while she took their place in the park. At another time the entire third-floor performance space was transformed into a carnival-like setting for College Art Association convention participants. Performance artists lined the walls in "booths." Activities included Nancy Angelo's nun swinging from the rafters; a kitchen confessional where you could confess food over-indulgences to housewife Mary Yakutis; Helen Harrison reading her meditations on California rivers while a woman in a wetsuit graffitied the parking lot; Laurel Klick auctioning personal items that had been in her house when she was raped; Vanalyne Green in a "portrait booth" revealing her impressions of the buyer's personality; Mother Art hanging a laundry maze; me as Cinderella occasionally dashing through, and

Barbara Smith's "kissing booth," where you could apply various colored lipsticks and kiss her body painted white like a canvas.

In other work, this participatory structure has been applied to a larger community, moving out of the space of the Woman's Building. When Suzanne Lacy had her first one-woman show, she called it *One Woman Shows,* and asked other women to participate with her by forming a word-of-mouth community the month before the exhibition. On opening night she performed for three women, and the community previously formed made its appearance through performances that evening. *One Woman Shows* was a visual expression of how our community is formed. It was also a portrayal of the Woman's Building's intent to democratize the artmaking process by broadening the definition of art to include a diverse women's culture, created by artists and non-artists alike.

In 1977 Lacy produced a series of events entitled *Three Weeks in May*, expanding the performance format to include the space of the entire city and three weeks in time. She documented rape in L.A. on a large public map, and enlisted the participation of artists and nonartists in bringing feminist issues to the attention of government officials. She demonstrated that rape is not indigenous to certain ages, classes, or races of women or geographical area, but strikes women everywhere, at any time, for any "reason."

During the five years since *Ablutions,* performance had matured through feminist education into sophisticated forms that provided for real social change. CR had moved simple personal expression and political analysis into a concern with how this information could create change. During the same time, performance had focused on creating forms for the transformation of mass consciousness.

In recent years, several exciting collaborative performance groups have developed out of the educational programs, groups that continue to explore the boundary between art, education, and political action. The Waitresses and Mother Art are issue-related collaborations in which the artists work out of the reality of their own social situation. The Waitresses was founded in 1977 by Jerri Allyn and Anne Gauldin with women who came together through the FSW. Their first series of events, *Ready to Order?*, included performing in restaurants and presenting panel discussions and workshops on issues around work. The Waitresses bring feminist issues to a truly general audience—unsuspecting restaurant employers, employees and clientele—

...broadening the definition of art to include a diverse women's culture created by artists and non-artists alike.

in a performance style that is accessible and fun. Through exploring their personal experiences as waitresses, they have found the waitress is a symbol for women's role in society, as nurturer, slave and sex object. The group is flexible and sometimes expands to include many other women as in The All-City Waitress Marching Band, that performed in a parade. In addition, they have performed in galleries, at conferences and fundraising events. Currently the core group in composed of Jerri Allyn, Anne Gauldin and Chutney Gunderson. Mother Art are mothers and artists who first met in the FSW. By "cleaning up" the banks and performing in laundromats, they bring the values of mothering into the public sphere. Mother Art is composed of Gloria Hajduk, Helen Million-Ruby, Suzanne Siegal and Laura Silagi.

An Oral Herstory of Lesbianism was a play conceived by Terry Wolverton, and collaboratively created out of the life stories of 13 lesbians: Jerri Allyn, Nancy Angelo, Leslie Belt, Chutney Gunderson, Brook Hallock, Sue Maberry, Louise Moore, Arlene Raven, Catherine Stifter, Cheryl Swannack, Christine Wong, Terry Wolverton and myself. Like The Waitresses and Mother Art, Oral... addressed important personal as well as political issues as interpreted by the people who experience that reality.

Feminist Art Workers—Nancy Angelo, Vanalyne Green, Laurel Klick and myself—directly express the philosophy of feminist education through performance art. Our work grows out of a deeply collaborative relationship and finds new forms to respond to continually changing political situations. We have performed a float in the streets, conversations with strangers on the telephone, airplane and bus tours—each time functioning as facilitators of a transformation with their audience/participants. The Feminist Art Workers' form-language has developed around a constantly changing responsiveness to women's needs.

Leslie Labowitz has contributed significantly to the communication of feminist concerns to a mass public audience through her exploration of the "media performance." In *Record Companies Drag Their Feet* she collaborated with Women Against Violence Against Women (WAVAW) to draw media attention to record companies' use of violent images of women in advertising. Staging the event beneath a billboard on Sunset Blvd., Labowitz created the piece to be seen by the general public through television news coverage. She

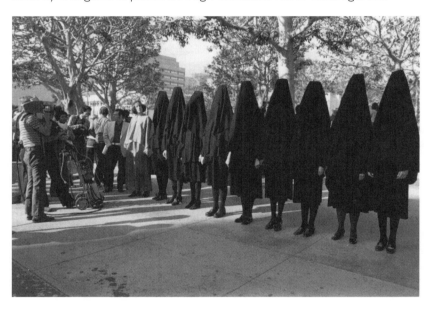

scripted the event, including offensive album covers, roosters portraying record company executives and women carrying protest signs to fit the design of a news broadcast. Her concern with the media performance was to portray women's political information that could pass the distorting mechanism of mass media.

Labowitz and Lacy collaborated in another piece for the media, *In Mourning and In Rage. . .,* a massive public mourning for the victims of the Hillside Strangler. Sensational media coverage of the Hillside Strangler murders was portraying women as random and inevitable victims without political analysis of violence against women. *In Mourning...* presented statistics about the pervasiveness of violence against women in all its forms and presented positive images of women fighting back. After this piece, Lacy and Labowitz cofounded Ariadne: A Social Art Network, as a conceptual framework for women artists, women in the media, government officials and the feminist movement to continue works on violence against women. *The Incest Awareness Project* is the most recent collaboration of this ongoing performance structure.

Feminist performance art has become an integrated part of life at the Woman's Building—used as a tool for education, community organizing and mass-media communication. It marks the flair with which all activities are carried out. At an opening, guests were surprised to see a middle-aged woman serving as a bathroom attendant—a performance student, Betty Gordon, carrying on the charade. When confronted with the storage problem for Kate Millets' *Naked Lady* sculpture, an eight-foot-tall Amazon of papier-maché, Sue Maberry and I came up with a plan: to hoist the *Naked Lady* to the roof of the Building as a beacon of women's power to the community. With the collaboration of media artist Labowitz, the hoisting was made into a media event, communicating the "performance" to L.A. and the world through a front-page photograph in the *Los Angeles Times.* Women's lives, the politics of their situation, how change can be implemented—all these are the material of performance at the Woman's Building, material that is shaping the direction of contemporary performance by bringing art/life/politics together to express a feminist vision of the future.

Fall/Winter 1980

Between the Diaspora and the Crinoline:
An Interview with Bonnie Sherk

By Linda Frye Burnham

*Bonnie Sherk was the founding Director/President of Crossroads
Community (The Farm) in San Francisco, 1974-1980. The Farm,
located beneath a freeway interchange in the heart of the city,
served as a series of community gathering spaces: a farmhouse
with earthy, funky and elegant environments; a theater and
rehearsal space for different art forms; a school without walls; a
library; a darkroom; a pre-school; unusual gardens—all providing
an indoor/outdoor environment "for humans and other animals."
At the time of this interview, excerpted here, Sherk had just
resigned as director of The Farm and was moving on to plans for
more site-specific environments in the world of everyday life.*

—Eds.

Between the abstract and the meadow hurls the chaos.
Between the Diaspora and the crinoline sits the poem.

—Bonnie Sherk

Linda Frye Burnham: *I guess one of the things everybody knows about*
The Farm *is that it's a farm in the middle of a bunch of freeways.
How did you find the site for it?*

Bonnie Sherk: Well, there were several things that led me to this site.
One thing has to do with when I was a child of about the age
of six. There was this recurring dream that I had, that I loved to
conjure up. It was the image of large, monolithic, technological,
clanging forms. Inside of them would be growing a fragile flower,
just a single flower. It was this incredible contrast that was very
much a part of me, and I was fascinated by this image. I would
literally conjure it up at night, and dream it. I don't know where
it came from.

As an adult this kind of imagery was very normal for me

to be working with. I was always aware of it. I was also very conscious of these buildings that were alongside this same freeway interchange, because I lived not too far from there. As I would drive by, I would see these buildings in the area. It was a very magical, mysterious place and always caught my attention.

During the period of late '73 and '74 I was interested in creating a public cafe environment. I was looking for a space where different kinds of artists and also nonartists could come together and break down some of the mythologies and prejudices between different genres, styles and cultural forms. All of this had to be connected with other species—plants and animals. It was very much a feeling that I had, a need to make things whole, to create situations through analogy. I was also working as *The Waitress* as a performance piece and a job. While I was looking for this space, at the restaurant, I met a musician who was interested in political theater. We started talking, and we both knew about this place, and decided to rent it. His name was Jack Wickert.

I felt that it was very important to create *The Farm* as a vehicle for connecting physical and conceptual fragments, for bringing together people of all ages from different economic and cultural backgrounds, people of different colors, and then people in relation to other species. *The Farm* was the product and process of hundreds of people. It emanated as part of a collective unconscious—a partial solution to urban and cultural error—some of which was specific to the site.

LFB: *So you really had this grand design from the very beginning?*

BS: Absolutely. You can look at the drawings that I made in 1974. The first proposal for *The Farm* was a drawing that I made, which shows the land (6.5 acres in all). Another element is that the buildings I had always looked at [during previous site-specific performance works] were adjacent to this four-and-a-half acre cement plaza, which had been the site of the Borden's Dairy Building. This —in relationship to the cluster of buildings, the freeway, the space in the middle of the freeway, which was about to be landscaped, and the four surrounding neighbor-hoods—was perfect to connect. The land fragments were owned by the city, state and private sources. The city-owned land was under the jurisdiction of several agencies. It was a true collage of spaces. It was also at the convergence of three hidden creeks, a magnet site of invisible energy. The timing was superb and *The Farm* was on its way.

I knew how to deal with the logistics of the project because of my work with the *Portable Parks*. At the time I did the *Portable Parks*, in 1970, I spent three months setting up the piece. It was a rehearsal for *The Farm*, because, with the *Portable Parks*, it was necessary for me to deal with certain established systems, communicate with them, and convince them of the rightness of the work. With *The Farm*, of course, the scale was much larger, but it didn't scare me because I had a sense of how to proceed and be effective.

I first contacted the Trust for Public Land, which was a fairly new organization, and was in the business of acquiring open space land for public use. I saw Huey Johnson, who's now the Secretary of Resources for the State of California. At that time he was President of the Trust. I brought the idea to him, the full plan, and he was fascinated with it, and so the TPL helped with the project. After two-and-a-half years of our work, the city did acquire the land. The land is currently being developed as a park with a rural feeling.

The creation of *The Farm* was an enormous series of simultaneous actions, which required hard work by many. On one level, I thought of it as a performance piece, but it was the performance of "Being." I was the "Administrator," "Politician," "Strategist," "Teacher," "Cook," "Designer," "Gardener," etc. In a sense, everyone who participated was a performer.

LFB: *Can you describe* The Farm *as it was when it began? How many buildings. . . ?*

BS: When it began it was completely barren. There was this four-and-a-half acre concrete plaza and a parking lot. There were these very dilapidated buildings with broken windows, boarded over and full of junk. The freeway interchange had just opened. In fact, part of the conception of the piece had to do with the unveiling of the interchange and the availability of public money. The city had just voted for there to be a fund for the acquisition of open space. Things were in synch. In a sense, it was very easy for certain aspects of *The Farm* to emerge as a concept because it was the right time. But it took incredible work and organization. Twenty-four hours a day was insufficient.

In many ways, some of the difficulties of *The Farm* had to do with the fact that it was also ahead of its time. In terms of concept, I was very interested, and still am interested, in creating works that relate simultaneously on many levels. For example, *The Farm*, to a large group, was merely a community center, where animals and plants and people could be together, with

...the theory and practice of art as a tool for cultural transformation and human survival.

each art activity separate. I saw the total integration as a new art form: a triptych (human/plant/animal) within the context of a counter-pointed diptych (farm/freeway: technological/non-mechanized), etc. But it also exists on metaphoric and symbolic levels. Of course, most things do. Years earlier, I had done experiments and works with very common objects, and I noticed that the most common object often was the most mysterious.

LFB: Describe the different elements that went into The Farm *and were part of it.*

BS: I was very interested in framing life and creating a frame for the diversity as well as the similarities. Toward the end of my tenure at *The Farm*, I was developing mechanisms (programs) and environments that would extend the multicultural diversity of the neighborhoods to an international level. Structurally, I saw possibilities by using analogous cultural forms and creating whole experiences—actions connected to a place. I was even negotiating with Japanese businessmen to bring a 300-year-old Japanese farmhouse to the site.

LFB: *Was it last year that you decided to resign as President and Conceptual Director of* The Farm?

BS: In October of '80 I left *The Farm* after almost seven years, because I felt that it was time for me to move on and develop some new projects. One thing I've learned about myself is that I'm not a maintenance person; I'm an initiator. From the beginning I made a vow to myself to stay at *The Farm* as long as it was interesting and fulfilling and to leave when it no longer satisfied me—that's what I did.

I was beginning to get bogged down and bored with a lot of the demands of running this institution. There were bureaucratic structures that were not allowing for certain kinds of things that I wanted to happen. There was also a lack of money. I felt held back and had an incredible desire to travel and experience movement. I felt that it would also be better for *The Farm* to grow on its own terms without me. It was a major "letting go," and I felt very good about it. It also coincided with an exhibition in London that Lucy Lippard had invited me to participate in, and I created a piece called *A Triptych Within a Triptych Within a Triptych Within the Context of a Counterpointed Diptych (Technological, Non-mechanized, Etc.).* A very catchy title.

LFB: *You can whistle it on the way home.*

BS: It had to do with the theory and practice of art as a tool for cultural transformation and human survival. The theory has to do with using art as a mechanism for creating whole systems—experiential situations for cultural change. For the installation I created a preface and three exhibits, two of which, Exhibits A and B, demonstrated different kinds of art. Exhibit A was a documentation of *The Farm.* Exhibit B was a piece which had an indoor landscape with a table of accoutrements and incorporated the Queen's Park across the street as viewed through binoculars. It had many elements which were personal as well as symbolic, including "food for mice" and "food for thought." Exhibit C, which related to the practice of creating and experiencing art, was my letter of resignation from *The Farm*, with my right and left brain cards indicating my respective roles as President and Conceptual Director.

The practice was stated: "Between the abstract and the meadow hurls the chaos. / Between the Diaspora and the crinoline sits the poem." In many ways this piece was my completion piece for *The Farm*, and an analysis of my work for the past ten years, as well as being a thing in itself.

Fall 1981

The Year of the Rope:
An Interview with
Linda Montano & Tehching Hsieh

By Alex and Allyson Grey

No two artists are more central to a discussion of the Life/Art Experiment than Linda Montano and Tehching Hsieh. For years, on opposite coasts, they had each cordoned off whole sections of their daily lives and called them art. When we heard that they were working together on a one-year piece, it seemed like a natural. When we heard they had vowed to spend a whole year in New York City tied to each other with a piece of rope, it seemed perfect—yet hardly possible. Alex and Allyson Grey were artists married to each other, and just as obsessively concerned with coupling at the intersection of art and life. In June 1984, while the Hsieh/Montano piece was still in progress, High Performance *asked the four artists to meet for a conversation about it.*
—Eds.

July, 1983

STATEMENT

We, LINDA MONTANO and TEHCHING HSIEH, plan to do a one year performance.

We will stay together for one year and never be alone. We will be in the same room at the same time, when we are inside. We will be tied together at the waist with an 8 foot rope. We will never touch each other during the year.

The performance will begin on July 4, 1983, at 6 p.m., and continue until July 4, 1984, at 6 p. m.

—Linda Montano
—Tehching Hsieh

With masterful simplicity of means, Tehching Hsieh and Linda

Montano created a year-long art epic. Each of the artists' past works had strangely prepared them for the endurance of the rope. The rope provided an extended and controlled shock to the patterns of their lives. Not separate, yet not a "couple," the two artists' work took on layer after layer of meaning. The reality of the rope became the symbol of relationship…the difficulty of relationships…the inescapability of interdependence… The rope made visible the psychic bond that exists between any two people in close relationship and told the truth that we are each alone yet connected.

One of the most highly publicized works of performance art, it retains an impenetrable privacy. No one will ever know "what it was like" but the artists themselves. Those who have seen or heard of Tehching Hsieh and Linda Montano's art/life performance will long remember it.

Alex and Allyson Grey: *When did you first meet and what inspired your collaboration?*

Linda Montano: I was living in a Zen Center in upstate New York. During a trip to the city I saw one of Tehching's posters and literally heard a voice in my head that said, "Do a one-year piece with him." I was free to do that, so I asked Martha Wilson [of the New York art space Franklin Furnace] for his number, called him, and we met at Printed Matter where we talked intensely for two hours. He said that he was looking for a person to work with…I was looking for him…so we continued negotiating, talking and working from January to July when we started the piece.

A&AG (to Tehching Hsieh): *So you were looking for somebody to work with before you met Linda?*

TH: Yes. I [had an] idea about this piece and I needed to find somebody for collaboration. After I met Linda, she told me that she had done a piece handcuffed with Tom Marioni for three days. Somehow I feel very good about collaboration because Linda had done something similar before.

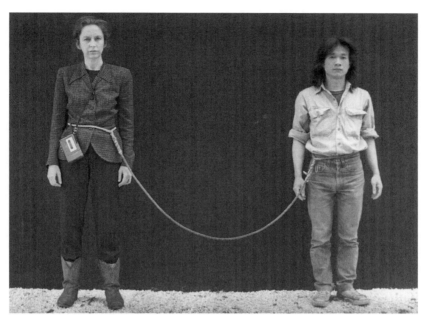

A&AG: *What inspired your idea for the piece?*

TH: You know, I've done three performances before connecting art
and life together. I like to create art about life from different
angles. Most of my work is about struggle in life. Like in *The Cage*
my life inside felt isolated—that's a kind of struggle. And in [the]
Punch Time Clock piece I [did] the same thing over and over, like
a mechanical man, and that's a kind of struggle. When I lived
outdoors it was about struggle with the outside world.

    I got the idea for this piece because there are problems
about communication with people. I feel this is always my struggle. So I wanted to do one piece about human beings and their
struggle in life with each other. I find being tied together is a very
clear idea, because I feel that to survive we're all tied up. We
cannot go in life alone, without people. Because everybody is
individual we each have our own idea of something we want to
do. But we're together. So we become each other's cage. We
struggle because everybody wants to feel freedom. We don't
touch, and this helps us to be conscious that this relationship
connects individuals, but the individuals are independent. We are

not a couple, but two separate people. So this piece to me is a symbol of life and human struggle. And why one year's time? Because then this has real experience of time and life. To do work one week or two weeks, I feel that it may become like just doing a performance. But I do it one year and then the piece becomes art and life—it's real connection and that has more power. Also a year is a symbol of things happening over and over.

LM: I think that's what interested me in Tehching's work; having similar interests—merging art and life. For many years I have been framing my life and calling it art, so that everything—washing dishes, making love, walking, shopping, holding children—is seen as art. Formerly, I would separate out activities—run to the studio and that was my "creative time." Gradually I found this separation unnecessary and felt that it was important for me to be attentive all of the time—not to waste a second. That became the Art/Life task that I have given myself until I die.

I made many pieces from 1969 on that experimented with this idea of allowing my life to be a work of art. I lived with different people and called that art. I wrote the *Living Art Manifesto* in 1975, and later turned my home into a museum so that everything I did there would be framed as art. I lived in galleries. I was sealed in a room for five days as five different people. All of it was an attempt to make every minute count. I knew that by working with Tehching I would experience his time frame, one year, and that kind of art rigor interested me.

A&AG (to LM): *Tehching has talked about what the piece symbolizes to him. What does the piece mean to you?*

LM: By being tied with a rope and not touching, I am forced to remain alert and attentive because I am doing something different from what I ordinarily do. That way I break down habitual patterns because the task of being tied is so difficult and absorbing that I can only do just that. Supposedly there are seven stimuli that can simultaneously grab our attention every second. This piece demands that the mind pay attention to one idea, not seven, and because being tied is potentially dangerous, the mind gets focused or else our lives are threatened.

Besides training the mind, the piece raises so many emotions to the surface that the soap-opera quality eventually gets boring. I feel as if I've dredged up ancient rages and frustrations this year and, although I'm glad that I went through with them, I now feel that holding any emotional state for too long is actually an obsolete strategy. On the other hand, because I believe that everything we do is art—fighting, eating, sleeping—then even the negativities are raised to the dignity of art. As a result I now feel much more comfortable with the negative. It's all part of the same picture.

> **...because I believe that everything we do is art...even the negativities are raised to the dignity of art.**

A&AG: *What is a typical day like?*

LM: We have this pattern. We go to bed around midnight, Tehching sleeps in the morning. I get up earlier, meditate, exercise, watch TV. Then he gets up. Sometimes we run. Three times a day we walk Betty, my dog. We take one picture every day and turn on the tape recorder whenever one of us is talking. Each month we switch off being responsible for either the camera or the tape recorder. If we aren't doing carpentry, teaching or part-time gallery work, then we go to our desks and sit back-to-back for about five hours.

A&AG (to TH): *What do you do at your desks during the day?*

TH: Thinking.

LM: We think about what we want to do and then we talk until we come to a consensus. So it takes many hours of sitting before we can do one thing.

A&AG: *You both seem to have different ways of thinking about the piece.*

TH: Yes, because we are two individual human beings and two individual artists tied together for 24 hours a day and so individualism is very natural to this piece. It's interesting to me because if we want to be good human beings and good artists at the same time, that's one kind of clash and struggle. Also if we want a relationship and independence at the same time, that creates a double struggle.

The piece has other levels that make us feel more individual—there are cultural issues, men/women issues, ego issues. Sometimes we imagine that this piece is like Russia with America. How complicated the play of power.

LM: This piece raises many questions. Like, how do two humans survive in such close physical proximity? A Russian journalist wanted to do an interview with us because she said that Soviet scientists were interested in exercises that their astronauts could do to prepare themselves for spending extended periods of time in space capsules. In many ways, the piece is valuable because I feel that it is necessary to learn new survival skills and to look at emotional conditioning and responses that are obsolete.

A&AG: *Waiting must be a big part of the piece.*

LM: We usually do a very simple thing, efficiently, so that we don't have to bother each other. Having 15 minutes in the bathroom is a luxury. If we are fighting then we do only the basic things like eating and going to the bathroom, and those things are done quickly.

A&AG: *The piece obviously has negative and positive qualities.*

TH: Most artists who collaborate want to try to be one. But we both have very different ways to work and have different ideas. For survival we have to work things out. This brings out a lot of negativity and fighting. It is part of [the] piece, so I don't feel too negative. The positive, we don't have to worry about. We just enjoy it.

LM: There are many people in worse conditions than we are—the person tied to a bad job or a bad place or a bad marriage. This piece is about the realities of life. They aren't always easy. Often we would just have to sit it out, sometimes for three weeks, until the "cloud of unknowing" passed.

TH: Some people think I am choosing to suffer—I don't think that I want to bring more suffering to myself, but the work is difficult and in some ways that brings suffering. As an artist I have a lot of pleasure [doing] my work. If I don't get any pleasure out of doing difficult work then I don't have to do it. I don't think I want [to] suffer for no reason. I am not masochistic.

LM: Artists choose forms that fit their internal image bank. Tehching has his own reasons for his images. Mine come from the ascetic, Catholic/spiritual world. I believe that if life is hard and I choose to do something harder, then I can homeopathically balance the two difficulties. Snake venom is used to cure snake bites!

A&AG: How do you feel about not having sex for a year?

LM: Actually, I'm beginning to reevaluate guilt, and lately have been more willing to sacrifice, not because I'm guilty but because it's an essential attitude. I also realize that not having sex is as interesting as having it. Besides, touch is highly overrated. In the past, I've often grasped without energy, charge or significance and called that touch.

TH: We do not touch. We are sacrificing sex, not denying it. We could, in theory, have sex with other people. But that would just be a way to try to escape. It is not right for the piece.

LM: Once you give the mind a command, then you watch the body carry out the process. When I went into the convent for two years, I informed myself that I would not have sex and noticed that the energy went to other things. This year I have a chance to experiment with desire. Am I turned on? To whom? When? How much? Also, since the body isn't touched, the mind is pushed into the astral.

  I believe that in the next 200 years, we will all be in outer space so why not practice outer-space sex now by letting astral bodies merge.

A&AG: *So you are using this piece as a kind of training?*

LM: Yes. One thing that interests me very much about this piece is that a work of art can be used to practice remaining conscious.

A&AG: *Is that part of your understanding of the piece, Tehching—training your awareness?*

TH: Yes, but it is secondary. The piece becomes a mirror showing me my weakness, my limitations, my potentials, and trains my will.

LM: Some artists choose difficult work. Other people do it in a cele- bratory way—Dionysian ecstasy, to get free enough to be them- selves and to be in the moment. It's really a matter of choosing the style that goes with our inclinations and then hopefully changing directions if the style isn't working, or if those old hin- drances aren't there any more. Then we can do something else. Maybe end up on a mountain, gardening.

A&AG: *Linda mentioned before that the piece is "potentially dangerous." How so?*

TH: I do not feel that the piece is dangerous. I have to know my limi- tations in a piece. So I do a rehearsal for a week to see what happens. That's just technical kind of help. But I don't want to do a piece that I feel is too risky—30% risk is okay. Accidents are possible in this piece, so we have to be very careful.

LM: For Tehching this is not such a big issue. For me it is, because I'm not used to taking large physical risks. Actually we were very lucky and only two dangerous things happened. Once Tehching got into an elevator…I was outside and the door closed. He pushed the "door open" button before the elevator went down, but for days I had images and nightmares of being smashed against the elevator door or else cut in half by the rope.

    Another time we were walking in Chinatown when a woman ran between us into the rope and almost tripped. So in that instance, the rope was dangerous for someone else. Riding bikes, one in back of the other, was more liberating than dangerous, but we had to be careful.

A&AG: *How does this piece go along with your spiritual outlook on life?*

LM: I come from a very strict, religious tradition and have been disciplined most of my life. I continue with discipline, but now I am using the artist's way to be spiritual.

TH: I have no interest in the spiritual but I am in some ways like a monk who is dedicated in a serious way. My dedication is to my art work. I am interested in the philosophical and in life experience. I try to make sense of who I am and what I am doing in my life without God. If I say I don't believe in God maybe it means that I am trying to find my own belief.

A&AG: *What are some of the influences on your work?*

TH: New York art, Dostoyevsky, Franz Kafka, existentialism—that influences me. Also, I am oriental. I grew up in Taiwan, and I have an oriental kind of technique and oriental kind of experience, that influences me too. Also, my mother influenced me—she is a very dedicated person.

LM: My influences have been—my grandmother, who took out her false teeth at most family gatherings and sang, "If I Had the Wings of an Angel"; my mother, who is a painter; Lily Tomlin; Marcel Duchamp; Eva Hesse, and St. Theresa of Avila.

I am also interested in using art therapeutically, probably because when I was 20 I was anorexic (82 lbs.) and it's only because I immersed myself in "art" that I came out of that experience intact. So for that reason, I will always be aware of the psychological/sociological effects of the creative process.

A&AG: *Now that you've been tied together for almost a year, how do you feel about each other?*

TH: I think Linda is the most honest person I've known in my life and I feel very comfortable to talk—to share my personality with her. That's enough. I feel that's pretty good. We had a lot of fights and I don't feel that is negative. Anybody who was tied this way, even if they were a nice couple, I'm sure they would fight, too. This piece is about being like an animal, naked. We cannot hide our negative sides. We cannot be shy. It's more than just honesty—we show our weakness.

LM: Tehching is my friend, confidant, lover, son, opponent, husband, brother, playmate, sparring partner, mother, father, etc. The list goes on and on. There isn't one word or one archetype that fits. I feel very deeply for him.

A&AG: *Talk more about how your relationship progressed through this piece and how you will face your separation.*

LM: We developed four ways of communicating. In the first phase we were verbal, talking about six hours a day. Phase two—we started pulling on each other, yanking on the rope. We had talked ourselves out, but yanking led to anger. In phase three we were less physical with each other and used gestures, so we would point when we wanted to go to the bathroom or point to the kitchen when we wanted to eat. Phase four—we grunted, and made audible, moaning sounds when we needed to go somewhere…that was a signal for the other to get up and follow the initiator. Communication went from verbal to nonverbal. It regressed beautifully.

It was also interesting to watch the overall energy of the piece. Eighty days before the end of the piece, we started to act like normal people. It was almost as if we surfaced from a submarine. Before that we were limited to doing just the piece.

TH: Our communication was mostly about this piece. Like, I have to ask Linda if I want a glass of water. It takes up all of our energy.

A&AG: *Your piece has been on the newswire. You've had a tremendous amount of media attention nationally. How do you feel about the publicity?*

TH: I have positive and negative feelings. Negative is that I don't really like that kind of publicity. But I would like for people to know. The problem is that they are more interested in the life issues and don't understand art. That bothers me. But I feel positive that people who know about it feel something even if they don't know about art. For example, mothers with young children often say to us, "You know, I've been tied to my baby for two years." That means she understands in some way.

LM: Pregnant women also respond because we are making the umbilical cord visible. We also get responses from policemen, feminists, religious people, S & M practitioners, people walking dogs…the image evokes many projections.

Actually the publicity has won over my father…He is a businessman and read about it in the *Wall Street Journal,* so now he's much more supportive of my work.

And being deluged by the media has helped me come to a new understanding of documentation. It seems that the primary document is the change inside the performer and audience. The results are felt and cannot always be photographed or expressed.

A&AG: *How does it feel to have the piece nearing an end?*

LM: We're so much easier on each other now that it's almost over, and there is a nostalgia that we couldn't have been this way earlier. But I've learned a good lesson…to give 100% all the time. Usually in relationships I have thought, "I'll open up tomorrow," or "I'll communicate tomorrow." Now I realize that life is short, and it's ridiculous to waste time.

I also feel a sadness that Tehching and I won't be doing an 80-year piece together…maybe we'll do it from a distance.

TH: On a philosophical level, I feel that the piece is not nearing an end. It's just that we are tied to each other psychologically. When we die it ends. Until then we are all tied up.

Fall 1984

D.B.D.—the Mind/Body Spa:
An Interview with Rachel Rosenthal

By Linda Burnham

Our interview with Rachel Rosenthal about her life-changing weekend workshop, D.B.D (Doing by Doing), opens the door on art as a vehicle of personal transformation. Rachel Rosenthal's performances deal with the universe on a grand scale, projected from the microcosm of the human ego. Her workshop techniques were derived from Instant Theater, an influential underground theater she established during the '50s, in which she developed a method for teaching whole groups of people to improvise magic on stage. She brings to The D.B.D. Experience years of research and meditation, facts and feelings about science, art, psychology, holistic health, body work and personal power. In this 1988 excerpted interview she talks about the workshop's chemistry and why art is so central to its transformational quality.   —Eds.

Linda Frye Burnham: *What's the most important activity for you now?*

Rachel Rosenthal: Trying to keep the faith. See, I kind of see my life and my work as being a continuum, I try not to separate things. Everything I do is really a quest, like I talk about in the workshops. I feel that I have to find my own relationship to the universe. I have to find the best way I can serve. Mainly I have to fight despair—in other people and in myself. I find sometimes that's very hard. I can't even see the light. So I try to approach from a different angle, the way I do in my performance. I pursue something for a while and then I get to a point where I reach either a cul de sac or a depression, so I try something else. So right now I've started to paint. I find when I'm very, very depressed, when my mind just won't stop going—I'm continually bombarded by things that just destroy me, mostly about politics, animals, the planet—I find now that painting is very helpful. The hours go by and I am very involved in a physical and sensual activity, which I haven't done for a long time. I realized that I was starved for the sensuality of making objects, no matter what happens to them.

LFB: You talk about depression and despair because of world problems?

RR: I know that it comes from spiritual emptiness. The spirituality of the universe is a real thing, but the problem is to remain connected with it. It's a cord that's severed by the way we live, the assault on our emotions and our intellect. The problem is that we are real orphans. There's a nourishment of the soul that is sadly lacking; we are all starved and we're over-eating and we're undernourished.

LFB: Because the input we get is all material?

RR: Of course. And our starvation is dangerous because that's where the spiritual adventurers come in, the cults and the Moral Majority, that's the breach for them. These people are not into spirituality, they are into control. The real problem is to be reconnected as a thinking, intelligent individual, and what I'm trying to do is take it in a roundabout way that isn't direct revelation or direct faith, but, let's say, scientific understanding. If you really read what is going on in the new sciences, you've got to come to the conclusion that there is a sea of spirit in which everything is bathed, because that's the reality. Reality is no longer material but spiritual. I feel I get my faith from this.

LFB: Is art for you a renewal of that connection with that spiritual pool?

RR: Yes. I really believe that. That's why I hate to see art used as an outlet for your own personal cruelties and your own worldly gains. I do have a really sacred sense of art. Art is the only place that's sacred. It always was, that's where it came from originally. Art today is not to promote the sacred conception of the universe; it's to promote the commercial and materialistic concept of the universe. It's also lost its moorings. It's also an orphan. It's been cut off.

LFB: Because we don't know what it's for any more?

RR: We don't know what anything is for any more. There is no certainty anywhere. Alan Watts said that the real reality is total inse-
curity, where nothing is what we want it to be and everything is
continually changing. The only way you can live in such a world is
if you don't build something solid on it. There is only an illusion
of solidity. So long as we try to live with these totally illusionistic
concepts, we are going to continue perpetrating the kind of
world that we are in now, which is a world that is hurtling
toward big, big punishment. We are being punished, in a sense,
for believing these untruths. We have to wake up to what the
real truth is and start rebuilding the world on a spiritual base, a
true spiritual base, which doesn't mean a religious base in the
sense of organized religion.

They are always telling us of the illusion of solidity, this is
this and not *that*, this is separate from this. And in reality everything is not only connected, but really flowing into one another.
We have probably evolved from a time when we were able to
take in reality in the real way,

Art is the only place that's sacred.

something closer to uncon-
sciousness as animals just
emerging from the animal king-
dom. We were probably very connected to all of nature and we
could really sense that continuum. But today it's 2 plus 2 is 4 and
that's it. We create language and then the functions of the brain
and the physiology of the brain sort of interlock. The more language creates these separate concepts, the more the synapses
of the brain become also very separate and divisive, and so,
anatomically, we are built in such a way that we sort of physio-
logically have to live in a state of illusion, which the Indians call
maya. We are stuck in that state, but some people who either
intuitively or through their reading know that there is something
else, that there is another reality behind all this illusion, they
make efforts through meditation and other things to go back.

That's what art does. Art is *about that*. When you make a

work of art, that's what you are really dealing with—what I call the continuum, which is really the abstract underpinnings, not the actual content or image, but it's everything else that goes into it. In other words, the way you use the space, the relationships between the forms, the equilibriums, the volumes, the rhythms, the oppositions, the interweaves. Some people try to reach this understanding through art and others use other means. My hope is that enough people will do this kind of effort before the end of the century, before it's too late.

LFB: *This sounds very much like your teaching in D.B.D. Is that one of your goals, to bring about that kind of spiritual transformation in your workshop participants?*

RR: With the workshop, I don't know if the artmaking is snuck in in all this strong spiritual transformation or if it's the other way around. It depends on how you are geared. Some people will see the workshop as a big artmaking ball and they will get the other stuff quite subliminally. Or the other way around; the people who are more geared that way will really sense the transformational quality and, in addition, they will be doing some nice improv and having a little fun.

LFB: *What would you say if somebody said, "Oh, D.B.D. is nothing but another California touchy-feely workshop?" What makes it unique?*

RR: The artmaking. It's different from psychodrama in that we don't use language and we are not trying to play out psychological problems. The work is much more spiritual and abstract and artlike, often on a mythical level.

LFB: *Do you see a healing quality in the workshop?*

RR: The healing quality comes from a larger context, not so much from the individual psychological knots that have to be untied. That you can do yourself. It's not even assuming that anybody is sick or has problems or blockages. It's assuming that, as human beings in this society, this day and age, everybody is in the same boat; we all have this unassuaged hunger and thirst, we all have these locks, we all have these knots inside of us.

Sometimes the connection that you see on stage is so…unpsychological! It's like two bodies beginning to move together magically as if they've learned a choreography that they've rehearsed a hundred times, yet it's totally spontaneous. They're doing it for the first time, but they are beginning to vibrate together. When those things happen you can't describe them in words. You can't say, well, there was a scene in which this guy goes to the grocery store and the store owner is angry with him—it's nothing to do with that. It has to do with colors and shapes, movement, putting on a costume. Somehow you've got four people in a piece and they don't watch each other get dressed, yet they come out and they're all wearing white and black, those marvelous synchronous moments that are sacred moments that create the artwork collectively.

You know, it's like a primal feeling, where I imagine in the days of primal culture people would get that connection without words. They would all come together and make art together; create those moments which are sacred moments and are absolutely filled with the creating juices, where you can really feel the power of creation, not only the individual but the whole schmear, the whole number. Those are the things that happen in the workshop. It's like a weekend of collectively trying to go beyond, to resolve things with a good massage, to soften all these hard strings that we have inside us and to make us vulnerable.

LFB: After five years, can you state the central idea of D.B.D., what makes it work?

RR: It's about erasing the borders, the demarcations between life and art. I do believe that whatever it is that you are will be transmitted into the art in one way or another. What is more the acme of behavior than art? You give form to something that didn't exist before. You are really fashioning your soul, an extension of your spirit. If you start tampering with that form, which is the materialization of your spirit, you can really reach to the most deep level of where your creativity lies, the whole source of your being. That's what it's about.

Now when I say that, people really get scared. They're thinking, oh boy, here comes this woman and she's going to tickle the core of my being! This is terrible! What if she tickles it in the wrong way? To that I can only say that we are always good and bad, we are always yin and yang, we are always black and white, a mess of opposites. I bring to the workshop my very best qualities and only my best qualities. For a weekend, two days and a half, I am a saint. My aim for that one weekend is to really take the spirit of the people who are there and give a bath to that spirit. I call D.B.D. now the mind-body spa. You go there and you clean out your body and your spirit, your imagination and your artmaking, it's all taking this terrific bath and it's coming out clean. Then you go out and you get soiled again, but you have had the experience of this real purity, the creative drive that brings the best out of you, not only as an individual, but as an individual who is part of a group, in society. So for that weekend, I am really there only and purely to be at the service of these individual spirits and I do what must be done. After the weekend I go home and I am still old Rachel, with all her weaknesses and stupidities and pettinesses, like everybody else. But for that weekend, I am a saint, or whatever you want to call it.

Spring 1984

Art and Ceremony

By Barbara T. Smith

Performance artist Barbara T. Smith's work has always been involved with ceremony, ritual and spiritual transformation. In 1987 Smith was investigating shamanic practices with a Native American teacher. Having made acquaintance with artist Jose Arguelles at the time he began articulating ideas about the Harmonic Convergence, she became interested in the real possibilities of using certain aspects of performance in healing practices and in "reconnecting humans with nature in a balanced way." This essay, excerpted from a longer article, puts forth many of the principles that link her work to spiritual practice and align it with the most radically ephemeral strain of California art.   —Eds.

The preconceived idea that all reality is a matter of cause and effect robs events of meaning. Healing requires an instant when time, which is ineluctably tied to entropy, is stilled or reversed.

—Gerald Epstein, *Brain Mind Bulletin*
May 1986

The emergence of performance art in the mid- to late '60s came from a bonding of Western art historical and cultural issues. Two particular ideas of the time were influential: the identification of the *act* of artmaking as the essence of creativity (as reflected in abstract expressionism), and the prominence of reductivism in mainstream science (as reflected in minimalism). Artists responded to these influences with an art expressed through the being of the artist, as both the carrier of the power and the expression of it. This new nontheatrical use of the body was both liberating and, paradoxically, the ultimate in super-individuated isolation. Reflecting, then, an instinctual longing for connection through meaningful ceremony and ritual long lost or trivialized, many artists began to create deep and profound self-generated ritual pieces.

Out of the pain of the early work, which was truly sacrificial and shamanic in nature, new forms emerged. As the feminist movement developed, the work of many of the women led into a search for connection into feminine spirituality. The new language was also fed by the study and experience of many ancient disciplines, as well as a rich and sustaining feedback loop that consisted of actual spiritual experiences. We found the light only as we took each step.

The gradual realization of the dangerous threat to life on the planet, precipitated by the dominant culture's greed, ignorance, insensitivity and territorial power practices, made the link between feminism, spirituality and ecology an obvious one. The widespread recognition of the need and desire for an entirely new perception and method of living has long been connected by and expressed through the visionary insights of such early writers as Teilhard de Chardin and Marshall McLuhan, and more recently through the nonmaterialist and holographic realizations of leading-edge scientists, mathematicians and Native Americans. In many

> **It is no accident that there is a widespread interest in remembering our ancient tribal past and connections to sacred ways long lost.**

ways we have been in a New Age for some time. By capturing the power of the sun and daring the exploration of space, we have birthed a new being with a new responsibility to Earth Mother. From having seen her in her totally interdependent state, where it is impossible to take from one place without sacrificing or giving in another, we see the urgent need for healing and know it. The Noosphere, Teilhard de Chardin's "realm of total consciousness," is approaching.

It is not surprising that another visionary has connected us with our ancient past and the impending future, and finds in the data a linkup experience that is happening, will happen and must be if we are trying to make the bridge to a viable future. Artist and art historian Jose Arguelles became that voice for many in his book *The Mayan Factor.* There he set the focal uplink date at August 16 and 17, 1987—the Harmonic Convergence of the calendar of days with the Mayan cycles of galactic time, and its perfect interface with the DNA of our genetic code. Thus we have passed into a new worldview where we have gone beyond our anchor in the solar system to an even more integrated connection in the galactic core. Whether or not this is accurately, objectively true relative to the Mayan calendar is not the point. It is metaphorically true, and a worldview becomes itself, with or without our tacit agreement, once there are enough people who hold that view. If it is a large enough macrostructure, with a deep enough resonant base in primal memory, it will gradually emerge to guide our salvation, especially as we live it.

Art functions, then, as the linkage between the archaic foundations with the macrostructure to which we are navigating, just as it did in the Renaissance—thus completing the law of "as above, so below," which *is* harmonic alignment. It is no accident that there is a widespread interest in remembering our ancient tribal past and connections to sacred ways long lost. Anthropologists used to call "quaint" and "superstitious" such beliefs that, without prayers and certain ritual practices, the sun might not come up. Now we see that we have for so long treated the earth as an inert thing to use and exploit, that she may in fact be dying and the sun might not come up for us.

·········

The power of this type of work is in its gift of participation, vortex-building, healing, release and alignment toward the creation of the Harmonic Convergence of a living global consciousness. The audience for such work probably far exceeds the limited parameters of the art context. The ethic is communal and invites participation rather than object-oriented criticism. The leaders, rather than being stars, create a tool that works, that functions as a balancing healer. These actions will not fix things once and for all; they are not meant to do this. They are meant as a way of life that is constantly and actively keeping the tribe in balance. They call upon nearly lost techniques and traditions, and in new ways seek a language that is transcultural and speaks to all. They direct us to the open land, there to speak with our plant and animal brothers and sisters in reciprocal teaching and harmony. The message is that the Earth is alive, sacred, has much to give and teach. If you ask her she will tell you how to be with her, and how to receive what you need. She is in love with you and wants you to survive, but we must learn that what we take we must give back. There is no trash heap that is not now acting on our lives. Recycling is the law of life.

The two most sacred laws of the Native Americans:

All things are born of woman.
Pass no law or take no action that would harm the children or the child within, both now and in the distant future.

Winter 1987

Ritual Keeper: An Interview with Anna Halprin

By Janice Steinberg

Anna Halprin's mid-'70s real-life bout with cancer forced her to focus on the power of the ritual material she was using in chore-ography and teaching. Her new ritual art work emerged in 1981 as a group dance to reclaim Mt. Tamalpais, the San Francisco Bay area landmark where Halprin lived and taught, and which had been the site of murders of women hikers by "The Trailside Killer." The result was a large group dance that was followed, a few days later, by the capture of the killer. The concept of the dance was expanded, and has been performed by large groups throughout the world, with the intent of experiencing and bringing about world peace. Halprin is interviewed here by Janice Stein-berg, a San Diego-based writer who participated in Circle the Earth: A Dance in the Spirit of Peace *when Halprin visited her city in 1986. This is excerpted from a longer piece.* —Eds.*

Janice Steinberg: *You had such skill in the peace dance, as if you're part dancer and part shaman, with the ability to take care of people's emotional needs as they arose. When you've got 100 people, how do you make it work for them emotionally, if you're working with material that's so real?*

Anna Halprin: This skill is the result of years of very careful develop-ment of process. To ask people to be authentic and to deal with real life issues, I had to develop real understanding about how to work therapeutically. I did a lot of Gestalt training. I did a lot of training in how to facilitate. I had to learn a lot about the nature of movement itself. I'm dealing with the power of movement and what happens when you move and you release authentic movement; how do you structure that? How do you work with structure? How do you work with the balance between struc-ture and freedom?

When I had cancer ten years ago I realized there was an

element that was being released that I wasn't processing and directing, I wasn't channeling it. I stopped performing, and all I did was develop the understanding of the kind of work I had been doing. This was now a message, part of the spirit world calling me. I wasn't just playing around with the little hardware in the theater; I was playing around with my life. I was playing around with spirits that were calling and saying, "Hey, knock knock? You're getting too deep, and what's going on?" I began to call on scientists, doctors, and just did a whole lot of research. I realized I was working with ritual, and didn't know it. I was working with the body as myth, and I didn't know it. I was working with parts of the body as symbols, and I didn't know it. I was working with symbols, myths and rituals, and I didn't know what I was doing.

Let me tell you, it's been hard work and I've almost died in the struggle. I've been my own laboratory. To be a shaman is not an easy thing. As far as I'm concerned, it's not psychic power. It's been a lot of hard work and a lot of research, and I take it very seriously. I don't release things with people unless I know how to process them.

JS: *On a similar note, I'm interested in the way you clearly became chore-ographer on the last day of the workshop—we were supposed to break for lunch at one, and you didn't let us break till three because we just weren't getting it the way you wanted.*

AH: Somebody made a beautiful remark—rather than choreograph-ing, being very clear about a structure that would liberate your creativity. By not having a structure, at a certain point you would just not be able to cooperate together. In order for you to feel totally confident and feeling your power, it needs to be really clear about what the structure is, so you're able to have the freedom to be creative and be totally expressive. I didn't feel that I was coming in to choreograph, as much as I was coming in to be your ritual-keeper and say: Here's your structure, let's make sure that you're all in agreement around it, and that this is a structure that will really work for all of us to get what we want. I don't wince a bit taking power and using it when I feel that that power will empower others.

JS: *There are a lot of things happening nationally and internationally for peace at this time. How do you see* Circle the Earth *in relation to them?*

AH: There's a lot going on now about dancing *for* peace, or for the benefit of peace. I think that what this is attempting to do, which I think is a little different, is that we're attempting to create a peace dance. The way people work together in learning to do this dance is itself an example of how a community can work together in a strong effective, peaceful manner. Nobody was put down; everybody was heard; everybody had a chance to express themselves. Isn't it astonishing that a full-length work of art for peace can be created in such a short time when people work peacefully together?

Then, the dance is dealing with how to find peace in yourself as well as injecting it in the world. First we emerge from the earth and we say, "Here we are, strong, and we come from the earth." Then we say, "Look at all our differences: How can we bring those differences together and become a strong unified community?" Then we say, "Now that we have the strength and the support and the trust, how can we look at the ugliest, the most evil part of ourselves?" That is hard. And we did. And we did it so totally that we were unashamed to cry in front of an audience.

> **I was working with symbols, myths and rituals, and I didn't know what I was doing.**

Do you know that people still think that crying was an actor's job? Isn't that unbelievable—that people would unfold themselves, be so vulnerable?

We fought, and then we released this evil. We were able then to take the same forces that create evil and transform those forces and create something more peaceful. We went through the bridge; we took the audience with us, and we said,

"We're ready now to move to another space." We did the Chief Seattle Run; we said, "We can all join together, we can run together and make our peaceful steps heard. We can put out our visions for peace. We have gone through our own ordeal, and then we can turn it into the song and send these peaceful messages out through the image of the bird."

The dance was itself an unfolding of a mythological peace statement, so it wasn't about peace, was it? We went through what it takes to go through to find peace within ourselves, and then unite to send that peace out. And we did it in a peaceful way. So the whole thing is around peace, not for peace, or about peace, but experiencing peace.

JS: *What comes next? Do you already have plans for a new project, or are you still totally involved in the peace dance?*

AH: I'm right here now with the peace dance: understanding it more consciously—being open to it growing and developing in richer ways, and being available to go wherever we're called to take it. Hopefully I see the circle growing, growing, growing—that's what I'd like to see—how can we nurture this process. Let's just be open and available to see where it will take us.

Spring 1986

Touch Sanitation: Mierle Laderman Ukeles

By Robert C. Morgan

When New York-based art critic Robert C. Morgan wrote this article, Mierle Laderman Ukeles had already been exercising the feminist art/life principal for more than a dozen years. Her own pregnancy sparked her long-term examination of woman's traditional caretaker role, extrapolating to larger questions about art, work and survival. Here Morgan gets to the bottom of the work's form, content and context.   —Eds.

Take out the papers and the trash
Or you don't get no spending cash
If you don't scrub the kitchen floor
You ain't gonna rock and roll no more

from "Yakety Yak," words and music
by Jerry Leiber and Mike Stoller
© 1958 by Tiger Music, Inc.

In 1969, Mierle Laderman Ukeles wrote a manifesto entitled "Maintenance Art—Proposal for an Exhibition," which challenged the delegation of housework to women. In this seminal document of feminist art, Ukeles was attempting to demystify the image of the "housewife" as someone locked into an irretrievable system of dependency. Being pregnant at the time with her first child, she was feeling biological and psychological changes within her body, as well as confronting social and political changes within the society, which were in turn affecting her attitudes about art. In deciding to become a "maintenance artist"—and by announcing her intentions through the manifesto—Ukeles wanted to reinterpret the conventional housewife stereotypes, not in imagistic terms, but through a systemic style of creative action.

The chores that accompanied the raising of children became meaningful as she refused to define her domestic role as being any-

thing more than a neutral work-system. Thus, by rejecting the standard "housewife" ideal, Ukeles hoped to revive the idea of housework
as a functional endeavor—a ritualistic series of activities that maintain
the hygiene of the family unit. Thus, she intended to confront the
apprehension and anxiety of falling into a role and of being handed a
social image she abhorred. Rather than disavowing her existential
dilemma, Ukeles chose to "perform" housework as a maintenance system—a literal art of work existing in real time.

Having read the Freudian historian Norman 0. Brown some
years earlier, the artist was able to identify her struggle between
housewife and artist as resembling the familiar life-against-death conflict used in psychoanalysis. By accepting the reality of her situation as
a necessary role in maintaining the household, she discovered the
reality of maintenance as a means to the survival of personal freedom, art and all other social institutions. In other words, maintenance
art was a necessary part of the human condition. Through this
approach to the problem, Ukeles began to extend the references in
her work outside of a purely feminist content in order to reveal the
conditions of work, and the stereotypes handed to maintenance
workers on all levels, whether in public, private, or corporate enter-
prises. Her mode of "doing" art became a series of actions that
acknowledged the basic human operations that supported various
institutions and perpetuated the idea of culture. In the course of
redefining her own domestic role, she caught the meaning of art as
action, art as gesture, art as circumstance within an appointed system
or any designated structure.

Initially, Ukeles acknowledged the tasks of maintenance as a liberating idea, a context for her art that she identified as a feminist position. As this position extended from the household system to that of
public sanitation, the artist performed in museums and office buildings
and eventually in the streets of New York City. In *I Make Maintenance
Art One Hour Every Day* (1976), Ukeles shifted her emphasis from the
personal or individual scale to that of a large-scale system. For two
months, she worked as part of a sanitation bureaucracy, cleaning
floors and elevators in a lower-Manhattan office building along with
300 janitors and "cleaning women" during regular shifts. Her recent

large-scale performance, *Touch Sanitation,* completed June 1980, involved more than 8,500 workers in the New York City Department of Sanitation. The performance itself lasted for a duration of eleven months. Her intention was "to face and shake hands" with each one of the 8,500 sanitation works while saying the words: "Thank you for keeping New York City alive."

While not oblivious to the biases that various news media held against the Department, Ukeles believed that most of these negative feelings were the result of irrational fears people had about garbage. As a performance artist, she wanted to emphasize the basically human side of the operation, that the activity of picking up trash was essentially no different than the disposing of it; the process was, in fact, one cycle. By shaking hands with a sanitation worker, or "san-man," she was demystifying another stereotype. There is a necessary task to be done and a necessary separation to be made between the task and those who perform it. Maintenance is a shared concern; there is both a private and public aspect to the

In the course of redefining her own domestic role, she caught the meaning of art as action, art as gesture, art as circumstance within an appointed system or any designated structure.

work cycle. Waste products are not created by "garbage men," but by individuals who designate leftovers as trash. "Are we to assume," Ukeles has stated, "that those who dispose of trash—being all of us—are the 'garbage people'?"

In *Touch Sanitation,* the artist has shifted the focus of her actions outside the gallery space as an implicit ideology, a container for her work. This is a more radical shift from her previous 1976 performance in which the exhibition space of the downtown branch of the Whitney Museum was used in conjunction with the performance in the building. The museum, in this case, was simply part of the larger system, the social network of maintaining the premises, regardless of where the art happened to be shown. In *Touch Sanitation,* however, the gesture of the handshake evolved as an action independent of any immediate spectatorship among art-world clientele. Not only was such an action independent of the gallery or museum space, it was also independent of the theater. Its lack of domination by any traditional aesthetic category puts it on the fringes of a support system with which it could easily identify itself as art.

In keeping with the ecological concerns pronounced in the earlier "Maintenance Art" manifesto, *Touch Sanitation* raises several important questions: What occurs at the other end of the production line? What happens after the utility of the material has been exhausted? What happens to the scrap? The refuse? The dangerous gases and toxicants? The chronically harmful effects of radioactive wastes? More specifically, who takes care of the 22,000 tons of waste produced each day by the factories, businesses and residents of New York City? And what is the current social attitude that surrounds the sanitation worker who is hired to clean the sidewalks and maintain the mobility of the streets?

The fact that Ukeles has operated within a bureaucracy from the standpoint of "real time" places her work within the scope of conceptualism; yet, it might also be acknowledged as a kind of sociological street-theater. Although the artist is questioning the rational aesthetics of modernism, as well as the groundless decorativeness of postmodernism, the art-historical concerns are rather diminutive in contrast to the larger cultural issues being addressed in *Touch Sanitation*. Given the perspective of a simple action, Ukeles has performed a subtle transformation upon the psychology of doing an otherwise humdrum routine. Although such an action might not be interpreted as dramatic in a theatrical sense, the handshake carries a powerful feeling of mutual interest and support among workers. It comes to signify a sense of trust, an instillment of a feeling about the social nature of work. In joining forces with the san-men, Ukeles was able to unite her feminist concerns with the general nature of the work which they perform. Furthermore, san-men tend to believe—and rightly so—that a certain disparity exists between the reality of their work and the public image that is presented negatively through the news media. The gesture, presented by Ukeles, offered an alternative to some of the bad publicity.

Consequently, the repeated series of handshakes literally became a chain reaction, a human support structure.

The definition of "nontheatrical performance"—stated earlier by Allan Kaprow (*Artforum,* April, 1976)—characterized certain types of work as "performing" a task well. Such performances given by garage mechanics, telephone operators or surgeons do not require an audience or a persona in the sense of constantly reinforcing what these performers do. They exist in their own right without audience support. Often such performances are related to maintenance and therefore seem appropriate to the underlying intentions in *Touch Sanitation.* In performing a collection maneuver, for example, a sanitation worker may have a personal style of choreography in the way he operates off the truck. In *Touch Sanitation,* this operation is further emphasized as having artistic merit while, at the same time, it is reinforced by a handshake—"pressing flesh," as the jargon goes. During this exchange, the worker is invited to step outside the normal routine for a moment, to lose his anonymity as a worker on the streets, and to become a person. This may account for a minor transformation of demeanor and attitude in the worker's mind. Yet the action cannot be forced; the sense of ritual is understood for the moment. No further motive is necessary. Although union ideology is an ever-present issue, to impose a specific ideological connotation upon Ukeles' action would give it an unnecessarily romantic edge. It is not an expectation of the job; yet by choosing to participate in the exchange, the san-man reaffirms something of the individual that he is. The decision to be one's own authority, given the anesthetization of the routine, persists while upholding one's end of the truck team, and while taking orders from the foreman. The sanitation worker is a basic support unit that keeps the system going, and the authority to do so is ultimately his own. The handshake further acknowledges that human hands do the work, and without them the work would not get done.

To comprehend the scale of maintaining a city as complex as New York is difficult. For Ukeles, it was necessary to have some insight into the reality of the system before she inaugurated her performance on June 24, 1979. The proposition of shaking hands with 8,500 workers throughout each of the five boroughs was one thing as an idea, and something else as an actual experience. The challenge, in addition to "walking out" the various sanitation districts and shaking hands with san-men, was to maintain oneself. Her performance also consisted of beating fatigue and depression, fighting off illness, nausea, discomfort, toxic odors and body aches. At one point, bronchitis landed her in bed for two weeks.

It is within this social/work context, outside of the conventional art/gallery syndrome, that the handshake and the spoken phrase assume another important connotation. When photographed by the news media, the image of a handshake serves to remind the public sector that sanitation is a team effort, that each worker and each citizen is valuable to the entire system. The affirmative message given by such an image is generalized as a public model. Pragmatically, however, not everything about the job or within the job deserves recognition or even positive reinforcement. It is inevitable, for example, that some workers will take advantage of certain situations and ignore parts of their job. The power of the commercial news media to blow such incidents out of proportion was one of the serious contentions that Ukeles sought to address. In performing a gesture of support, she hoped to reveal the more favorable, though often ignored, attributes of the majority of workers employed by the Department.

Ukeles' performance of *Touch Sanitation* was primarily an attempt to exorcise the stereotypes affiliated with employees in the New York City Department of Sanitation. The notion that one who handles garbage works at the lower echelon of society was the stereotype Ukeles saw revealed time and again. Such a notion is possibly in evidence when a culture has not yet vanquished its puritanical work-ethic as a criterion for godliness. Garbage could be considered a metaphor as much as illness is. Thus, in advocating "the human part of the system," Mierle Laderman Ukeles has further extended the notion that feminism and maintenance are intertwined; to overcome the stereotype remains a challenge. She has further advocated that maintenance is the "underbelly system" of urban life and culture—a work-a-day system that keeps people alive and things functioning, whether on a public or domestic level.

Fall 1982

Two Lines of Sight and An Unexpected Connection: The Art of Helen Mayer Harrison and Newton Harrison

by Arlene Raven

The work of Helen Mayer Harrison and Newton Harrison con-sists of deceptively simple solutions to complex ecological prob-lems. Their process is embedded in layers of discourse, poetry, sci-ence, politics and passionate concern for human life. Here art his-torian Arlene Raven, a long-time contributing editor to High Per-formance, *delves into the collective mind of the Harrisons, one layer at a time.   —Eds.*

What is art in the environment supposed to be or do? Can such art just sit there, surrounded by nature? Or hang in galleries in the art environment and simply refer to ecological issues? Does envi-ronmental art have to be ecological? If so, what—in practical terms—does that mean? By what standards should it be said to have accom-plished or not accomplished its purpose? And by whom? Art critics, environmentalists, scientists, or the public?

Helen Mayer Harrison and Newton Harrison make no claims to answer these questions, to fit into any established categories of art and environment, or to fulfill any standards but their own. They insist that their work, at its core, shifts fundamental designs in human per-ception and calls an observer to participate in recreating a dynamic, healing balance between nature and people. The Harrisons are artists who rediscover and recreate physical, social, philosophical and mythic environments—with artistry, originality, and with exemplary integrity

I.

Helen Mayer Harrison and Newton Harrison began a conversa-tion in 1970. After 18 years, their discourse continues uninterrupted. Mutual thinking, the basis for all of their collaborations, contextualizes works to such an extent that they titled a recent interview about new projects, "Nobody Told Us When to Stop Thinking." They embark "…when we perceive an anomaly in the environment that is the result of opposing beliefs or contradictory metaphors," they said recently in an artists' statement. "It is the moment when belief has become outrageous that offers opportunity to create new spaces, first for the mind and thereafter in everyday… always compose[d] with left-over spaces and invisible places."[1]

II.

"We did a work for an exhibition called Land Art…at Bard College…we took a look at the coffee pot," they told me in an interview in 1987.

> You know, we like good coffee. The inside was so encrusted with salts from the drinking water that the pot was inlaid with gray-green whitish crud. So we developed a work about cleaning water. A still was made which would be situated right there in the gallery. Ironically, the only place on campus where you could get pure water would then be in the art gallery.[2]

The Socratic dialogue that distinguishes the Harrison relationship appears as myth and metaphor in their work *The Lagoon Cycle*, created over a period of twelve years, opened at the Los Angeles County Museum of Art on November 18, 1987. It is a poetic meditation of asking questions, and mulling over these questions together as "Lagoonmaker" and "Witness." As Carter Ratcliff observed,

> One meets the Witness and the Lagoonmaker in the introductory panel of the Cycle. That is the first of numberless occasions for wondering to what degree the Witness is Helen Mayer Harrison and the Lagoonmaker is Newton Harrison.… From the start the Lagoonmaker and the Witness treat large questions of creation and self-creation, will, and belief and action.… The Witness and the Lagoonmaker have learned to improvise. As they create the Lagoons through which they travel, they accept the "discourse of lagoon life" as a metaphorical guide. Or at least they struggle toward that acceptance. If our culture undertakes the same struggle and accepts the same guide, perhaps we'll find ways to adapt even to

ecological disaster. Our adaptation may even be, in the Harrisons' word, "graceful."[3]

But the relationship of Harrison to Harrison is also a concrete comradeship within a marriage that has endured 35 years. Domestic, everyday. And an intriguing aspect of the two personas of *The Lagoon Cycle* is their clarifying fidelity to aspects of male and female, nature and culture. They weave their colloquy to reconnect these personas and thus initiate a healing that stands against the antagonism of mechanistic culture for unruly nature. As metaphor and example, their collaboration also reconsiders the plunder of world ecology and the fissure between men and women. Their eco-feminism and eco-aesthetics spring from this point of departure.

III.

In light of their unusual approach to artmaking on the one hand, and their commitment to artistic identity on the other, the Harrisons' view of the function of art in contemporary society is complex. For Helen, "The structure underlying our work is different because the assumptions underlying our work are more complicated."[4]

Referring to an historical example, Newton reasoned that "if you go to look at the Parthenon, you see a truly astounding work of art. But those artists were totally at the service of the culture's imperialistic impulses. If I took the Parthenon as a model, I'd say it was the job of the art to glorify that culture."

"Conversely," Helen adds,

earlier art was probably at the service of religious cults or impulses, although we can only theorize what such impulses might be that could lead to such diverse expressions in time and space as fecundity figures like the Venus of Willendorf or delicately carved miniatures like the head of Our Lady of Brassempouy or the Bull and Vulture figures of Catal Hayuk or the covered skull from Jericho with its inlaid cowry shell eyes.

Commenting on modernism, Newton said,

Art, like all aspects of modernism, is fractured, bifurcated and re-bifurcated, in little bits and pieces. We have decorative art, deconstructionists,

Duchamp leftovers. Various forms of realism, conceptualism. Our work is influenced by all of them. In truth, we go back to the story of the place's becoming and if we can be part of that story, enhance it. I don't know or care if that is "far out."

In contrast to the current emphasis on product, he explained that,

I don't think about our art as product at all. As a guiding thought, "product" is counter-productive. Every once in a while we will make an array of images. We hope people buy them. But generally we make installations which stand for the place and as meeting ground for discourse, which are models for how to perceive and enact our work. We pack our 'products' in boxes and tubes and hope some day somebody will put them up somewhere. But the most important parts of our work are non-products. In the reshaping of a place, our work exists in bits and pieces of the planning process of the place. In a gallery, those parts are attributed to us. But when enacted in the real environment, we become anonymous. We are both bigger than our plan, and more anonymous.

Helen Harrison underlined that, in contrast to city planners, the two had no vested interest in, nor any sense that they must choose between, loyalty to either art or the environment. "One of the things that happens to people, even the best of the planners, is that they have a vested interest in getting something done."[5]

Rather, the question of conflict "comes up when money is made available," said Newton. "We will take that project over a little better project which is unfunded. And that's the only conflict—when someone else is trying to modify our participation."

The Harrisons have been compared and contrasted in almost every interpretation of their work to earth artists, survivalist artists, conceptual and performance artists, and even the Hudson River School of landscape painters active in the 19th century and earlier 20th century social realists. Musing about Michael Heizer, Helen admired "the vast energy put into those early big cuts and shapes in the desert that are inherently gestural, simply primary structures in another context. They are transactional with museum spaces not with the earth. They are involved primarily with forms."

In "Earth Art: A Study in Ecological Politics" (*Art in the Land: A Critical Anthology of Environmental Art* edited by Alan Sonfist), Michael Auping says of Heizer: "Heizer has often argued that it is naive to criticize his work from an ecological standpoint, given the fact that modern industry is rearranging the landscape on a scale that dwarfs any of his endeavors."

Quipped Newton: "No art is as intrusive as a freeway intersection. I'd love to see Heizer take up 10% of Los Angeles. I'd vote for him."

"Christo's contribution was to re-define how big you can get," added Helen. "His Running Fence didn't do more to the environment than a picnic. The ecological balance can readily restate itself. James Turrell makes a very small move, not taking your now for granted. That's economy of means at a very high level."

IV.

The Harrisons have a new idea for San Diego, where they live and work. *Cruciform Tunnel*, now in the proposal stage, would extend under Genesee Drive, rejoin two nature reserves (the Torrey Pines Reserve and the UCSD nature reserve), the Penasquitos Lagoon and the Pacific Ocean. Water from the UC San Diego campus would now be channeled to the Penasquitos Lagoon. And a new bicycle path from their campus at UCSD to Sorrento Valley would be created.

Cruciform Tunnel is, indisputably, "ecological art"—art concerned with (improving) the environment. But the Harrisons are not primarily motivated by the need for a bicycle path or even increasing the overall ecological value of the site for *Cruciform Tunnel*. Nor are they mainly concerned with the aesthetics of the tunnel or the resulting beauty of the landscape, though these might be desirable and even necessary results of their work. Rather: "We go to a place—anywhere!—and engage in the story of the place. We make a representation of the story, of its own becoming. We add our story to it. Our work is, as best we can make it, the poetry of the whole."

Newton Harrison's explanation of concerns is headily abstract, and poetic itself. Yet the Harrisons' works have practical applications, require careful research, and have often had a measurable impact on their sites. How do their concerns differentiate their works from standard ecological research? Newton responded:

> When did standard ecological research begin with a medical metaphor, turn itself into poetry, turn back into a proposal, shift into a performance, and then begin a process of nagging a city council? Standard ecological researchers made a series of experiments with the canyons of San Diego. We then did a work based on this research, and proposed *Cruciform Tunnel*. A lot of our work depends on illuminating ecological research by others, which sits in limbo, in an untransformed state.

V.

   Newton said:

> We have also done standard ecological research. For the second lagoon [*Sea Grants*, for which an artificial environment for crabs was constructed], we did environmental and habitat studies, as well as observed and concluded through observation that cannibalism [in crabs] reduces itself when the environment is complicated.

> Our 1973 *Sea Grant* crabs laid out experimental grounds [for the development of a commercial aquaculture system for the crab]. Our method is available and can be used. We believe in theoretical research. Although our work points in theoretical directions we haven't engaged in theoretical research,

> *But*
> *the tank is part of an experiment*
> *and the experiment is a metaphor for a lagoon*
> *if the metaphor works*
> *the experiment will succeed*
> *and the crabs will flourish*
> *after all*
> *this metaphor is only a representation*
> *based on observing a crab in a lagoon*
> *and listening to stones.*[6]

However, when it becomes necessary to do original research, we can and have. Nonetheless there is a big difference between original research and a work of art and our focus is on the work of art. But we define art broadly.

VI.

The fluidity of professional roles and tasks with which the artists are able to move through researching, planning, proposing and carrying out their projects in their own minds has very often become problematic when the process of their work is thrust into the nuts-and-bolts world of sponsors, agencies, sites and workers. When the Harrisons attempted to make earth and plant a meadow on top of 40 acres of rock pile—in their words "a physical act of reclamation" called *Spoils Pile* and planned for the old refilled canyon quarry that was Artpark—they were forced by Artpark authorities to stop after 20 acres were covered with soil, ostensibly due to the (too large) scope of their project.

Meditations on the Sacramento River, the Delta and the Bays at San Francisco (1977) was based on the same principle of reclamation. Said Newton: "We made a work projected to impact the level of public awareness."

"Our work was an extended argument in many media," added Helen, "from billboards to posters to radio and newspaper spots, to a museum mural. Heads of environmental agencies later quoted our own words in the newspapers without crediting us."

In 1982, they created *Thinking About the Mangrove and the Pine* (their working title for *Barrier Islands Drama*), a site-specific work for the John and Mable Ringling Museum in Sarasota, Florida. They considered the pines that were brought in from Australia to Florida and used for decorative reasons. The pines had knocked off the native ecology, and taken up mangrove root and sun space. As the mangroves disappeared the pines took over water's edge. To quote from the text:

Take Longboat Key, for instance
Where

That pushy shallowrooted immigrant
That exotic and graceful pine from Australia
Colonizes behind that manyrooted earthholding mangrove
Colonizes behind that oceanic nursery of mangrove roots
When
Displacing the mangrove
Gaining water's edge
It topples in the wind.[7]

How can their voices be consistently aligned with their values when they are not in complete control of the process by which their projects are realized? In fact, they cannot. Also, as Helen noted, "We cannot really know the consequences of our actions. That is why we really need environmental impact studies, even on creativity."

VII.

The Harrisons' art participates in the "New Age" and in its optimistic belief that transformation of the environment and human consciousness is necessary and possible.[8] With eco-feminists and environmentalists, they reexamine the European scientific revolution and simultaneous rise of our modern market culture. But while utilizing contemporary technology, they question the model of the cosmos as machine rather than as organism, a (machine) model that has for centuries sanctioned, de facto, domination over nature and women. The existence of their work calls for the contributions of the "fathers" of modern science—Francis Bacon, William Harvey, Rene Descartes, Thomas Hobbes and Isaac Newton—to be reevaluated in light of the mechanistic roots of their modernism. Most important, the Harrisons' work both presents and suggests alternative organismic paradigms that must temper the catastrophic contemporary consequences of the long-running machine age if humans and nature are to survive and thrive.[9]

VIII.

Their particular blend of aesthetics and politics evolved from their working process and their focus on conceptual, artistic, and ethical issues. "An aesthetic" they've said, "exists always in interaction with, and in commentary on, a larger social context…to isolate an aesthetic and attempt to make it unrelated to other things is impossible."[10]

With their connections between their aesthetics and the social context for producing art in mind, it seems natural that they would name as imperialist and unjust the disruption of social intercourse and physical movement as artistic "problems" to be confronted. Their propensity for making and altering maps—appropriately enough, a preoccupation of visual artists during the Renaissance—can also be traced to their aesthetics, from which originates the impulse to restore the relationship between the physical ground and the physical humans inhabiting that ground. They want to create actions that not only stand beside but work to undo the domination and manipulation of nature in the service of man-made hierarchical systems.

The environments for their environmental art are, therefore, the human and societal environments, in a dialogue with physical environments. The Harrisons are never motivated by a sentimental love of trees or animals or unspoiled rivers but of justice, balance, good sense and people. When addressing problems of city planning in San Jose, Atlanta or Baltimore, they observe when basic human activities—in these cases, walking—have been disrupted because urban planning served other needs. They unearth the cultural values embedded in systems of domination that make "other needs" priorities, rather than simply battle in the realm of politics and law.

In the service of their central concern—reestablishing discourse—they proposed a promenade for Baltimore based on their conviction, put forth in their statement for the project, that

> a promenade is both an activity and a place, a stage on which people in a community meet and mix.… A promenade is marked by people physically tuning to common movement and rhythm. A promenade is an activity common in all urban ecologies, a basic homeostatic or self-regulating mechanism by which the community as a whole maintains awareness of the well-being of the individuals who comprise it, and by which the sense of community is reaffirmed collectively.[11]

The city's Baltimore Harbor project was already established when the Harrisons took up their analysis. They proposed connecting the Harbor Project to the city's cultural center in one direction, and to a park, which already existed, in the other. As Susan Platt put it,

> They visualized this connection by simply pointing out that, by means of two 20-minute promenades, people could move out of the self-contained nucleus of the harbor, surrounded by its eight-lane noose of highways, to the surrounding city. All that the artists suggested was a walk that made use of the city as it already existed—they simply drew a line on a map to mark the walk. The total cost to the city was that of moving one bridge and adding a stoplight, and the result was "Baltimore Promenade/a concept for making Baltimore walkable (again)/a proposal inviting involvement and action…."[12]

And, as Helen Harrison says, "The ideas about redevelopment that we had went into the city plan and are occurring in city time—that is in scores of years—but they are happening."

IX.

If one accepts (and I do) the fully artistic and fully ecological nature of the art of Helen Mayer Harrison and Newton Harrison, then they are legitimately creative resources for identifying the most pressing environmental concerns and suggesting the opening phrases of our communion with our Earthly surroundings. "We have focused a fair amount on water," they said.

> Water is a very critical bio-indicator. If water remains pure, and rivers are maintained, then many other good things happen. Pollution into oceans can be reduced, for instance. One can just as well spend time on trees. Or the stork, as we did in Kassel [Germany, for Documenta 8, 1987].

> We're really not messianic. We're just two people putting one foot in front of the other, asking for reasonably ethical behavior. We've empowered *ourselves* through our work. And our greatest concern is establishing models wherein *anybody* can start *anywhere* and radiate out change and transformation by engaging the discourse. The most important thing is to begin anywhere, and get cracking.

Notes

1. Statement, Helen Mayer Harrison and Newton Harrison: New Projects, March 17-April 18, 1987 (New York: Grey Art Gallery), reprinted in "Nobody Told Us When To Stop Thinking," *Grey Matters: The Quarterly Bulletin of The Grey Art Gallery and Study Center*, (New York: New York University) Vol. 1, No. 2 (Spring, 1987).

2. Helen and Newton Harrison, interview with Arlene Raven, October, 1987. Quotations unless otherwise cited are from this interview.

3. Carter Ratcliff, "A Compendium of Possibilities," *The Lagoon Cycle*, (Ithaca: Herbert F. Johnson Museum of Art), 1985, p. 13.

4. Helen Harrison, *Grey Matters.*

5. Helen Harrison, *Grey Matters.*

6. Text from *The Lagoon Cycle* by Helen and Newton Harrison.

7. Text from *Barrier Islands Drama* by Helen and Newton Harrison.

8. See Linda McGreevy, "Improvising the Future: The Eco-aesthetics of Newton and Helen Harrison," *Arts*, Vol. 62, No. 3, November, 1987, p. 68, for a discussion of "New Age" philosophies and the therapeutic aspect of the Harrisons' work.

9. See Carolyn Merchant, *The Death of Nature: Women, Ecology, and the Scientific Revolution*, (San Francisco and New York: Harper and Row), 1980.

10. Newton Harrison, interview with Michael Auping, in *Common Ground: Five Artists in the Florida Landscape*. (Sarasota: The John and Mable Ringling Museum of Art), 1982.

11. Helen and Newton Harrison, from their statement about Baltimore Promenade.

12. Susan Platt, "Helen Mayer Harrison and Newton Harrison: An Urban Discourse," *Artweek*, Vol. 14, No. 20, May 21, 1983, p. 1.

Winter 1987

The Streets: Where Do They Reach?

By Guillermo Gómez-Peña

Street performance may be the oldest form of cultural expression. It has existed in every culture in recorded time. Here Mexican performance artist Guillermo Gómez-Peña, in a excerpt from an article about performance art in Mexico City, looks at the theater of the street in the biggest city in the world, in a time of severe economic crisis. Art and life collide for survival, the creation of new languages, catharsis, social change and public expression.
—Eds.

Mexico City has been the cultural mecca for Spanish-speaking countries since the 1950s, operating as the meeting place for the Latino and Spanish intelligentsia. It seems contradictory that such a culturally dynamic place should present such a nightmare of daily existence. The nature and scale of its urban problems border on science fiction. Mexico City leads the world in, among others, demographic growth (one million people per year), smog (it has far surpassed the level of tolerance), unemployment (over 40%) and traffic jams (in the rainy season, they last more than six hours).

Despite these apocalyptic circumstances, art is livelier than ever. It is omnipresent in the mass media (artists and writers appear daily on TV and radio), in the streets and in the hundreds of active cultural institutions throughout the city. Here, art and crisis live hand-in-hand, and artists use the contradictions of urban life as material for their work.

At the same time, the economic breakdown that the country is currently experiencing, with a 90-billion-dollar national debt plus exorbitant inflation, is definitely affecting the arts. Federal funding has been cut, and the little available is distributed only among the most recognized. Sophisticated equipment, except for that of certain museums and universities, is not available for independent projects. This forces the artist to exercise resourcefulness, to recycle, to borrow, to invent, to substitute, to trade and to depend more and more on one another. In this process of bustling, new languages are found and artists' networks are developed. Performance artist Marcela Ortiz de Zarate comments: "Now in Mexico, there is a very strong solidarity among young artists. We are helping each other as the only means to survive." Basic survival, in the context of "*la crisis*," paradoxically favors the creation of a more audacious non-objective art, outside of the virtually paralyzed art market.

Merolicos, Carpas and Naïve Performance Artists

Mexico is an extremely theatrical country, and Mexico City is its most effervescent example. The contradictions of its cultural, social and political life have always found a "free stage" in the streets for extravagant events that resemble performance art. Though not motivated by conscious artistic forces, these street events are extremely elaborate, truly interdisciplinary and show a deep understanding of dramatic devices.

Walking along the Alameda Park on a Sunday morning or cruising the Pink Zone (the arty quarter) in Chapultepec Forest or at a crowded metro station, one encounters an incredible variety of *merolicos*. These naïve but extremely effective guerrilla actors measure the pulse of the city. Their style is farcical and exaggerated. Their pieces are filled with "magical realism" and outrageous cultural contradictions. Their speeches are automatic texts that mix political, religious, social and sexual information, and that play off the people's taboos, fantasies and frustrations. Their costumes are shocking: shabby tuxedos, tribal make-up and cardboard masks. Their gimmicks are foolproof. One embarrasses a "gentleman" from the crowd with genital jokes, while his son (a miniature clone of himself) walks around stealing wallets or selling aphrodisiacs. Another one promises to show "the pre-Columbian beast" (a creature convulsing inside a bag) if the audience gives him enough money and applause. His detailed description of "the beast" takes almost an hour. When the impatient crowd is just about to lynch the *merolico,* he literally disappears. Other street performers use animals (monkeys, armadillos, snakes, tropical birds) to attract attention, as they deliver endless speeches about the apocalypse of Mexico City, blaming it on priests, congressmen, television heroes or millionaires.

Freak shows are common in the barrio during *fiesta* days. Frederico Fellini and George Cukor would love these mini-extravaganzas. Outside a 30-year-old school bus covered with motifs from popular mythology (anthropomorphic animals juxtaposed with media slogans), a *merolico* invites the audience to witness "the amazing iguana woman, daughter of a Seri Indian and a reptile." Inside the bus, 20 people crowd under a bright red light. The *animateur* opens a curtain, revealing the head of a beautiful mulatta with a pulsing iguana body, inside an aquarium. The image is completely realistic. The "iguana woman" tells her story, spicing it with elements of the Indian, Spanish and North American pop cultures. *Cumbia* music plays at the wrong speed on an old-fashioned turntable while she dances. People are inevitably touched by this shamanistic vision that shatters their sense of the commonplace and reminds them of other realities. This and other freak shows—a frog-kid, a gigantic rat, a *chaneque* (elf), a winged old man and a bearded woman who claims to be the *primogenita* (first daughter) of a Catholic priest—function as ten-minute protohistorical dreams, a sort of instant catharsis within the incommensurable urban pathos of Mexico City.

A more elaborate form of street performance is the 300-year-old tradition of living theater called *carpa*. In a vacant lot, a plaza, or the middle of the street, performers erect a huge circus tent, while someone screams through a megaphone the magical word: "*carpa!*" Word of mouth brings the entire neighborhood. The emcee, an awkwardly gallant character—half Cantinflas and half Valentino—wearing an absurdly large pachuco jacket, announces the coming repertoire. Most of these supposedly world-renowned performers have surreal names like "Telma from Tahiti and her Portorrican gorilla" or "The Patagonian Brujo." One by one, the audience is confronted with these masters of verbal improvisation, imperfect but expressive mimes, *albureros* (dirty talkers) and, above all, first class *provocateurs*. Their monologues are confrontational, vulgar and filled with anarchist subtext. Their main targets are Catholic puritanism and corrupt politicians. They laugh at themselves, at death, poverty and military abuse. The *carperos* love to offend their audience, who always answer back and sometimes even jump on stage. Everyone laughs, releasing their existential demons. A two-bit tropical trio or an "invisible orchestra" accompanies this strange celebration of life on the edge. It is raw theater at its best, art in its primeval force, a ritual of love, impotence, resentment and renewal. People walk out ready to face the world again.

Carpa has been the main school for Mexican comedians. Such film legends as Cantinflas, Resortes and Clavillazo were once *carpa* animateurs. Here even the most sophisticated artforms—experimental theater, independent cinema, mural painting and more recently performance art—have been influenced by this microcosm of human idiosyncrasies. It is sad to have to state that *carpa* is slowly sinking into oblivion.

Another Way of Singing the Lottery

Ricardo Anguía has consciously adopted Mexico's folk theater traditions and taken them one step further. Once a painter, now an installation/performance artist, Anguía constructs *espacios lúdicos* that resemble the wagons of the freak shows. His installations are decorated with popular sayings, trucker's slogans and *pulquería* graphics. Here, the raw traditions of the *merolico* and the *carpa* are deconstructed and recycled into new models. The icons of urban mythology are twisted to give place to a new set of mythical beings that comment on politics and culture. The "frog-kid found in mental lagoons," the snake-woman, *El Goloso de Rorras* (a *barrio* Casanova) interact with contemporary political figures such as the president, López Portillo.

> **The art audience was enlarged to include the general public, and the streets became the creative context.**

Anguía's performances often incorporate a version of the traditional *lotería,* recontextualizing and transforming its images into threatening icons: the suicide, the hungry, the politician-thief, *el aviador* (the bureaucrat), among others, become caustic illustrations of city pathos. When the game is over, he gives the winner samples of his own art work.

"Los Grupos"

Like Paris and Berkeley, Mexico City in 1968 was the scene of student riots that were brutally repressed by the para-police. This conflict profoundly transformed the attitudes of Mexican artists. The students of the art schools and the UNAM (National University) began to make art within and about *el movimento esudiantil*. Their objective was to distribute information in rapid and effective ways. To express their political beliefs they used banners, *mantos* (painted fabric), mail art, mimeographic prints, impromptu murals and spectacular demonstrations incorporating avant-garde theater. The city boiled with public art activities.

The movement generated a freer use of media, artistic materials and languages. Such criteria as availability, immediacy and effectiveness determined the medium. The art audience was enlarged to include the general public, and the streets became the creative context.

This new attitude toward art and society persisted throughout the '70s. Perhaps the most significant artistic phenomenon of that decade was the creation of "*los grupos*"—independent associations of artists working with different media but similar goals. Photographers, performers, book artists, poets, sculptors, muralists, installation artists and filmmakers gathered under the premise of collective/interdisciplinary work to explore sociocultural issues. The most influential groups were *Proceso Pentagono, Suma, Peyote y La Compañía, Mira, No-Grupo and Tepito Arte-Aca.*

The tradition of the groups is still alive in Mexico City. Some have eclipsed, and others, with new concerns, have emerged. *Grupo Sin Nombre* (nameless group) is a collective of twelve sculptors/performers whose main concern is "to utilize sculpture, not as a decorative element, but as part of a space." For them, the art work is only a tool to provide the spectator with the means to react and interact.

At their *Casa Del Lagá Ambient Ambivalente* installation, I attended one of GSN's participational performances entitled *Lara, Manzanero, Beethoven*. The audience of workers, artists, families and students was led into a completely dark labyrinth of wire and told to remain still. Soon, we realized we had to exercise our will, to disobey and explore. I began to walk through the overcrowded structure. In one corner, I was staring at a neon outline of popular composer Austin Lara, when suddenly a '50s *cabatera* grabbed me to dance a bolero. In another part of the labyrinth, a chanteuse was wrapping people with colored ribbons to the prerecorded music of Armado Manzanero. In the opposite corner from Lara, a bust of Beethoven was illuminated intermittently, while the Fifth Symphony faded in and out.

Placed in this dark, confined and unfamiliar environment, we were forced to establish tactile and verbal relationships with each other. At the end, searchlights accompanied by an ominous sound-track of war planes abruptly changed the tone of the event, reminding us of political realities. When the lights came up, we all felt a strange sense of sympathy for one another.

María Guerra's *La Dirección* is composed of two painters, one photographer, one art critic, one musician and María herself, a per-former and video artist trained in a Chicago art school. The group lives downtown, where it is part of an emerging punk scene. "We like to perform in the *zocalo* for the unemployed. We often have con-frontations with the authorities," María explains. *La Dirección* gained notoriety three years ago when they planted 1,000 crosses along a strip during the Day of the Dead celebration.

The Museums

In the last few years, Mexico City's art museums have become "living spaces" involved in interdisciplinary programming. Helen Escobedo exemplifies this new mentality. As an artist, she is responsi-ble for a solid body of work that encompasses small and monumental sculpture, "total environments" and architectural projects. She and oth-ers are also responsible for the conception of *Espacio Escultórico*, the amazing multipurpose neo-pre-Columbian architectural site that has been the setting of many significant performance pieces (Stelarc per-formed there). When she served as director of the Museum of Mod-ern Art (MAM), Escobedo never missed an opportunity to demystify her own space.

Perhaps the most outrageous event that the museum has ever produced was *La Calle ¿A donde llega?* (*The Streets. Where do they reach?).* Escobedo invited French art sociologist Hervé Fischer to transform the museum into an extension of the streets. Here, people could speak loudly, scream, sit around and laugh, and even create. Materials were available for anyone to paint and write on the walls. Under Fischer's premise, "We all are creative, we all are artists," MAM became the site for two months of a wild celebration of art and life. Dozens of theater, dance and music groups performed with the public. Some grupos created participatory environments where people voiced their opinions on the show, the government, ecology, public transport and world issues. The goal was clearly to make the participant understand that the museums, like the streets, can be public arenas for expression, and MAM was able to see itself reflected in a multiple mirror.

Winter 1992

The Artist as Activist

Ideologies can usually be found at the crux of activist art—both ideologies that artists hold dear and ideologies that artists seek to change—so an awareness of the construction of ideology can be essential to the activist artist's work. We begin our section on the artist as activist with Adrian Piper's 1981 essay "Ideology, Confrontation and Political Self-Awareness," in which she puts forward an understanding of how ideologies are developed and maintained, and how the activist artist can recognize and address them. Piper's conceptual performance work of the '70s included street performance focused on the interchange between the "self" and the "other," in which she appeared in public with her clothes smeared with food, paint and bubble gum, or carried tape-recorded burps with her to the library. There were also stage performances confronting audiences with their own roles as manipulated spectators. The essay operates as theory, rooted in Piper's background in philosophy and her interest in human behavior, and, as we discover toward the end, it is also an essay-as-artwork that practices her aesthetic as a politically aware conceptual artist.

In California, Latino artists were among the first to come to activist art. Latino politics was a growing presence in the state throughout the '80s, and many artists cut their teeth on activism in collaboration with the United Farm Workers. Our interview with playwright Luis Valdez traces the rise and influence of El Teatro Campesino, from its birth in the fields of the San Joaquin Valley to opening night on Broadway. Emily Hicks, in an article from our 1986 *"Nuevo Latino"* issue, profiles four extremely influential artists working in southern California, Mexico and the border region in between: border animateur Guillermo Gómez-Peña, community muralist Judith Baca, guerrilla organizer Felipe Ehrenberg and Chicano activist David Avalos. Hicks details the activist-art strategies of these binational postmodernists to change their culture and broaden the definition of "artist."

In the mid-'80s, the domestic and foreign policies of the current U.S. administration caused artists to rise to activism in rapidly increasing numbers. In 1984, we published a special section of *High Perfor-*

mance called "Artists & Issues," featuring articles about the New York movement "Artists Call" and its focus on U.S. Intervention in Central America; Venezuelan artist Rolando Peña and his work about oil politics; Vietnam veteran Kim Jones' street performances as Mudman, an image about the experience of war; and a tour of Northern Ireland and artists' attitudes about the conflict there. Nancy Buchanan had just returned from a tour of Nicaragua, and here we excerpt our interview with her about how the trip would impact her work.

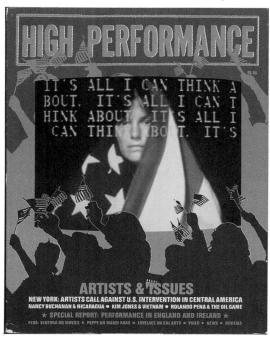

Contragate was dominating the news when Robbie Conal began blanketing the cities of the U.S. with his political posters. These satirical portraits of celebrities and political figures, underscored with one-liners, became interactive artworks, with comments and additional art adorning them everywhere in no time. Here Conal talks about his motives in the one-man postering campaign, and his excitement in getting people to think about people in power.

High Performance was the first art magazine we know of to devote an issue to AIDS. Among our writers was Max Navarre, a New York playwright (now deceased) whose "Art in the AIDies: An Act of Faith" brought up issues that still resonate more than ten years later: What is the artist's best response in a time of personal, cultural and planetary crisis? Is art an appropriate tool for education, for grieving, for healing? What are we willing to look at on stage?

Five years after our 1986 AIDS issue, ACT UP (AIDS Coalition to Unleash Power) had come out full force in support of more research and funding for AIDS. During that same period computer technology proliferated and became much more accessible to artists and to everyone. It was only a matter of time before the artists in ACT UP starting using the new technologies to attract attention to their cause. Lucy Lippard wrote for us about Michael Nash, an artist member of ACT UP Denver, who used billboards and a computer disk to open up issues he thought the country ought to be discussing related to the epidemic.

Artists were using many different forms to register protest in the '80s. The Korean-American artists of Theatre 1981 added a new element when they created a shamanic theater of protest against the massacres of students in Korea, and the use of mass violence against peoples everywhere. Our interview with them reveals that images of protest can vary widely from culture to culture. It also has some unexpected things to teach us about the nature of shamanism, so popular among artists of the west-coast U.S.

By the end of the decade artists' concerns were becoming intensely culturally specific. We were going out of our way to learn a great deal about each other. Pearl Cleage's "No Time for the Blues (Aesthetic)" appeared in our "Blues Aesthetic" issue of 1990. The idea for the issue arose from "The Blues Aesthetic: Black Culture and Modernism," the title of a show at Washington Project for the Arts in Washington, D.C. Guest-edited by Los Angeles-based artists Keith Antar Mason and Wanda Coleman, our issue included articles, comments and artwork by African-American artists examining the blues not just as music, but as painting, photography, fiction, politics, social condition and cultural force.

1992, for many artists and their communities, was a year of infamy: the 500th anniversary of the year Columbus "discovered" America. The discovery was being celebrated across the country, but not by everyone. We published a number of accounts of the artists' response: protests and demands for a recognition of the real history of our hemisphere, in all its shame and ancient glory. Many institutions who wanted to comment on the issue did so by involving American Indian artists, in a special brand of "outreach." In our interview here with California performance artist James Luna, "Call Me in '93," Luna echoes the frequent complaint by minority artists that they are kept on a special ethnic shelf in art history, and only brought out during Cinco de Mayo, Black History Month, Hiroshima Day and other ethnically appropriate times, instead of being treated like artists at all times. In Luna's interview, he responds to his distorted popularity during the Columbus anniversary year as a spokesperson for American Indians.

As artists became more and more vocal, and more effective in their activist art strategies, the power structure began to take notice, and take action. Soon the so-called Culture Wars were raging in earnest, with artists and artspaces being attacked by right-wing politicians for blasphemy, desecration of religious symbols, insult to family values and promotion of homosexuality.

The attack on the work of Andres Serrano was one of the first shots across the bow. In *High Performance* Coco Fusco interviewed him about the death threats, loss of funding and notoriety he was experiencing—and what brought him to photograph members of the Ku Klux Klan. Serrano was a reluctant soldier in the Culture Wars. By his own admission, there was no activist intent to his work, and taken at his word he is an unusual inclusion in this anthology. Yet the public reaction to his work by the public made him a symbol in the "freedom of expression" debates, and his reflections on the impact of that phenomenon are useful in the examination of the mixture of art and politics.

Performance artist Karen Finley was another artist who received the wrath of the right. One of four artists whose NEA grants were rescinded for what appeared to be political reasons, Finley stood out in her ferocity and contempt for the games politicians play. A regular in the pages of *High Performance* since its early issues, Finley has for 20 years been confronting audiences with the taboos of our culture. Ironically, the provocative nature of her work has often made Finley herself taboo as a performer. Her unwillingness to compromise her material has excluded her from all but the bravest late-night clubs and alternative spaces, and yet her reputation stretches far beyond those who have seen her in person. Media reports of vile language, nudity and orifices filled with foodstuffs have led some to assume her work exists for its shock value. But this is not exhibitionism, this is anger. Voyeurs who like to see women humiliated could find safer places to indulge their prurient interests. This performance isn't done for them, it's done at them—with a vengeance. Karen Finley is an archetypal example of the artist as warrior.

The Culture Wars did more damage than expected. When the dust began to settle, artists found themselves isolated from and unsupported by their culture. The climate for art in America was chilly. Many artists began addressing this gap of understanding by turning to their own communities to try to rekindle the fires of creativity. They joined a small cadre of artists who had been doing that job, in communities everywhere, all along…

Ideology, Confrontation
and Political Self-Awareness

By Adrian Piper

Adrian Piper is a conceptual artist with a background in sculpture and philosophy. Her performance work and writing during this period asked the observer to consider the construction of his/her own beliefs and their relation to action in the world. Art historian Moira Roth has written that Piper's work of this period "deals with confrontations of self to self and self to others, exposing the distances between people and the alienation that exists in our lives—personally, politically, emotionally." Here she puts forth some basic considerations about ideology.   —Eds.

We started out with beliefs about the world and our place in it that we didn't ask for and didn't question. Only later, when those beliefs were attacked by new experiences that didn't conform to them, did we begin to doubt: e.g., do we and our friends really understand each other? Do we really have nothing in common with blacks/whites/gays/workers/the middle class/other women/other men/etc.?

Doubt entails self-examination because a check on the plausibility of your beliefs and attitudes is a check on all the constituents of the self. Explanations of why your falsely supposed "X" includes your *motives* for believing "X" (your desire to maintain a relationship, your impulse to be charitable, your goal of becoming a better person); the causes of your believing "X" (your early training, your having drunk too much, your innate disposition to optimism); and your *objective reasons* for believing "X" (it's consistent with your other beliefs, it explains the most data, it's inductively confirmed, people you respect believe it). These reveal the traits and dispositions that individuate one self from another.

So self-examination entails self-awareness, i.e., awareness of the components of the self. But self-awareness is largely a matter of degree. If you've only had a few discordant experiences, or relatively superficial discordant experiences, you don't need to examine yourself very deeply in order to revise your false beliefs. For instance, you happen to have met a considerate, sensitive, nonexploitative person who's into sadism in bed. You think to yourself, "This doesn't show that my beliefs about sadists in general are wrong; after all, think what Krafft-Ebing says! This particular person is merely an exception to the general rule that sexual sadists are demented." Or you think, "My desire to build a friendship with this person is based on the possibility of reforming her/him (and has nothing to do with any curiosity to learn more about my own sexual tastes)." Such purely cosmetic repairs in your belief structure sometimes suffice to maintain your sense of self-consistency. Unless you are confronted with a genuine personal crisis, or freely choose to push deeper and ask yourself more comprehensive and disturbing questions about the genesis and justification of your own beliefs, your actual degree of self-awareness may remain relatively thin.

Some people have to believe that the world of political and social catastrophe is completely outside their control in order to justify their indifference to it.

Usually the beliefs that remain most unexposed to examination are the ones we need to hold in order to maintain a certain conception of ourselves and our relation to the world. These are the ones in which we have the deepest personal investment. Hence these are the ones that are most resistant to revision; e.g., we have to believe that other people are capable of understanding and sympathy, of honorable and responsible behavior, in order not to feel completely alienated and suspicious of those around us. Or: Some people have to believe that the world of political and social catastrophe is completely outside their control in order to justify their indifference to it.

Some of these beliefs may be true, some may be false. This is difficult to ascertain because we can only confirm or disconfirm the beliefs under examination with reference to other beliefs, which themselves require examination. In any event, the set of false beliefs that a person has a personal investment in maintaining is what I will refer to (following Marx) as a person's *ideology*.

Ideology is pernicious for many reasons. The obvious one is that it makes people behave in stupid, insensitive, self-serving ways, usually at the expense of other individuals or groups. But it is also pernicious because of the mechanisms it uses to protect itself, and its consequent capacity for self-regeneration in the face of the most obvious counterevidence. Some of these mechanisms are:

(1) The False-Identity Mechanism

In order to preserve your ideological beliefs against attack, you identify them as objective facts and not as beliefs at all. For example, you insist that it is just a fact that black people are less intelligent than whites, or that those on the sexual fringes are in fact sick, violent or asocial. By maintaining that these are statements of fact rather than statements of belief compiled from the experiences you personally happen to have had, you avoid having to examine and perhaps revise those beliefs. This denial may be crucial to maintaining your self-conception against attack. If you're white and suspect that you may not be all that smart, to suppose that at least there's a whole race of people you're smarter than may be an important source of self-esteem. Or if you're not entirely successful in coping with your own nonstandard sexual impulses, isolating and identifying the sexual fringe as sick, violent or asocial may serve the very important function of reinforcing your sense of yourself as "normal."

The fallacy of the false-identity mechanism as a defense of one's ideology consists in supposing that there exist objective social facts that are not constructs of beliefs people have about each other.

(2) The Illusion of Perfectibility

Here you defend your ideology by convincing yourself that the hard work of self-scrutiny has an end and a final product, i.e., a set of true, central and uniquely defensible beliefs about some issue; and that you have in fact achieved this end, hence needn't subject your beliefs to further examination. Since there is no such final product, all of the inferences that supposedly follow from this belief are false. Example:

You're a veteran of the anti-war movement and have developed a successful and much-lauded system of draft-avoidance counseling, on which your entire sense of self-worth is erected. When it is made clear to you that such services primarily benefit the middle class—that this consequently forces much larger proportions of the poor, the uneducated and blacks to serve and be killed in its place—you resist revising your views in light of this information on the grounds that you've worked on and thought hard about these issues, have developed a sophisticated critique of them, and therefore have no reason to reconsider your opinions or efforts. You thus treat the prior experience of having reflected deeply on some issue as a defense against the self-reflection appropriate now, that might uncover your personal investment in your anti-draft role.

The illusion of perfectibility is really the sin of arrogance, for it supposes that dogmatism can be justified by having "paid one's dues."

(3) The One-Way Communication Mechanism

You deflect dissents, criticisms or attacks on your cherished beliefs by treating all of your own pronouncements as imparting genuine information, but treating those of other people as mere symptoms of some moral or psychological defect. Say you're committed to feminism, but have difficulty making genuine contact with other women. You dismiss all arguments advocating greater attention to lesbian and separatist issues within the women's movement on the grounds that they are maintained by frustrated man-haters who just want to get their names in the footlights. By reducing questions concerning the relations of women to each other to pathology or symptoms of excessive self-interest, you avoid confronting the conflict between your intellectual convictions and your actual alienation from other women, and therefore the motives that might explain this conflict. If these motives should include such things as deep-seated feelings of rivalry with other women, or a desire for attention from men, then avoiding recognition of this conflict is crucial to maintaining your self-respect.

The one-way communication mechanism is a form of elitism that ascribes pure, healthy, altruistic political motives only to oneself (or group), while reducing all dissenters to the status of moral defectives or egocentric and self-seeking subhumans, whom it is entirely justified to manipulate or disregard, but with whom the possibility of rational dialogue is not to be taken seriously.

There are many other mechanisms for defending one's personal ideology. These are merely a representative sampling. Together, they all add up to what I will call the *illusion* of *omniscience*. This illusion consists in being so convinced of the infallibility of your own beliefs about everyone else that you forget that you are perceiving and experiencing other people from a perspective that is, in its own ways, just as subjective and limited as theirs. Thus you confuse your personal experiences with objective reality, and forget that you have a subjective and limited *self* that is selecting, processing and interpreting your experiences in accordance with its own limited capacities. You suppose that your perceptions of someone are truths about her or him; that your understanding of someone is comprehensive and complete. Thus your self-conception is not demarcated by the existence of other people. Rather, you appropriate them into your self-conception as psychologically and metaphysically transparent objects of your consciousness. You ignore their ontological independence, their psychological opacity, and thereby their essential personhood. The illusion of omniscience resolves into the fallacy of solipsism.

The result is blindness to the genuine needs of other people, coupled with the arrogant and dangerous conviction that you understand those needs better than they do; and a consequent inability to respond to those needs politically in genuinely effective ways.

The antidote, I suggest, is confrontation of the sinner with the evidence of the sin: the rationalizations; the subconscious defense mechanisms; the strategies of avoidance, denial, dismissal and withdrawal that signal, on the one hand, the retreat of the self to the protective enclave of ideology, on the other hand, precisely the proof of subjectivity and fallibility that the ideologue is so anxious to ignore. This is the concern of my recent work of the past three years.

The success of the antidote increases with the specificity of the confrontation. And because I don't know you I can't be as specific as I would like. I can only indicate general issues that have specific references in my own experience. But if this discussion has made you in the least degree self-conscious about your political beliefs or about your strategies for preserving them; or even faintly uncomfortable or annoyed at my having discussed them; or has raised just the slightest glimmerings of doubt about the veracity of your opinions, then I will consider this piece a roaring success. If not, then I will just have to try again, for my own sake. For of course I am talking not just about you, but about *us*.

Spring 1981

The Artist as Citizen:
Guillermo Gómez-Peña, Felipe Ehrenberg,
David Avalos and Judy Baca

By Emily Hicks

Complicated times call for new strategies. In the '80s artists from Mexico, the border region and southern California were illuminating issues of Latino politics. Some were doing more than that by actually employing art strategies to get involved in the binational political struggle. Their issues included the survival of Mexico City in a time of terrible crisis; the outlaw status of undocumented workers in the U.S.; the cultural visibility of Latinos and other ethnic groups in southern California; and the reinterpretation of reality in the borderland region between the two countries. Here San Diego-based scholar and border artist Emily Hicks positions four noteworthy activist artists in the postmodern cultural battlefield.
—Eds.

A flamenco surfer surrounded by waves of blood / a tourist donkey cart strategically placed and later perceived as a threat to public safety / a rock concert in the midst of the coffins and debris after an earthquake / a portrait of the man who discovered blood plasma and later died of lack of blood in a Southern hospital.

These images appear in the work of Guillermo Gómez-Peña, Felipe Ehrenberg, David Avalos and Judy Baca. Some artists in Mexico City, Los Angeles and the U.S.-Mexico border region are producing work that is profoundly political and linked to "performance" in its largest sense. Their work may offer a narrow conceptual passageway between the Scylla and Charybdis of performance [art] and mass culture. To negotiate this passageway is to broaden the definition of the artist.

The notion of art as cultural intervention—or what Mexican

muralist Arnold Belkin, in his attempt to define Mexican interdisciplinary artist Felipe Ehrenberg, calls "the artist as citizen"—stretches the definition of art beyond even the flexible boundaries of postmodernism.[1]

As the critic Fredric Jameson has pointed out, postmodernism has many variants, some that are progressive and others that are not.[2] And yet, it is within the debates of postmodernist criticism in North American and European art journals that performance artists like these are again redefining themselves. Among the features that link their work to a postmodernist critique are: 1) the medium changes according to the requirements of the cultural intervention—it can be community organizing, mural art, journalism, radio, criticism, multimedia performance, etc.; 2) works may be collaborative, even anonymously so; 3) works may be changed or compounded by other artists; 4) the meaning depends on the active participation of a politicized audience.

Most importantly, many North American performance artists have experienced the isolation of small, specialized audiences and the pressure to do more accessible work. Postmodernist critics have christened this dilemma as the problem of high culture vs. mass culture. Artists experience it as a problem of performance vs. entertainment.[3] But consider instead the alternative response of an artist like Felipe Ehrenberg and his project of the reconstruction of Mexico City after the 1985 earthquake. For him, the goal is not to be a pop star, but a responsible citizen/activist. At the moment, his community is Tepito, the devastated neighborhood in the city of his birth, Mexico D.F.

For muralist Judy Baca, who grew up in Pacoima, California, the definition of community includes the relationships of ethnic groups, the interrelationships of social problems, and the question of who occupies a public space. The community for her mural projects began in East Los Angeles, but then expanded to include blacks in South Central Los Angeles, Filipinos in Echo Park and Japanese in Little Tokyo.

For David Avalos, who grew up in National City, California, 20 miles from the U.S.-Mexican border, the creative context is the Chicano community, which he calls "a community outside the law." Using site-specific works and media-art strategies, he explores the notions of "citizenship" and "identity" in relation to the labor provided by the undocumented worker, a "citizen" whose civic rights are systematically denied.

For Gómez-Peña, a performance artist and writer from Mexico City, the community is the border region of Tijuana-San Diego, where

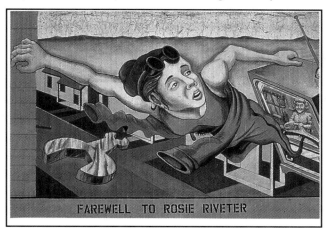

FAREWELL TO ROSIE RIVETER

he has lived since 1983, and which, for him, represents a microcosm of U.S.-Latin American relations. Through collaborative, interdisciplinary art projects, involving people from both countries, he attempts to create a binational dialogue that supersedes mass-media-produced misconceptions and transcultural fears.

These citizen-artists, involved in cultural projects that often include performance, get excellent media coverage and reach very large audiences without striving to be pop stars. The recent activities of Felipe Ehrenberg in Mexico City have received wide coverage in the international press. A performance by Gómez-Peña appeared in a Louis Malle film on new immigrants to the U.S. that aired nationally on HBO. Baca's *Great Wall* is perhaps one of the most widely viewed and discussed Chicano murals, and Avalos' donkey cart sparked a national media scandal involving a federal judge. What do these artists have in common?

In a recent site-work, after being authorized by city officials, Avalos brought his own version of a Tijuana donkey cart to the Federal Building in San Diego, where the Immigration and Naturalization Service (INS) office is located. Traditional Tijuana donkey carts are decorated with hats, serapes and images of Aztec warriors and buxom Indian princesses. Tourists, including middle-class North American families and U.S. military personnel, pose for photographs on the carts. Avalos' cart, instead, is painted with the image of an undocumented worker being frisked by a border-patrol agent. While the traditional carts give the tourist a romanticized taste of Mexico, Avalos' version gives the viewer the opportunity to identify with a daily experience of an undocumented worker. Declared "dangerous" and "anti-American" by a federal judge, the cart was ordered removed immediately. When Avalos refused to remove the artwork, it was confiscated and detained in a storage area of the Federal Building. This resulted both in television interviews and national feature articles in which Avalos was paradoxically allowed to address the social contradictions embodied in the artwork and often avoided by the media, and to expose the authoritarian censorship of the judge. At this point, we can say the piece was completed.

Gómez-Peña creates border stereotypes in order to deconstruct their underlying oppositions: a *cholo*/punk, a wrestler/shaman, a Latin American general/movie star, a *"bruja"*/maid. His works involve a continuous recycling of images and texts. A recent text that began as a radio art show on the U.S.-Mexico and the U.S-Canadian borders entitled *Border-X-Frontera,* later inspired a performance by Poyesis Genética around Avalos' donkey cart in front of Sushi Gallery (San Diego). Another version then appeared on a local cable station. This sparked *Cabaret Babylon Aztlán,* a multimedia work performed at the Centro Cultural de la Raza. Malle filmed a segment of this version, with the donkey cart as the set, and juxtaposed Gómez-Peña's performance describing thousands of "Waspbacks" illegally crossing the border into Mexico, with anti-undocumented worker statements by Harold Ezell, Western Regional Commissioner of the INS. The same text appeared on the cover of the bilingual art journal *La Línea Quebrada,* in *Uno-más-uno,* the most important newspaper in Mexico, and in two art exhibits accompanying an upside-down map of the continent. This strategy of recontextualizing image and texts has much in common with postmodernism. It undermines the sanctity of the single creator, the finished piece, and the work of art as a commodity.

Baca's work, in its mixture of the mural tradition and community organizing, also undermines the sanctity of the single creator. In 1976, Judy Baca began the *Great Wall Mural Project,* the largest of its kind in the world, in the Tujunga Wash Channel of the San Fernando Valley. Baca envisioned the channel, which had been built by the Army Corps and was being developed into a park, as a wall that could bring the diverse mural groups she had been organizing together at one site. It began with 80 teenagers and nine artists. The mural depicts the history of California, from pre-Colombian times to the present. Images include Tomás Alva Edison;[4] Jeanette Rankin, who opposed WW II; Charles Drew, who discovered blood plasma; David Gonzales, recipient of a Congressional Medal of Honor; Pulitzer Prize-winner Gwendolyn Brooks; zoot suiters, athletes and many other recognized and previously unrecognized historical figures. The opportunity to paint murals was not the only benefit for participants in the *Great Wall Project*. They also received counseling on the draft, sexuality, drugs, incest and other social problems. For Baca, art is merely a catalyst for the regeneration of the community.

In the case of Ehrenberg, cultural intervention took the form of entering the disaster area of Tepito in Mexico City immediately after the earthquake. Ehrenberg took some artists, friends, and his own family into Tepito in order to organize brigades to comfort survivors, who had been left without homes, electricity and social services, and to distribute food and clothing. Volunteers who made up the brigades included psychologists, musicians, teachers, actors, university students and painters.

While the Mexican government prevented supplies from reaching Mexico City by insisting that they go through government channels, Ehrenberg and the Tepitenos began to raise money and opened bank account #228333 at the Banco de Crédito Mexicano. To administer the account, he organized the Committee for the Reconstruction of Tepito, which included community representatives, well-known cultural activists, scientists and specialists in fields from urbanism to finance. Between September 25 and October 1, his group managed to give food, medical attention and drinkable water to nearly 5,000 people a day. On October 6, Ehrenberg organized a "Festival of Life," which included music by rock groups, to celebrate, in Ehrenberg's words, "that we are alive, that Tepito didn't fold, and to be aware that we have to help ourselves." In addition, children's theater, concerts and a library were organized. Citizens of Tepito have recently appeared in the press carrying banners saying "*No nos moverán de aquí*" ("They won't move us from here"), referring to their desire to reconstruct Tepito rather than be relocated by the government. In a sense, these activities can be considered an epic performance installation, in which an entire city functions as a gallery space.

While the above artists' work shares several of the previously mentioned features of postmodernist critiques, what they do not share with some of those critiques is their ultimate goal: the transformation of social conditions. Socially committed artists commonly have very broad backgrounds, and they point to the other influences on their work as more important than their experiences in art schools.

Ehrenberg was a painter who had worked with Margaret Randall on the legendary bilingual journal *The Plumed Horn*. After the massacre of students in October, 1968, Ehrenberg and his wife left the country. He lived in England for several years, directing the famous Beau Geste Press. He later returned to Mexico where, during the 1970s, he nurtured both a widespread movement of alternative small-press publications called *Neográfica*, and the creation of a network of art collectives that opposed the gallery system. In 1982, he ran for office on the United Socialist Party of Mexico ticket (PSUM). Ehrenberg's decision to participate in *la reconstrucción* was inspired by the work of his brother, who went to Nicaragua during the revolution as a cameraman and joined the southern guerrilla front.

David Avalos is a product of the tradition of political activism in the border region. Jose Montoya, one of the godfathers of the Chicano movement, sees Avalos as a Chicano artist who "hasn't succumbed to the false, hedonistic tendency of so many Hispanics who consider being Chicano to be one of the unpleasant realities of these times, and who have eagerly embraced Reagan's redefinition of our national character...the I'm OK, you're poor, poverty sucks bunch." Avalos, who studied communications at UC San Diego and Stanford, is a self-taught artist and has been, since 1976, a member of the Committee on Chicano Rights, which monitors the activities of the INS in the border region. In 1982, he and a group of artists including Gómez-Peña formed BAW/TAF (Border Arts Workshop/*Taller de Arte Fronterizo*). This group includes Chicano, Mexican and Anglo artists, and offers a successful example of multicultural, multidisciplinary artmaking.

Gómez-Peña came to the United States from Mexico City, where he studied linguistics and was a student activist at the Autonomous National University of Mexico (UNAM). He entered CalArts in 1979, and two years later cofounded with Sara Jo Berman the *Poyesis Genética* troupe in order to explore artistic and political contradictions between the United States and Mexico. The troupe toured Europe in 1982 and relocated to the Mexican-American border in 1983. Gómez-Peña's art projects include bicultural journalism for radio and newspapers and binational interdisciplinary art projects involving people from both countries. Both activities proceed from the same set of concerns, but utilize different formats in order to reach different audiences.

Socially committed artists commonly have very broad backgrounds, and they point to the other influences on their work as more important than their experiences in art schools.

Judy Baca attended Cal State Northridge and received a master's degree in art education. Her decision to define herself as an artist came halfway through her career, because she "couldn't align art with her sense of political commitment." Her community organizing as a director of mural projects has resolved this conflict; she has been personally involved with more than 150 murals. Furthermore, her cultural activities in Los Angeles have created a bridge between feminism and the Chicano movement.

In the Mexican and Chicano art worlds, the relationship between art and politics is a much more widely shared reference code. This is particularly true in the case of Ehrenberg, Baca, Avalos and Gómez-Peña, who are bicultural, have identified with the upheavals of the 1960s, and have been involved in social activism outside the art world. In the context of the economic crisis and the earthquake in Mexico, politics and art are clearly connected for many artists in a way that they are not in the art scenes of New York and Los Angeles. When one is of Latino descent living in the border region, confronting everyday violations of human rights, media distortions and the ethnic insensitivity of the general population, one has no choice but to engage in some kind of social/political discourse.

It is unfortunate, but probably true, that the best reaction many North American mainstream artists may hope for is that a painting will sell or a performance piece will be reviewed. This is a less satisfactory response than the attainment of the more ambitious goal of the activist: a profound cultural impact outside of the art world. The question of why many artists settle for less than being understood, and for merely a career, may have something to do with their inability to conceive of themselves in historical terms and therefore to understand the world as a political structure.

The vast majority of North American artists have not experienced the political repression in El Salvador and Guatemala, the fear of invasion by Reagan in Nicaragua, the war against "subversives" in Argentina and the U.S.-Mexico border region, police brutality in Chile or in the Chicano barrios, or the ecological deterioration of Mexico City. Instead, their primary experiences are likely to be art school, art openings, "relationships" and mass culture. Their sense of belonging in the world is mediated by mass-media images. And their problems are "personal," not social. Few have engaged in cultural activism. Those who have most likely have experienced other cultures and other political regimes.

For artists not currently involved in socially committed activities, there may be something to learn from cultural activists. Will art schools encourage students to form multicultural groups and begin to produce a new generation of artist/citizens? There are isolated examples like Rutgers University and UC San Diego, but a mass movement is very unlikely. However, at least we can recognize non-New York, non-master-discourse-packaged art forms in whatever contexts they occur. Mexico City, the border region and the Chicano barrios of California are three such contexts. A multicultural redefinition of the "art world" and a willingness to become fluent in many art languages could facilitate an interchange among artists from a variety of contexts, including those mentioned above and the Anglo art world.

Notes

1. When this article originally appeared, I failed to thank Philip Brookman for his help with information about the work of Felipe Ehrenberg.

2. Fredric Jameson, "The Politics of Theory: Ideological Positions in the Postmodernism Debate," *Critical Inquiry*, January, 1985, pp. 53-65.

3. Jacki Apple, "Commerce on the Edge," *High Performance*, no. 34, vol. IX, no. 2, 1986, pp. 34-38.

4. Better known in the United States as Thomas Edison.

Fall 1986

El Teatro Campesino:
An Interview with Luis Valdez

By Carl Heyward

El Teatro Campesino was the cultural wing of the United Farm Workers union, a popular theater that took its material directly from the lives of its audience in the bean fields of California's central valley. With a pointed political mission, the theater, and its driving force Luis Valdez, went from agitprop to Broadway. San Francisco writer Carl Heyward met with Valdez in 1985 to talk about the theater and its radical activist history.   —Eds.

Luis Valdez is out of the fields, but the heart and sentiment of his El Teatro Campesino remain true to its original vision: performance that addresses the Chicano experience in America in a context meaningful to all Americans.

In the mid '60s, flatbed trucks provided their first forum in the fields, adding a creative element to the struggles of farmworkers in Valdez's native Delano County. The immediacy of these *actos*, agitprop improvisations, communicated eloquently to many workers, who could neither read nor write, but recognized themselves and their values in what were essentially morality plays. El Teatro created site-specific installation in the truest sense of the format, transforming the fields into sociopolitical arenas, furthering the cause of the United Farm Workers union in their fight for human dignity. If Cesar Chavez was the upfront political figurehead of the farmworkers, then Luis Valdez provided its cultural wing with a flair and artistry that, in tandem, realized a solidarity unprecedented in relation to such emotional issues.

Years later, during the enormous success of *Zoot Suit,* Valdez observed that "until we had the artists who could express what the people (farmworkers) were feeling and saying, we wouldn't really register politically. Art gives us the tools of that expression."

El Teatro is popular theater with a deference to technical proficiency, to professional and performance excellence, all geared toward expression of social, political and cultural perceptions. It is a theater rooted in the American streets, early California history, Mayan/Aztec mythology and Mexican folklore and spiritualism. It cannot be ignored. Valdez, like Artaud, believes in a total theater—one where an elevation of sensation is achieved through a trinity of music, dance and drama to stimulate a "New American Audience."

In the 20 years since El Teatro's inception, the political erosion of many of the gains of the UFW has made a need for revitalization of the movement obvious. Though autonomous and independent of the union for a long time now, the unpretentious yet eclectic theater group still bases itself in its community, and preserves and rediscovers rites of identity of Mexico and the region.

During the past four years El Teatro faced both bankruptcy and the roller-coaster effects of sudden Hollywood and New York fame, forcing a reordering of priorities. Some of those priorities are the training of Third World directors, playwrights, actors and technical people. Other concerns include the development of that "New American Audience," plays centered around early California history and the evolution of the unique "Campesino aesthetic" through a body of new works.

My first conversations with Luis Valdez began in the summer of 1981 while completing a National Endowment for the Arts Fellowship for the Expansion Arts Program. I documented national NEA grantees whose organizational and artistic performances stood as models for the continued federal support of such groups.

Arriving in the old mission pueblo, San Juan Bautista, I walked the short, cactus-covered distance from the Greyhound stop to their new playhouse, a sprawling former packing plant. Valdez, understandably flush with the celebration of the opening of the space, their first real home, struck me as an articulate, committed artist, centered, yet excited at the prospect of establishing a place for his plays and his company. This building would house a training center and showcase for People's Theater. He is a highly talented man; actor, playwright and poet, concerned with the conditions he experienced as the son of migrant workers. That ability to feel and communicate is essential to understanding the source of his drive to touch easily and deeply.

My last visit to San Juan Bautista marked the 20-year celebration of El Teatro, and the retrospective of two of Valdez's early surrealistic "popular classics," *Soldado Razo* and *The Dark Roof of a Scream*. The

...our artistry had to sustain our politics...

collective's mood is less ecstatic after the sobering experiences in the "bigtime," and dwindling foundation and federal support. Still, they believe in the magic of exploration of the human being and the ability of their work to teach and delight. The following is an excerpt of those conversations.

Carl Heyward: *What does it mean that El Teatro has been in existence for 20 years?*

Luis Valdez: Twenty years is a long time and not such a long time. What it means in a word is that we are on the verge of institutionalization. We have laid a foundation that will insure the survival of the company, not just in terms of a physical building, but also in terms of having an aesthetic, developing an approach to our work that has evolved from practice. We have also identified a need for this work that gives us confidence that we will be here as an organization 20 years from now.

CH: *El Teatro and your work are interesting in terms of the mix of cultural information that is offered. What is that aesthetic?*

LV: We are after the truth about America. I guess that it's time that America came of age and got a little sophisticated about itself. We are a lot more varied, as a country, than we like to pretend to be. I mean, we give sort of a nodding recognition that the country is multiracial, for instance, but do not do a lot to really integrate, in a cultural-artistic sense, the real currents that flow in this country. That sort of thing has to happen of itself through the daily life of the people, through the daily cultural life.

As a theater company, we are consciously and deliberately trying to provide certain kinds of images. When you talk about what California really is, the truth can be so penetrating that it changes perceptions of history. When you view the Anglo-Hispanic crux of this country, you are talking about two different views of people, especially in terms of racial culture. La Raza, if you look at the whole of Latin America, integrated all the races of mankind, it mixed everyone really—Blacks, Anglos, Asians, Indians, everyone. In that sense, Hispanic culture has not had the problems that Anglo culture has had, and our job is to stop some of this hard-core, blue-nosed racism; we have always been fighting and addressing that.

CH: How have you grown and matured as an artist? How have the goals of El Teatro evolved over the years?

LV: I have been challenged in a number of different ways with the way that El Teatro has developed. When I first started, we were the only ones. I had an image in mind, when I went to Vallejo, that I wanted to work with people. I had to introduce basic concepts. I was working with farmers, some of whom could not read scripts, so we had to use improvisation, which made presentations very lively. We had a willing audience, a message, and that was the raw material, to better structure the drama, improve the acting and get a better organizational grasp of our own reality so that there was a roof over our heads. I have developed into a playwright and director through the work of El Teatro. I was its first student, and to teach is to learn. In the old days, we rehearsed on the run and performed on the picket line. This was in the middle of the great strike.

While we had the strength and urgency of the struggle, our artistry had to sustain our politics. Ultimately it is artistry that makes the point and cuts across the barriers to understanding. There is a certain quality of excellence that we have discovered over the years, that a lot of people assumed that we didn't have to have, you know? They assumed that we could be rough and untutored and primitive, and still maintain our charm.

CH: What are some bright moments in the history of El Teatro?

LV: For a long time, a milestone in the history of El Teatro was a milestone in my personal life as well. Going back to Delano was a milestone. My family had left the valley to get away from that

whole life of working on the farms—migrant labor. It was hopeless. We went to school, me right behind my brother, the first of
the family ever to have gone to college. My people were
shocked to see me show up back in Delano. I saw the social
movement of the time, 1965. I felt that this movement was right
at the center of things, that this is what I should be doing. I went
back on so many levels…. El Teatro was located a block from
the place where I was born. I was in the belly button of reality
(laughs). A milestone for the company and one also for me. The
next came with the separation from the UFW. It was a classic
argument, we were doing art and doing politics: At what point
do they meet and at what point do they diverge? It seemed like
a contradiction in terms in that we were a part of the union, but
we came to that point.

   The union was interfering with our organizational growth.
They were not focused on the arts, they *allowed* the arts to
happen. It was viewed as a tool and not a service. So the chaot-
ic birth of our independence began. Another milestone might
have been *Zoot Suit*. It marked my rededication as a playwright.
Without El Teatro I would not have been able to write *Zoot Suit*.
I know that our work reaches into the streets. We attract young
people, people who are confronted with rather stark realities.
They have to hope for something, man. If they don't have the
arts telling them about the essence and meaning of life, offering
some kind of exploration of the positive and negative aspects of
life, then there is no hope. I was a very angry young man not
too many years ago, and I was able to channel that anger into
the arts.

CH: *Talk about the experience of doing* Zoot Suit.

LV: It was an American experience. I had no notion of what that kind
of success was. We have always been successful in terms of the
work, and the audience telling us that they like the work, but
that thing just took off. We were here in San Juan in the spring
of 1978, trying to pay attention to going to L.A. and the Mark
Taper Forum. By the spring of 1979, we were packing to go to

New York. All this in one year. All the madness came to the limit around opening night. Celebrities, people that you don't know—all there, wishing you luck, covering their bases in case you were a hit on Broadway. I had a very sobering moment in Sardi's when Phil [production chief Phil Esparza] came in and told me that the N.Y. critics knocked it very badly. At that exact moment I felt home again. I touched the ground. People think that tremendous success is very good, but it takes you off the deep end. Being successful again and again, you can get used to it. The first time, [success] can knock you for a loop, and destroy the thing that you love most, your stability. Not too many opening nights in N.Y. for you, buddy! [laughs]. [*Zoot Suit* played for 46 weeks in L.A. for more than 40,000 people. Valdez became the first Chicano director to have a play presented on Broadway. The film version was nominated for a Golden Globe Award and won the 1982 Cartagena Film Festival's Best Picture Award in Colombia.]

CH: *Talk about your relationship with your audience—the idea of the "New American Audience."*

LV: Since we started as a theater company, the audience has always been crucial. In Delano, we had a mixed audience to begin with; largely Mexican and Filipino, with Berkeley volunteers and black farmworkers from Bakersfield. The combination was always varied. That set the pace for us. The audience has always been looked upon as the main factor in our presentation. Once you have a mixed audience in that way, which is a true cross-section of the country, there is a dynamism and electricity that helps each performance. It is just as important for us to cast the audience, as it is to cast the play. We have found that playing just for Chicanos evokes certain things, just as playing for Anglos…neither is correct. What we call "The New American Audience" is a cross-section of the country that brings us to the future. We have to respond to the whole audience, the whole country. You are protected against your own racism and narrow-mindedness, and are urged, due to the make-up of that audience and the need to reach them, to reach a higher place. That is the truth that needs to invade Broadway—get in touch with the world.

Winter 1985

It's All I Can Think About:
An Interview with Nancy Buchanan

By Linda Burnham and Steven Durland

Nancy Buchanan is a Los Angeles-based visual and performance artist whose work has pointedly examined social and political issues such as the status of women, the Cold War, U.S. policies toward the Third World, and the war in Nicaragua. In January 1984 she visited Nicaragua with a group of artists from the San Francisco Bay area called Artists Tour Nicaragua. The tour was guided in Nicaragua by a Sandinista artists' union. In this inter-view excerpt we asked her to relate this intense experience to the art she makes every day.   —Eds.

Linda Frye Burnham: *The last few years most of the work you've done has dealt with political issues—the CIA and so forth. How do you think this trip [to Nicaragua] is going to affect your work? Have you felt a real impact?*

Nancy Buchanan: One of the things I've been interested in is trying to fit myself in as a social being somehow. And that was the exciting thing about Nicaragua. You had this sense that people felt they actually had a place, that they actually belonged, and all the aspects of their life sort of made sense. I think in our society that's not the norm. You have one role here, and one role there, and you juggle your life, your beliefs and your work. I don't want to do that. I also think that my personal feelings are very inti-mately tied up with where I am as a member of society; that there's a level of personal concern about political issues. That's a personal choice. I've never felt that everybody should make political work. I think we need the full spectrum of things that are very beautiful, things that are very intimate or spiritual…and what I do is simply a result of who I am. For a long time I sepa-rated the information about issues that I cared about from my work, until I finally figured out that I didn't have to do that, and it was a real delight.

Steven Durland: *What would you say your first piece was after that realization?*

NB: Some of the earlier, more feminist pieces. *Please Sing Along* [in which men danced nude and women wrestled] was a reversal of male-female roles. I didn't really expect that anyone would tolerate that. One of the ways I've always worked is to move along some kind of an edge and see what I could get away with. I couldn't think of anything more appropriate to have in the Woman's Building than beautiful men, naked and dancing. I didn't know how people would take it. I was real surprised; I got a positive response and realized I didn't have to be afraid of pushing boundaries, that just to be clever was perhaps not interesting enough. I think I'm moving back toward that. The piece I'm working on now is real personal, and right on the edge of being in totally bad taste. What I want to deal with is the idea that runs through a lot of work, which is the manipulation of consciousness by the government or the ruling class—down to a real personal level. A lot of my recent videotapes have been about that too. The new piece is called *Sex and Freedom, Who Can Ask For More?*

> **For a long time I separated the information about issues that I cared about from my work...**

SD: *But I assume that the references won't be just to your personal life?*

NB: No, in fact, I think that only certain people will figure out the personal references.

SD: *Do you think you'll use any of the information or attitudes you formed during this trip?*

NB: I will be collaborating with Robbin Henderson, a Berkeley painter, to make some montages about our trip for a show of the group with whom we traveled. I'm also collaborating with Doug Wichert on a little book. I want to put information in a form that parodies media news and advertising—humor plus non-mainstream information.

SD: *What do you think that does?*

NB: I hope that it might make people interested in things that they might otherwise overlook or not face. I think it's unpleasant to face the fact that your government is participating in massacres or manipulation of the politics of entire nations around the world. I find that a very staggering fact. I find it very hard to take, because—the Nicaraguans are right—the people of this country are not callous or bloodthirsty; they're simply not informed. Oftentimes we're not used to participating fully in the political process. I hope that I might encourage people to become more involved, at least to educate themselves, to become interested enough to want to find out more and maybe be active.

LFB: *Do you think Americans are reluctant to get involved because they feel helpless to change things?*

NB: I think there's a lot people can do. This brings to mind the papers I went through of my father's. In 1945 they were studying the air defense of this country, and there were some people at that time who wanted to bomb the Soviet Union and get it over with. One of the findings of the study my father was involved with was that public opinion would never adjust to that kind of barbarism. Public opinion does count. I think you can find arguments on both sides, but the protest movements of the '60s and '70s really did influence what went on in this country. The Vietnam War might have been different if there hadn't been an incredible popular response. And look at Reagan. Now he's even starting to say that he would like to eliminate nuclear weapons. I think that's quite incredible, and it's only public pressure that brings that about. We're taught to believe that it's fruitless, but I don't think it is.

SD: *To take that a step farther, in the '80s there's been a lot of reactionary audience response to political art, and it seems like one is* *frequently left preaching to the converted, so to speak. How do you go about getting past that?*

NB: One of the ways is to make videotapes and try to disseminate them to a wider audience. That's why I'm interested in video. It's portable, it's easy to send or play or cablecast.

LFB: *I imagine, from the way you talk about what you're trying to do with your work, that the more exposure you can get for your tapes—to any kind of audience—the happier you'll be.*

NB: Yes, I really believe that one of the great things going on right now is the possibility for expansion of the number of channels that one can receive. As pitiful as it often has been, the public-access programs around the country are incredibly important, and also local cable, because it really is a voice of a community. And just the fact that it can exist and that people can be themselves, no matter how bad their camera work might be—it's exciting to me that the medium itself can be demystified by being used by your neighbors.

I have a great interview on my next tape with a Marxist computer expert. He feels that technology is no longer labor in any sense, it's strictly information. Control of information is really the important thing in terms of power and market and reorganization.

LFB: *The new class system. There will be two classes: those with electronics and those without.*

NB: This man has been involved with teaching grassroots organizations to employ computers. I think there is a second wave of the computer revolution that is humanizing computers more, and using them for things that perhaps they weren't intended to be used for. It's the same thing with—going back to Nicaragua, I guess—not being controlled by the technology. There's a group of people in Nicaragua called "The Innovators." They figure out how to make all the spare parts to keep everything going!

LFB: *What kind of response are you getting from your students back in*

Madison [University of Wisconsin]?

NB: Very positive, particularly in a seminar that I did last fall about art
and politics. It was very broad-based. I didn't allow anyone to
talk about their own work. We only discussed the issue of
whether art could be political or had to be "free of any pollution from the real world." It was exciting, the kinds of information the class came up with, the kinds of discussions we had...

Spring 1984

Robbie Conal: Taking Back the Power

By Claire Peeps

The Reagan-Bush era set many an artist's teeth on edge. During the summer of Contragate, 1987, Los Angeles artist Robbie Conal began wallpapering cities with his satirical portraits of figures in power, including Caspar Weinberger, Nancy Reagan, Oliver North and Margaret Thatcher. Here he talks with L.A. writer Claire Peeps about what inspired him to do it.   —Eds.

At a construction site on Beverly Boulevard in Los Angeles, between posters for new movies and record albums, four familiar faces are glued to the wall with a caption that reads "Men With No Lips." They are Ronald Reagan, Caspar Weinberger, Donald Regan and James Baker, all portrayed as haggard and prune-faced men. "What's 'Men With No Lips,'" asks a teenage passerby, "a rock 'n' roll band?"

Around the corner on the traffic light switching box is a companion piece: the four smiling faces of Nancy Reagan, Margaret Thatcher, Jean Kirkpatrick and Joan Rivers, with the boldly printed title "Women With Teeth."

A third poster, of Oliver North, appears repeatedly on the wall of a nearby vacant building. Under North's frowning, tight-lipped portrait is the single directive: "Speak." Two passengers in a car point at the poster and, nodding and laughing, they begin to speak animatedly to each other as they drive away.

Since October, these posters have appeared quietly along heavily trafficked thoroughfares throughout Los Angeles—in Venice, Santa Monica, Beverly Hills, downtown, Watts, East L.A. They have also appeared from Wall Street to Tribeca in New York City, and on Capitol Hill in Washington, D.C.—right across the street from the State Department. Because of their unknown origin, some viewers have speculated that the posters are part of a strategy of the Democratic Party to curry favor in the election year. Others are simply bemused by their humorous, poignant messages.

"Authorship is not the point," says artist Robbie Conal in

response to the issue of the posters' anonymity. "The primary goal is just to get people to *think* about people in power—to think along with me."

Conal conceived of the posters as a cost-effective way to take his work out of the studio and onto the street, where he could engage the largest possible number of people in the process of inquiry. Since 1983 he

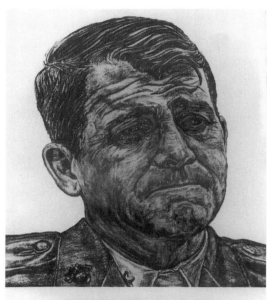

SPEAK

has been amassing a body of paintings of key figures in international politics. Intended as "adversarial portraits," the paintings call attention to the physical manifestations of the pursuit of power on a group of politically successful men and women. More often than not, these physical effects—wrinkled brow, shrivelled lips, squinting eyes, bared teeth—translate into imposing, thickly painted black-and-white canvases ranging in size up to eight feet. Not an easy sell. "I mean," Conal concedes, "who wants a sour Caspar Weinberger on their dining room wall?"

As the series grew in number, and as the early warning signs of Contragate began to unfold, Conal decided to test the waters. He felt increasingly compelled to express his concern about the diminishing accountability of our government representatives to their constituencies, and to express it *immediately* to an audience both within and without the traditional art mainstream. He selected a group of portraits that were individually the most recognizable, and presented them with a simple line of text to catch the eye of L.A.'s harried commuters.

Conal asserts:

> There's a large audience outside the galleries. The gallery is for commerce.
> I think the artist would be foolish not to engage it—it's the system, we're
> in it. But there's also an opportunity to circumnavigate it, go beyond it, and
> I think one could consider that a responsibility.

Judging from the popular response to the posters, Conal would
appear to be right in his estimation of the existence of a "nonart" audience. The posters have become a public forum for the critique of government policies; graffiti and written commentary are generously and
frequently added. Articles about Conal's work have appeared in various daily newspapers. His most recent poster, *Speak*, is the first that
addresses specific political circumstances on Capitol Hill. For Conal, the
synchrony of current political events and the evolution of his artistic
ideas couldn't be better. "This is going to be my wonderful summer," he
says. "I paint with the hearings on. If there's a ball game on, I paint with
the ball game on TV with no sound, and the hearings on the radio."

And what will come after Contragate? The elections, he says,
pointing out the parallels in the issues of power and accountability.
Since the elections are the one time in the electoral process when
politicians are directly responsible to their constituencies, Conal
believes that we should exercise
our rights to exact that accountability. "I think there is a tremendous danger for people, when
they get wise," he says, "to become
cynical and feel 'there's nothing I
can do about it.' I really don't
believe that. We need to feel

> **"The primary goal is just to get people to *think* about people in power—to think along with me."**

empowered to take back the power that's been taken away from us."

So he paints. As things get hotter in the political arena he just
paints faster. Conal thinks he might actually be ahead of Contragate at
this point—if his predictions turn out to be accurate. He's also con-
templating billboards as another venue for his ideas. The only thing he
feels he lacks is sufficient dialogue in the art community—despite the
fact that the posters have begun to win him critical acclaim, a one-man

exhibition at Robert Berman Gallery in Santa Monica and even a few sales. "I think it would be great if more artists addressed issues like this and didn't feel that this kind of subject was beyond the province of art," says Conal. One scenario, he suggests, might be for a group of artists to pool their resources to collectively produce, say, five posters. Acknowledging the important work of such artists as Barbara Kruger, Leon Golub and Jenny Holzer, among others, as well as the recent success of such cooperative efforts as Artists Call—evidence that political ideas are being explored in art—Conal says he feels optimistic about the future impact art may have on public opinion. Nevertheless, he's still looking for a debate partner on the streets. Any takers?

Summer 1987

Art in the AIDies: An Act of Faith

by Max Navarre

By 1986 the AIDS epidemic had claimed a shocking number of artists. Here New York playwright Max Navarre imparts personal feelings about making art in the face of death, and talks with other prominent artists with AIDS about their issues related to art, survival and political fury. Navarre was vice president of the People with AIDS Coalition, as well as the first publicly identified PWA to serve on the executive board of the Gay Men's Health Crisis, at the time the largest AIDS-related service-provider in the world.   —Eds.

Life has changed completely. Things will never be the same again.

We are confronted daily with the media image of the helpless victim, covered with lesions, watched over by the equally helpless, praying parents. We have the other side of that image, the side we see infinitely less of, which is the living with AIDS, the day-to-day showing up of having it that owes nothing to the concepts of victimization or salvation: the going on with life.

When I was diagnosed with AIDS—July 12, 1985—making art was the last thing on my mind. I was too freaked out, too hysterical, too ready to believe that I was at the end of the line to spend much time wondering if there might be a book or a play in it. Not once did I think, "Gee, this might be great for my career," or "Gosh, this might be rough on my health, but I bet it does wonders for my writing."

I thought I was dying. Shit, I thought I was dead. Offstage, I could hear the fat lady tuning up. I was too busy deciding who would get my suede jacket and my bicycle to think about how the artists of the world were interpreting the worst disaster since the Black Plague.

I was not interested. I had become a universe of one.

When the dust settled, when I realized that I still had all my arms and legs, that I was not dead, that I was, in fact going to survive, at least for a few days, I peeked out over the top of the blanket.

It took awhile, but eventually I was ready to crawl out from under the debris and check out the landscape. When I did, the first thing I reached for was a pencil.

In the 16 months since my diagnosis, work has been my primary resource in evaluating and (you'll excuse the expression) sharing my experience. Learning how to listen to my body and to trust my instincts over and above the unrelenting media image of the "AIDS victim" has been a real exercise in faith, an exercise that parallels my life as a writer.

I am not an AIDS victim because I say I'm not. I turn to my work because I always do. Any opinions I have about the effect of AIDS on art are colored by the effect of my AIDS on my art.

In the popular view, there's this prevailing idea that, in the health crisis, there are issues, side issues and nonissues. For example: providing health services, legal, financial and counseling services for people with AIDS and those around them are issues. Getting federal funding to provide those services is an issue. Quarantine is an issue. HIV testing of "risk groups" is an issue. Confidentiality is, however, a side issue. Self-empowerment, self-help and the active role of the person with AIDS are all side issues. Art, evidently, is a nonissue.

Of course, as with most priorities, it all depends on whom you talk to.

And who talks. Some wouldn't. Not necessarily because they thought the question was beside the point, but because they were just too flipped out to think about the issue long enough to answer me. Some folks wanted to talk, but absolutely could not articulate their thoughts. People are reeling. Why should artists be any different?

There was the performance artist, a friend of mine, who had a wonderful conversation with me. She talked about learning to be responsible about her sexuality and how she saw that responsibility reflected in her work. Then, when I saw her a few days later, she was bent out of shape because of what she'd said, and she was anxious about being quoted, and she couldn't believe how confronted she'd felt and how much agitation she'd experienced just talking about AIDS. *Then,* still later, she called me up to give me a quote.

She said, "It's the maturity effect. If you're forced to face an issue that affects every angle, and if people are forced to confront, it affects your work. That's the way you make pieces. You're forced to take risks." But I'm not using her name.

I have another friend, a well-known performance artist who has AIDS. His health is iffy, and he's so well-protected by the people around him that I couldn't get close enough to him to talk. I'm not pointing fingers, if I were sick I'd want my friends to protect me too. But it's the ferocity with which people defend themselves that puzzles me. I've had a hundred conversations with this man. I may have a hundred more. But not for publication. Is it about the stigma of AIDS, or the social taboo of being unwell? Is it about denial?

Vito Russo, author of *The Celluloid Closet*, gifted screenwriter and a spokesperson for the gay community for many years, said to me: "I am emotionally and psychically devastated by this disaster. I am too busy living through it. I do not want to write about AIDS. I refuse to. I will not write about this. When it's over? Maybe."

He went on to say, "Everyone is threatened. Not a lot of people are in touch with their feelings, and the people who have created works are not sick."

Someone who is "sick" who's creating work is Michael Callen. Diagnosed in 1982, Callen is an activist and a founder of the People With AIDS Coalition, which is the leading proponent of self-empowerment for PWAs. He is also a singer and songwriter, author of "The Healing Power of Love" and coauthor, with Marsha Malamet and Peter Allen, of "Love Don't Need a Reason." With his band Lowlife and his status as one of a handful of high-profile, publicly identified people with AIDS, Mike is the very epitome of someone whose art provides a beachhead for his life.

His song "Living in Wartime" was used in Larry Kramer's controversial play *The Normal Heart* during its run at the Public Theater.

"AIDS made me get serious about life and about singing," Mike says. "It wasn't until AIDS gave me that cosmic kick in the ass that I said to myself—OK, with whatever time you have left, what do you want to do? The answer was to make music, queer music."

For Callen, being publicly identified as a PWA is essential, but it also poses a dilemma on the career front. "What record company would invest money into a band when they think the singer is going to die?" [Callen passed away in 1993.]

This seems like the moment to ask, "Max, what do you want from people?"

Answers, I guess. I'd like someone brilliant to appear on the scene who would create something—a performance piece, a play, a painting, an opera—that would put the whole health crisis into perspective for me. That's what I want. Tidiness. I want order in a situation that seems more and more devoid of order.

I remember sitting in a parked car in Los Angeles having an argument with Philip Minges about Tim Miller's piece *Buddy Systems*. I'd seen the piece in New York in the fall of '85, and we had just come from seeing it again. "Why isn't Tim making a piece about AIDS?" I crabbed. "I love Tim and I love his boyfriend and I love the piece and I'm glad they're having a relationship, but *who* cares? People are dying."

If you ever want to make a point about AIDS, just say "people are dying."

Philip, none too patiently, pointed out to me that Tim Miller and his lover Douglas Sadownick were both very aware that people are dying and that, if I would just shut up, I would realize that. "When a gay man makes a piece these days that is about trying to maintain a monogamous relationship with another gay man, then that piece is certainly reflective of the health crisis." So there.

He was right, of course. Even if the health crisis is not the topic of an artwork, that does not mean that the creator of that work is not up to his or her ears in AIDS and its meaning.

David Schweizer directed *Plato's Symposium*. It's a contemporized (sort of) retelling of the Platonic dialogs. I got a lot of hope from the piece and I called David to see if other people had responded in the same way.

"We got started because we know people are dying," he said. "Everyone has their own personal way of trying to be of help, to mobilize, to contribute instead of shutting down. The atmosphere of the project was about turning a creative instinct and a concern into an affirmation of life and a potential for some kind of transcendence."

About himself, David said, "I might be able to do something that presents a view of life that is of some comfort during this time when life is so precarious. The material in *Plato's Symposium* is perfect because it says, 'Here is something beyond this moment.'"

For Schweizer, his proximity to AIDS has made living and making art a self-conscious, special privilege. He said, "I don't take life for granted." A common theme.

Someone else who doesn't take life for granted is Michael Kearns, director of *AIDS/US* and founder of Artists Confronting AIDS.

AIDS/US was an L.A. production that took 13 people, some with AIDS, some with AIDS-related complex (ARC), some who are bereaved, and put them on a stage to tell their own stories. To say that it was a sensation is to understate badly. "This is the genuine article," said the *L.A. Times*. The *L.A. Herald Examiner* said, "In their refusal to be victims, we witness the collapse of theatrical artifice before emotional truth." The piece sold out for months.

Concurrent with the success of *AIDS/US* grew Artists Confronting AIDS, a collective of artists whose goal is to address AIDS-related issues head on.

"We can't afford to be protective of our feelings," says Kearns. "Artists have been gifted with a way of seeing the world. The question is how best to face the challenge."

For Kearns, the best way is to generate awareness among the artist's community, and, through that community, to the public: an awareness of feelings, an awareness of fears, an awareness of coping. This extends particularly to the realm of works created by PWAs. We have the same problems other artists have, but there is also the question, in some cases, of physical impairment. Some

> **I'd like someone brilliant to appear on the scene who would create something—a performance piece, a play, a painting, an opera—that would put the whole health crisis into perspective for me.**

people simply don't have the stamina to work, regardless of their need to create.

There is a need to move away from our cultural obsession with physical perfection. It is time for an across-the-board reassessment of what we, as a society, are willing to look at on a stage. And art by PWAs, particularly performance art, must be presented with love, sensitivity and respect: The last thing we need is a P.T. Barnum sideshow.

Kearns says, "We need to allow PWAs to be seen as something other than just their bodies. If there is something we're going to learn from this hideous disease, I would hope that it is that we're not our physical beings."

Artists Confronting AIDS is committed to the idea that people who are affected by the health crisis find a public source of expression. The fact that this notion may confront ingrained ideas about professionalism and threaten the public's firmly held aesthetic beliefs leaves Kearns undaunted. "The idea that someone would have something to offer and would be cut off from that by fear, or by a need to comfort an audience, is in opposition to the work of Artists Confronting AIDS."

AIDS is not always pretty, but it is always a challenge. I see more and more people reaching beyond themselves for expression. For those people who are writers, the mechanism is already in place, and dealing with AIDS becomes a question of being willing to explore the feelings behind the impulse to create. For those people with AIDS who are not artists, learning to create art can help them to rediscover themselves and can provide a vehicle as they wend their way through an increasingly complicated and confusing emotional landscape.

Art is a lot of things: it's an educational tool, a grieving tool and a healing tool.

When you talk about healing in relation to AIDS, there's an automatic cringe response. All kinds of people are promising all kinds of results based on all kinds of ideas. When I write of healing I do not necessarily refer to physical healing. There is more to the concept of wellness than physical recovery.

Healing is more fleeting and satisfactory. It comes from experiential and emotional truth that soothes and eases pain, as it stimulates and clears the way for what is to follow. Grief is healing, as are joy, sorrow and celebration. Sometimes death is a healing.

I don't know the future of art in the face of the health crisis. I believe that we can all only profit by continuing to risk beyond our limits of safety. If AIDS challenges us to go beyond those limits, then we can begin to see past the devastation and accept the gifts that are available to us all through this experience.

I want to survive. I want my friends to survive, my culture and my planet to survive. The best way I know how to do that is by loving myself as I am and expressing my joy, my pain and my vision.

Winter 1986

Silence Still = Death

By Lucy Lippard

Extremely provocative art about a very hot issue got the full treatment from art critic Lucy Lippard in this 1991 essay dealing with the work of Michael Nash. Even though the artist, and his cohorts in ACT UP, claimed to care more about the politics than the art, Lippard views Nash's ACT UP campaign as an artwork. She takes her critical analysis all the way, including citations of historical precedent, awareness of the work's social context and understanding of the technology employed.   —Eds.

What I am doing is not ART.
I don't care about making ART as a final product.
I don't care if it is not looked at as ART.
My images are about FUNCTION.
My images are about INFORMATION.
My images are about VISIBILITY.
My images are about PRESSURE.
My images are about CHANGE.
My images are about ACTION.
My images are about COLLABORATION.
My images are about COOPERATION.
My images are about AIDS.

—Michael Nash

In the last two years, Michael Nash has collaborated with ACT UP/Denver on a striking, and ongoing, series of visual interventions on the AIDS crisis. The partnership began after Nash, a Boulder photo-activist who was working on his MFA thesis at the University of Colorado, had a blood transfusion. Although HIV-negative, he became enraged when he learned what the government wasn't saying and doing about AIDS. He contacted the Denver group, and found a task that has come to obsess him and fuel his work.

The first product of this righteous rage was a unique, interactive computer publication, the impressive centerpiece of Nash's 1990 thesis show that was billed as an ACT UP project called "Silence Still = Death," rather than as a Michael Nash exhibition. The second was a series of extraordinarily ambitious and provocative billboards in Denver last fall.

The computer disk was produced to establish interaction and alliances among activist groups and community-service organizations dealing with the AIDS crisis. Its Macintosh Hypercard format is an indexing and cross-referencing tool that allows input from readers. The information comes on electronic "cards," rather like a series of

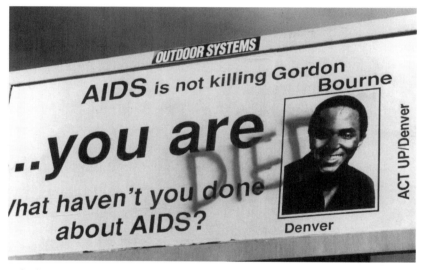

rolodexes, all interlinked with others, so the event spreads out into the community as the information is read, and/or reproduced, on a printer and further distributed in hard copy. It is a lively program, hard to escape. When you try to disengage, it is likely to say something to the effect of "Wait, you don't really want to go yet, do you? How about the bibliography? Another article? A letter to your senators?"

The disk, with its simultaneous commitment to information dissemination and retrieval, provides an incredible amount of practical visual and textual information, including model letters to public officials or offending corporations, complete articles and analyses, statistics, local newspaper items, press releases, activist ideas, resources and addresses, and lists of issues and groups needing attention through political action and support. There are also hard-hitting photo-text poster and flyer models, that can either be printed and xeroxed from the disk, or acquired in higher resolution on request—altered to include specific information about local events anywhere. The unique part of the project is that it is distributed on disk with its participatory element intact, and the hard copy is only a by-product.

"Silence Still = Death" was to be evaluated by community groups and health agencies, then sent out quarterly as a publication, with amendments and additions from regional and national partici-pants. Although this idea was superseded by other projects, the disk has been passed around to some extent, and the group still hopes to update and continue its dissemination. Groups would be encouraged to add information of their own to the files, which would then be incorporated into master files. The publication would act as a source for information exchange about HIV testing, safer sex practices, drug trials and current AIDS and health-care legislation. Critical responses to the AIDS crisis would be solicited, "critical dialogue being a neces-sary part of the search for an eventual cure."

Hoping to form alliances in order to reach "those communities that seek identities of their own," and to dispel the "us versus them" line of thought prevalent in government and media coverage of AIDS, Nash and ACT UP/Denver also planned to put the publication in pub-lic settings for "real-time access." No computer knowledge is neces-sary. The basic idea, says Nash, is that "it may be too late for AIDS information to be given if it is given in *response* to a question. It must be readily available, and stated in understandable terms before initial questions arise."

Colorado is a conservative state, isolated from the coasts, with a classic urban/rural split (Denver vs. the people "out there on the plains"). But AIDS affects 35 of its 65 counties. When Governor Roy Romer referred in late 1989 to AIDS as a "coming crisis," ACT UP replied loudly and strongly that the crisis is already here and it's every-one's crisis; we are all "living with AIDS." Their computer project encourages the exchange of thoughts and ideas with an emphasis on unique local issues, while making an acceptance of "local differences by the wider audience a 'routine part' of this audience's thinking." Jan Zita

Grover has written that the government continues to generalize on geography, race and culture, while specific local analysis is the key to progress: "What works well in volunteer services in San Francisco does not work well across the bay in Oakland; what works well for a gay white man in Manhattan's Chelsea neighborhood does not play equally well in Riverside or the Bronx, much less in Franklin County, Ohio."

Nash has chosen a "de-aestheticizing" form, along the lines suggested by the Gran Fury collective in New York, and by video artist Greg Bordowitz. Greg Bordowitz has challenged artists to articulate the crisis, "to deal with AIDS in whatever form they want, but to do it in a way that reveals what their stake is—to do it in a way that doesn't pose as objectivism, that doesn't pose as removed for any academic reasons, or reasons of aestheticism."

For years now, ACT UP has been using the continually updated line "With 108,949 Dead, Art is Not Enough." But as critic Douglas Crimp has said, "Art does have the power to save lives.... But if we are to do this, we will have to abandon the idealist concept of art. We don't need a cultural renaissance; we need cultural practices actively participating in the struggle against AIDS."

But there are many who find this dichotomy unnecessary. To see expressive, expressionist, ironic, beautiful or "idealist" art on AIDS in a positive light takes nothing away from the effectiveness of ACT UP's preference for graphic, media-competitive activism like the "Silence Still = Death" project. At Nash's show—which symbolically took place in the more public hallway of the art building rather than in the gallery—his graphically effective flyers were available on pads, to be torn off, taken away and posted, duplicated, used in the broader community. Other visuals included a postcard to those supporting the products of Burroughs-Wellcome, manufacturers of Neosporin, Sudafed and the AIDS treatment drug AZT. Although AZT is providing Burroughs-Wellcome with obscene profits off of PWAs (People With AIDS), the company continues to deny access to the drug to those who can't afford it.

Among the flyers on the disk are images of kids or families with the caption, "What Do People With AIDS Look Like?" The question is borrowed in response to Nicholas Nixon's "Faces of AIDS" exhibition at the Museum of Modern Art in 1988, attacked by activists for its relentless pathos and "victimization" of PWAs. Another features the image of a plump, braided, bespectacled Girl Scout and the question, "Dear Mr. President, can my friends and I catch AIDS?" The most chilling, however, had no image. In a straightforward public service format it read, "Here is a simple AIDS test." There are two boxes, a choice between "I care about my health and value my life" and "I don't." The questionnaire ended: "Get informed, get tested, get real. If you don't care, good luck."

At one point during the project an AIDS testing team was available in the art building. The university was a particularly important place to mount a project designed to create dialogue about AIDS and its impact on the community. Statistics from the American College Health Association show that a projected one in five hundred students on campuses across the nation are HIV-positive. The 1988-89 survey was based on unrelated blood samples at 20 major universities including the University of Colorado; teenagers tested more recently, when entering the military, turned up a ratio of one in 3,000; women aged 17-18 tested higher than their male counterparts and also die more quickly.

> **"Art does have the power to save lives...But if we are to do this, we will have to abandon the idealist concept of art."**

In the spring of 1990, ACT UP/Denver took a highly controversial stand regarding AIDS on college campuses by using gender and class analysis to an ironically extreme degree. After having been invited to Colorado State University in Fort Collins, where they were met with indifference, ignorance, denial and even ridicule, ACT UP members developed a startling position: They would not take their AIDS flyers to any more college campuses.

> These college kids are the sons and daughters of the power structure in Colorado...Why help this future generation of leaders stay free of HIV so they can continue to believe the myth that AIDS is only a problem for the

underclass? Fuck 'em! Let these kids get infected and die and then maybe their parents will decide to outlaw AIDS….Yes. Fuck a suburban teenager today. Pass HIV along…Share it with a college student. And tell them to pass it on. Want to bet we'll see a cure before a few hundred of them have died…. It feels right and sounds like fun! ACT UP has lots of leftover flyers. Any ideas on what to do with them?

Their position created a furor and, as they intended, drew more attention to the issues. "Hate us for our methods," they say, "but think about AIDS."

In November, 1990, Nash and other members of ACT UP/Denver embarked on another ambitious project. With support from the Chinook Fund, they produced five images and spent $3,300 to display them on 51 billboards around Denver. The images were portraits of local men with AIDS, three white, one African-American, one Latino. A call had been put out for people willing to declare their status publicly, and the five were selected from the pictures received. Hoping to reach the broadest possible audience, they worked hard to include a woman and a child, but the few willing to consider going public with their diagnosis withdrew at the last moment to protect relatives. The texts—"AIDS is not killing David Esquibel [for example]…YOU ARE. What haven't you done about AIDS?"—were printed in English and Spanish. The photographs ranged from family snapshots (one with wife and child, one with a cat) to handsome studio portraits. None pictured the emaciated "victim" that has become the AIDS stereotype.

Some of the billboards remained up after the contracted four months, during which time four of those pictured succumbed to the disease. The billboard company was supposed to write "DIED" across the appropriate boards if this happened, but they didn't, so a spray-paint team from ACT UP did it themselves. "Rationally," says Nash, "I know that the billboards had nothing to do with their deaths, but three of the four deaths actually seemed quite sudden. In the last few weeks, I just wanted to pull it down."

At a vigil and rally in late April, David Esquibel was the only PWA left to speak. Few of the invited mayoral and City Council candidates showed up. "It seems government agencies would rather see these people disappear than to address communities they do not understand," says Nash. "Genocide comes to mind." While the Chinook Fund received favorable mail about their part in the billboards, ACT UP received a death threat from the father of one of the PWAs.

Somewhere down the line, Nash would like to establish an "electronic co-op" for computer image production by activists, consisting of a central site, with a few terminals that would allow members of any group to produce work on a regular basis. In the meantime, Nash and ACT UP continue to assail the authorities and the people of Denver with variations on the themes of denial and memory. They feel it's a matter of life and death—rather than art—to compete with the major media, and to incorporate electronic production with greater originality and sophistication in their visual work.

Fall 1991

On the Side of the Deepest Soul on Earth: An Interview with Ja Kyung Rhee and Hye Sook of Theatre 1981

By Steven Durland

Gok. It is the sound of wailing. It is a cry from deep in the heart. In Korea for thousands of years it has been a way of expressing sorrow over the death of a beloved one. In Los Angeles it was the name given to a series of performance works created by Theatre 1981 that explored themes of suffering and the sorrow of war and nuclear destruction. —Eds.

Theatre 1981 evolved out of the Korean American Avant Garde Theatre: Korean-American artists dedicated to feminist and antiwar themes. The pieces were written by Ja Kyung Rhee and directed by her husband, filmmaker Ik Tae Rhee, the group's only male. Other founding collaborators included painter and performance artist Hye Sook, the principal performer in the series, playwright So Hyun Chang, filmmaker Hye Sook Yoo and fashion designer Kimmi Song, along with a number of other participants.

In 1982 the group presented *Gok-I: We wail for all the spirits of the dead,* in 1985 *Gok-III: The death of water,* and in the Fall of 1988 *Gok-IV: The death of the earth.* (*Gok-II* was written but never produced.) Their style combined traditional Korean theatrical and ritual forms with experimental performance techniques to express political and spiritual concerns. The performances had none of the didacticism one might expect from political theatre. Instead, the group chose to explore the deeply personal and human issues inherent in global political maneuvering.

The *Gok* performances were all very similar, especially to Western eyes unfamiliar with the traditional Korean references. On the stage, an environment was created with lengths of white rags, typical of Korean shaman theatre. The performers produced the chilling and unworldly sounds of Korean funeral wailing. Universal symbols such as water and fire were combined with symbols such as the raven—representing power and death—to create allegories of suffering and eventual transcendence. They find the road to transcendence in the feminine. "Throughout our history, we've [Korea] always been attacked by people," Hye Sook said in a recent newspaper interview. "But we never attacked others, so a different soul developed within us—like a woman's—one that can contribute to the world's soul."

I interviewed Hye Sook and Ja Kyung Rhee in 1989 about their work with Theatre 1981. Sook had recently returned from a visit to Korea where she had several exhibits of her paintings and did a solo performance. Rhee, who writes art criticism and cultural commentary for the Korean press, has been doing research on a group of Koreans who left their country early in this century to escape Japanese domination, only to end up as slaves in Mexico with no homes to return to and no country to protect their rights.

Steven Durland: *How did the* Gok *series develop?*

Ja Kyung Rhee: In Korea in 1980 there was a big massacre of students who were protesting against the dictatorship. At the time you knew about it, but you couldn't talk about it. It was a dilemma for Korean people. What should we do about it? We wanted to mourn for them, but we weren't allowed to acknowledge the massacre. In *Gok-I* we were mourning for those students. But I also wanted to make it in a universal tongue. These kinds of massacres happen all over the world. We were mourning for Iran and El Salvador and other places as well.

In *Gok-III* I elevated it into a more aesthetic level. I used fire to symbolize destruction and water to symbolize peace. *Gok-III* was less specific than *Gok-I*. *Gok-IV* was a warning about nuclear destruction.

SD: *In Gok-IV you gave significant attention to aesthetic, political and shamanistic issues. Is any one of these areas of particular importance to you?*

JKR: We wanted to make a very powerful piece in which the three elements worked well together. We wanted an overall powerful work. In Korea shamanism is used to express and soothe the pain of the people. So we used shamanism in that way.

SD: *Do you see the shamanism in your work as more actual or metaphorical?*

JKR: It's actual. Even in high religion—Christianity or Buddhism—the shamanistic element is very alive. It's a driving force in civilization.

SD: *There's an underlying focus on feminism in your work. Do you make a direct connection between shamanism and feminism?*

JKR: Realistically, there is no connection between shamanism and feminism. But in the sense that shamanism and ritual are used to comfort and lift people's souls who are oppressed, it counters the authoritarian and masculine culture that does the oppressing.

SD: *Are shamans usually women in Korea?*

Hye Sook: Yes. And usually they are very low-class. People don't want to meet or marry them. There are two kinds. One becomes a shaman because of some kind of sickness she goes through. The other is descended from a shaman family.

When I was young Korea was very interested in the new Western culture and tried to abolish shamanism. Now that it is almost gone there is becoming a new interest. Koreans have always had their own shamanistic religion but I think they've been denying it for a long time. But I don't think you can erase it just by taking on a new culture.

SD: *Hye Sook, the singing or wailing you and the other performers do in Gok-IV provides much of the work's power. The sounds you produce seem almost primal. How did you develop that?*

HS: One evening after we'd first met and were deciding to do something, I got really drunk, and I was lying down and making this weird sound. The others recorded it. They said, "You made this sound while you were drunk. Let's try to improvise with this sound." It was the sound you hear me make during the performance. That's how I started.

I never learned singing. But everyone has a sound inside them. When you're really touched you weep or laugh. Or when you have sexual ecstasy you scream. It's all the same thing you have. I feel really lucky that I found the voice inside of me.

SD: *Even though the dialogue is in Korean, it seems you've structured the work to eliminate any language barriers.*

HS: Yes. Ik Tae Rhee [the director] kept telling us that this sorrow is so universal that when we are truthful to it we can convey our feeling to other people. There's no better language than emotion. He was focusing on that. At the same time we wanted to stress how beautiful another language could be when you hear it.

SD: *How does the Korean audience in Los Angeles react to your work?*

JKR: There are some taboos among Koreans about shamanism so Korean audiences don't really like it that we do this.

HS: Koreans are very religious people but now they believe in Christianity. It's interesting. Christianity has never worked in Japan. They believe in Shinto. But the Koreans are very much against Shinto because Korea was under forced Japanese rule for so long. Catholicism has a lot of power with the young people because of its liberation theology—liberating the people, fighting dictatorship, working for the poor, not the rich. But Korea also has deep roots connecting it with shamanism.

SD: *Do they get more upset about the shamanism or the politics?*

HS: The shamanism. Sometimes they call us and say, "Don't ever do that again."

SD: *So they're sympathetic to the politics of the work?*

HS: Yes. Korean people are very interested in politics now because political changes are happening so quickly. Our role is to expand their political concern toward the survival of the human race.

SD: *Is there any theatre in Korea that is similar to the works you're creating here?*

JKR: There's a similar shamanistic search in Korean plays. But it is specific to local Korean concerns. We wanted to penetrate into Western culture so we focused more on universal issues.

SD: How does Korean politics affect your work?

HS: I live in Los Angeles but I read the Korean newspapers. I'm very connected with Korea in my heart. There are many radical youngsters in Korea who are very interested in seeing the government change. The issue now has become the unification of Korea. There has been a lot of torture and killing. Last year several students burned themselves to death. It's a situation that drives people crazy. It is not uncommon for young people to end up in mental hospitals. It's like their schizophrenia reflects the divided country they live in.

But things are getting better. I went to Korea this year and the whole thing was changing, becoming more dramatic. There is more freedom of the press. I did a performance that was on national television. If I had gone there five years ago I would have been banned or they would have taken my passport away.

SD: What's the art world like in Korea right now?

HS: There's an art scene just like the American scene—galleries, money, markets. Then there are younger artists who are doing important things who aren't getting much attention. Their work is about challenging the government. It's political art, people's art.

But there's also a problem with some of this work. Some really goes to the core of humanism and is still aesthetically so good that you can be really touched by it. But often you see bad performances with a lot of propaganda. Many political artists don't believe in aesthetic high quality. I read the same thing about North Korean art. They make really great propaganda on a grandiose scale, but it's not too good aesthetically.

SD: There's a lot of talk these days about cultural appropriation, the dominant culture claiming the cultures of Third-World countries. How do you see this issue as a Korean-American?

HS: It's kind of funny. You come to America and you talk about "why my art is not here." But this is America. If you really want you can go back to your own country and make a great statement.

Sometimes I feel awkward about it. Korean art is often about expressionistic lines using brush strokes. It's a natural line, we didn't "invent" it. Now, when this generation of Korean artists show work, the critics say our art looks like Sam Francis or Robert Motherwell. But Sam Francis looks like us. So Korean artists have a problem because we didn't go beyond Motherwell. There is another realm of creation using our line and personality that can go beyond Sam Francis or Motherwell, but we haven't reached that yet because our history of modern art is only 30 years old. Artists came to Asia to get inspiration in Zen art and we didn't even ask for credit.

> # We've got to create our own version of modern Asian culture.

I think a lot of the responsibility is ours. We were trying to somehow melt into the tradition of Western art and got lost. But it's also unavoidable. I'm brought up on TV. I'm wearing this jacket. The world is one place now, and Third-World people have a lot of catching up to do to create their own unique, modern culture. I feel very strongly about it. I am the type of person who tortures herself about history. So if you are beyond history, then it's good. I feel we have a mission as the new generation from Asia. We've got to create our own version of modern Asian culture.

SD: *Then what are the issues for you two as artists working outside your native country?*

JKR: Where an artist lives is very important. We live in Los Angeles. This is where our reality exists. And Los Angeles is very interesting. America has had a very short history to cultivate its own culture. New York art developed by buying up preexisting Western art. In Los Angeles, people are coming here and it is happening here. An actual pattern of history-making, rather than just accepting pre-existing culture.

HS: I think Asian artists have to be at the very core of their existence. They can use their costumes or their voices or something, but it's not the time to take advantage of the fact that you're Asian because it's different. The Japanese art of Kabuki is good because it's good, not because it's chic. Artists have to be on the side of the deepest soul on earth.

Spring 1989

No Time for the Blues (Aesthetic)

By Pearl Cleage

Pearl Cleage is an Atlanta-based writer and performance artist, columnist for the Atlanta Tribune, *and founding editor of* Catalyst Magazine. *We commissioned this essay for an issue of* High Performance *called "The Blues Aesthetic."* —Eds.

I don't know if I want to think about a Blues Aesthetic. It might be too dangerous. Or too scary. I am, after all, a 40-year-old black woman writer, living in the Deep South with a 15-year-old daughter, and a way of making a living that depends largely upon the kindness of African-American strangers, the accessibility of the public dole, the benevolence of corporate America, and the availability of white critics to review my work.

What I mean is, I don't know if it's psychically safe for me to pause and consider my blues aesthetically. I don't think so. I'd probably have to spend the rest of the day weeping, and I've got too much stuff to do. Thinking about my blues doesn't help me get my work done, which is, after all, the point.

We are at war, right? Fighting for our lives, right? Struggling ceaselessly for our freedom? Taking our blues underground to teach it how to be a demolitions expert? Right?

I do, after all, live in a place where women are routinely beaten, tortured, mutilated and murdered by men and almost nobody talks about it. A place where the jails are full of black men, and the housing projects are full of black women and children, and nobody seems to notice. A place where there is rape. The kind of place where blues is always the dominant state of mind for anybody who's got half a brain and an ear to the ground.

I am, after all, a member of a group that is in a state of serious and probably terminal crisis, caught up in a weird, high-tech, MTV kind of crack-fueled genocide that we don't even understand yet. It soon come, as the Rastas will tell you. Soon come. And it will be easy to recognize that terrible moment because the realization of where and what and who we are really will be so overwhelming that we will all stop working or hanging out or making love or raising children or cooking dinner and just wail, moan, holler, beat our breasts and tear our hair and ask the goddess to please explain what the hell we did to deserve to be black in the belly of the whale, locked into a decadent goose step toward the decline and fall when we never even got to run the damn thing.

> **I want an aesthetic that is based in struggle, energized by commitment, deeply rooted in and reflective of our own specific community, crisis and culture.**

And if we're not careful, somebody will hear all that terrible, hopeless, helpless, angry sound, clean it up, put some biking pants and dread extensions on it and sell it to our enemies and less-enlightened comrades for a bundle. Langston already told us they had taken our blues and gone and you know Langston did not lie.

See what I mean about a Blues Aesthetic? It has a good beat but you sure can't dance to it.

I don't want to think about the blues. I want to think about victory chants and warrior wails, the stuff my people should sing when they go into battle and kick ass and right the wrongs and sing the songs of our own black loveliness.

I want an aesthetic that is based in struggle, energized by commitment, deeply rooted in and reflective of our own specific community, crisis and culture. I want an aesthetic where slavery is not one of the acceptable options and a good review in *The New York Times* is cause for serious self-criticism and major regrouping.

I want an aesthetic that screams and hollers and tells people it's time to *rise*. I want an aesthetic that is stockpiling weapons in the basement and books in the attic. I want an aesthetic that is not afraid of politics or propaganda or popular culture or women's wisdom or the phases of the moon. I want an aesthetic that will not go gently into this or any other good night. I want an aesthetic that doesn't simply describe the problem eloquently, but proposes some solutions, some perspective, some points of view that lead to clarity, not confusion.

What I mean is, I know I've got a right to sing the blues. I just don't have the time right now.

Winter 1990

Call Me in '93: An Interview with James Luna

By Steven Durland

Performance artist James Luna, of Luiseno Indian ancestry, talks about what it's like to be pigeonholed as an ethnic artist, and called upon only when his ethnicity is timely—as during the Christopher Columbus anniversary in 1992. He also addresses his place as an artist in his own community.   —Eds.

James Earle Fraser modeled *End of the Trail* in the 1890s and enlarged it to monumental size for display at the Panama-Pacific Exposition of 1915 in San Francisco. The exposition marked the completion of the Panama Canal and a watershed in California history, separating the state's pioneer past from its future as a center for Pacific commerce. Fraser's sculpture is, in effect, a bow to the modern world. Body drained of energy, the Indian slumps lifelessly, his spear, once raised in war and the hunt, hangs downward, as if about to slip to the ground. This particular formulation of the ill-fated Indian has projected a powerful stereotype through the 20th century. It can be seen today on belt buckles, in advertisements and commercial prints, and, in perhaps its most ironical manifestation, on signs designating retirement communities.

—Julie Schimmel[1]

If James Earle Fraser's sculpture *End of the Trail* was a "bow to the modern world," then James Luna's photographic tableau *End of the Frail* is a message to the modern world 75 years later. The message is simple: The "ill-fated" Indian, so mythically portrayed on belt-buckles, is not dead. Indians are part of contemporary culture. Only the enemies they struggle against—poverty, alcoholism, identity—have changed.

In his tableau variation on *End of the Trail,* Luna mimics the same lifeless pose, but the pony has been replaced by a weathered sawhorse, and the spear by a bottle of liquor. Nobility has been replaced by pathos. The exhaustion is no longer that of effort but that of despair.

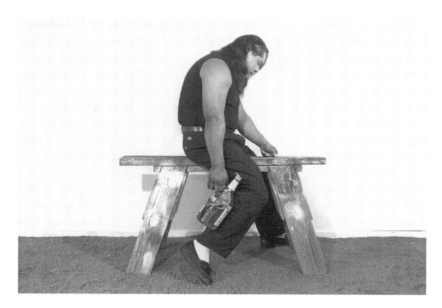

The piece reflects the range of concerns Luna brings to his body of work. It plays directly on art-historical reference, parodying an American masterpiece. The humor is informed by the conceptually based, art-referential parody typical of so much recent art, but has deeper roots as well. "My appeal for humor in my work comes from Indian culture where humor can be a form of knowledge, critical thought and perhaps used to just ease the pain. I think we Indians live in worlds filled with irony and I want to relate that in my works," he notes.[2]

Luna was born on the La Jolla Indian reservation in 1950 to a Luiseno Indian mother and a Mexican father. He grew up in Orange County and graduated from the University of California Irvine with a degree in art in 1976, a time when the school was a hotbed for the development of conceptual and performance art in southern California. He received a masters in counseling at the San Diego State University in 1983 and currently works as a counselor for Palomar College in San Marcos. He moved back to the La Jolla Reservation in 1976.

Originally a painter, Luna now refers to himself as a conceptual artist and works primarily in installation, performance art and video. He has found a comfortable place to create in the space where contemporary art and its concerns with parody, ritual and autobiography intersect with the traditional attitudes of Indian culture. The forms he uses are familiar to a contemporary gallery/performance audience, yet when he infuses those forms with information from his own culture, it exposes some of the ancestral roots of the forms themselves.

Luna claims his work is not political. "In doing work about social issues I use myself to explore conditions here on the reservation. It is not my place to tell people how to act," he says.[3] Yet, in the hands of an outsider, it would be hard to see his work as not being political. He is challenging our tendency to mythologize and historicize Native American culture. He is breaking taboos by directly addressing his own, and his culture's battle with alcoholism. (It is telling that he discusses his work and the struggles facing contemporary Indians using words like "dysfunction" and "recovery.") It is work that can produce a certain amount of discomfort for non-Indian and Indian alike.

Luna's work has been appearing in shows throughout the country during the past several years, and his installations in the Whitney Museum's "SITEseeing" exhibition and The New Museum's "Decade Show" recently earned him a Bessie Award. He has declined offers to exhibit outside the country, feeling that his audience and the issues he works with are particular to North America.

I did the following interview with Luna in September, 1991.

Steven Durland: *When I first approached you to do an interview, you quite pointedly told me your motto was "Call me in '93." How did that develop?*

James Luna: I'm quite disillusioned with the multicultural movement. I really feel like education is the key and we still haven't addressed that. For instance, I would be very proud to be in a book of contemporary American Indian artists. But I think in the end what would be most satisfying would be that I would be in the art-history text used in a regular art-history class as James Luna, artist. Period. James Luna, artist who happens to be an Indian. I wouldn't want to be in one and not the other.

This '92 thing is sort of coming on the tail end of that. Curators want a certain kind of Indian and a certain kind of Indian art. They want you to be angry, they want you to be talking it up. It's the same rush to say 'let's have a multicultural show.'

Now everyone is saying 'let's have an Indian show' or 'let's have a colonialism show.' So when people call me I have to ask 'Why didn't you call me before? You're calling me now, but are you going to call me in '93?' It's a way to show but it may be a dead end if you don't do that kind of work. This last year has been real good for me. I am showing at different places and I am

...there was one guy there who was accusing me of using my culture. Using it. And I thought, "Well, what the fuck am I going to use?"

real happy to be in this *Shared Vision* show, as much I was really happy to be in the *Decade Show* with all types of artists. But I don't know if I want to take a step back and be in that kind of titled show. So I have this personal thing that if it's colonial, call me in '93.

SD: You started as a painter. How did you get involved in performance?

JL: When you go to a school like [University of California] Irvine, and you come from a small place and you're not into the names and the movements, you might as well be on Mars. In my paintings I was trying to match colors with designs and do movement, very simple geometric forms going one way and other things going another, that were doing a lot of things on the canvas. I felt I was stymied with the paintings because I couldn't be vocal. I couldn't express feelings.

Then I stumbled into performance with Bas Jan Ader, an instructor from the Netherlands [at Irvine], and Jim Turrell, another instructor there. I found a whole new place to be vocal. I wanted to show transition, like the *Drinking Piece*. That was a transition from the normal state to the unnormal state. I did a piece about an unwrapping of a bundle where eventually I became the bundle. It was an offshoot of the Lakota ceremony where the guys wrapped themselves in blankets. I did another one about a dancer, where I had the dancer's objects nailed to the walls, and I came in and as I undressed I put something on, till I was a dancer. Then I danced and went back through the transition and put on my street clothes and walked out. It was a real simple thing.

SD: *How was your work viewed at the school?*

JL: When I introduced some Indian imagery into my geometry paintings, which was real popular at the time, I found I could use my culture in my art and it was OK. People liked the paintings, but because they were "ethnic" it was very hard for them to be critical. With the performance work they were more frightened and put off. We had a critique class and there was one guy there who was accusing me of using my culture. *Using* it. And I thought, "Well, what the fuck am I going to use?"

SD: *Before and even during the time you were there, UC Irvine was really a hotbed of experimentation and performance. Were you influenced by other students like Chris Burden?*

JL: Yes and no. I'd heard he was around there. I never saw him or his work. I just felt aloof from the whole school. On the other hand it offered me the opportunity and training to know how to do this. It wasn't until later that I put it all together, that I realized that I'd brushed shoulders with someone who was to be famous later on, or that I was being shown something that a lot of other departments weren't doing. I didn't go to a lot of shows and I didn't hang out with the art crowd. I didn't do all these things these other people did. I feel it's somewhat unfortunate, but at the same time I think I was probably saved. I have a full-time job as a counselor and there's no way I'd ever quit it, because of the security it offers me and even more so because of the connection it gives me to people. I feel like if I were in art full-time, as an artist or an arts administrator, that I would lose touch. Maybe that's not true, but that's what I feel.

SD: *What did you do after you finished school?*

JL: I went dormant. Then [in 1986] David Avalos, the curator at the Centro [de la Raza in San Diego] and Philip Brookman heard about me and they brought me down from the mountains because they realized that there must be something out there happening other than the typical Indian art. So I brought some ideas and some old stuff and they liked it and turned me loose. It was probably one of the biggest things that happened in my life was to be let loose, to have a budget and to be given these two big rooms. It just felt real good.

SD: *You have a vocabulary that incorporates Indian traditions as well as the relatively recent history of process performance. Do both of those things enter in when you create your work?*

JL: It was during the creation of the Intar piece, *Two Worlds,* where it really hit me hard that that was my strength, that I was a man of two worlds. It sounds kind of hokey, but that was really the moment, as I was walking through that doorway, fixing the piece, I realized that this is my strength, not just that I'm a man of two worlds, but that I do it with ease. And every Indian who lives long enough, it comes to them.

SD: *How do you relate your performance to traditional Indian rituals?*

JL: Well, other people talk to me about rituals, and I don't think I could do that. I couldn't show a ritual. I couldn't get a ritual and tear it up and show it as art. That would go against all of my personal beliefs. But, on the other hand, the performances *are* rituals, because they're a process, and they involve a lot of things that are in ritual that people don't realize. There's a lot of patience involved. There was a lot patience involved in the WPA piece [*Tell Tale Heart,* 1990]. If people leave in the middle, maybe they'll get part of it. The people who stay the longest have gone through the ritual. When I'm running [in the piece], that's another part of ritual, endurance. It has that strenuous feel of dancing. The feet against the floor, the sweating, the whoosh when I run by.

I presented concepts of ritual without presenting ritual, Indian ritual. It's part of the message I have for my Indian audiences. Here is a medium [performance] where you can do all those things—you can do ceremony, you can do dance, you can do singing, you can do what you do every day—and in the right context it's art.

SD: Do you intend for your work to address both Indian and non-Indian audiences?

JL: I think that what keeps me rooted is that I try to think of my audience as being all Indians. That doesn't mean that I do all my work for approval by the Indian people, but the biggest thing is that they'll get it; whether they like it or not, they'll get it. Being simple is much harder than being complex.

SD: Does the fact that you're an artist give you any particular position in the community?

JL: Well, it's kind of funny. I told you I made my art for Indians. But Indian people, reservation people, don't go to galleries. That's educational. Why should you go to a gallery? So that's been a real dilemma for me. And it's not just my Indian community, it's all Indian communities. So a lot of people haven't seen my work. But the people who have have been blown away by it. It's broken their whole concept of what art is. I showed the video [of *Tell Tale Heart*] to a few people and they were stunned. They go, "God, it has everything in it. There's watchmacallit's house, there's a picture of my great-grandmother in there, one of the old Indians, there's songs." And it blows people away because there's all this history. There's a sequence, not only in the past, but in the present.

SD: You cross back and forth across cultural borders a lot. Does that produce any antagonism?

JL: I've gotten some criticism. But it's been from people who really haven't seen the work or the body of it. Like the drinking piece—after I did it people came up and patted me on the back and what they were saying was, "I'm glad you talked about it, because we can't keep quiet about it." As a trained counselor and an alcoholic, you know that the first item in recovery is talking about it. I just try to show by example the agony of it, the pain of it, using myself as an example and the reality of it.

SD: *You've referred to yourself as a contemporary traditionalist. What does that mean?*

JL: You always see these Indian paintings and people refer to them as "traditional Indian paintings." That's bullshit because the only Indian painters we ever had did body painting, and hides, and pottery. That's Indian painting. All this other stuff is contemporary. The traditional part [in my work] is the ritual part. It's traditional thought, traditional process. It has nothing to do with these stoic paintings of Indians. That has something to do with memory, or not even memory but just passed-down visual imagery.

SD: *Last year the Los Angeles Festival presented a number of works that were representative of traditional performance and ritual from a variety of cultures. Afterward there was a lot of discussion around questions of authenticity. Can traditional ritual exist in the context of an avant-garde festival? Why were the Matachine Indians wearing tennis shoes? What's your feeling about issues of authenticity?*

JL: Aren't we allowed to progress? Yeah, things are handed down, but things change. People die, things are forgotten and you just carry on as best you can. And probably that stuff they think that happened has gone through a process, too.

And there's the issue of what's an Indian? Who's an Indian? If you're part Indian, what's the other part? How does that influence you? Does it make you less, does it make you more? I don't have an answer for that but that's part of my work, questioning that.

Then there's this whole group of people out there who want to be Indians, that want to be the "good" part of the culture. But for me being an Indian from a reservation is more than that. And it really bothers me that there's all these people wanting to *take*. And what pisses me off is they only want the best. You can't have just the best.

That's why I dislike the movie *Dances With Wolves*. It did nothing but glorify all the good stuff. It didn't show any Indians mad, or any Indians upset. It didn't show any Indians cry. It didn't show any Indians fucking up. We're still beautiful, stoic and pretty. You see the movie and you go out and see a fat, overweight, acne-covered, poor, uneducated person—is that the real Indian you want to see? Not that we're all either one of those. But it just isn't one way.

Notes

1. "Inventing 'the Indian,'" from *The West as America: Reinterpreting Images of the Frontier, 1820-1920*, 1991, Smithsonian Institution, p. 173.

2. From artist's statement in *Encuentro: Invasion of the Americas and the Making of the Mestizo*, a catalog for a show of the same name presented at SPARC (Social and Public Art Resource Center), Los Angeles, 1991.

3. *ibid.*

Winter 1991

Shooting the Klan:
An Interview with Andres Serrano

By Coco Fusco

Andres Serrano was an apparently unwilling soldier in the Culture Wars of the early '90s. Here scholar and performance artist Coco Fusco asks him what he intended to do when he made Piss Christ, *what he thinks he's doing photographing the Ku Klux Klan, and how things have changed for him as a result of all the hoopla.   —Eds.*

It was *Piss Christ,* Andres Serrano's photograph of a crucifix immersed in his own urine, together with Robert Mapplethorpe's homoerotic images, that in 1989 set off the attack against art from the far Right. In a short period of time, Serrano was transformed from a relatively successful but reclusive New York artist and member of the collective Group Material into a celebrity/pariah under perpetual public scrutiny.

He has received death threats and hate mail and has lost grants on the one hand, and on the other has enjoyed dozens of laudatory articles and a sizeable hike in his prices. Furthermore, the fuss caused by Christian fundamentalists has hardly dimmed Serrano's fascination with religious iconography. His apartment, nestled in a semi-industrial area near downtown Brooklyn, is full of antique ecclesiastical furniture. It would give the impression of a Mediterranean antechoir were there not also numerous skulls, artworks and other unusual knick-knacks.

The combination of indirect approach to issues, cool conceptual technique and emotionally charged focus on symbols that resonate outside the vocabulary of the art world has been Serrano's trademark since he began to produce mature work in the early '80s. In his first pieces, he concentrated largely on reworking Catholic iconography in highly stylized tableaux. Later he moved into more abstract images that also touched on social and religious taboos, using bodily fluids such as milk, menstrual blood and semen. *Piss Christ* emerged

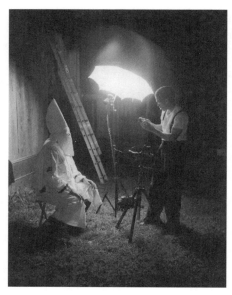

out of a transition between these periods and was originally part of a series in which Serrano photographed several statues, which had varied connotations, immersed in different fluids. Nonetheless, just as the artist has come to stand for the biggest controversy to rock the art world in the '80s, so has one photograph come to stand for his entire oeuvre.

Many other artists whose funding and freedom of expression were threatened by the National Endowment for the Arts (NEA) controversy have since made their "censorship" the subject of their work. Serrano, however, has avoided focusing on the far Right's attacks as much as possible, and has ostensibly ignored it in his recent work.

In November, 1990, Serrano opened a new chapter of his career with an arresting exhibition of 20 cibachrome portraits, 13 of homeless people in New York entitled *Nomads*, most of whom are African-American, and seven members of the Atlanta, Georgia, chapter of the Ku Klux Klan entitled *Klansman*. Presenting us with an encounter of extremes, Serrano uncovers disturbing paradoxes. The homeless become the symbols of the outcome of life for people of color in a racist society, while the Klansmen stand as the symbols of racial hatred; but they are both outcasts, both marginal in relation to the presumed audience. Even the most liberal "other-loving" spectator or collector would have to contend with the impossibility of assuming a racially or socially neutral position in relation to these subjects.

These images confront us with the moral and political dilemmas stemming from racial tensions in this country. Yet Serrano's style, though frontal, is far from declaratory. His pictures are emotive and elliptical, puzzling, frightening and beautiful at the same time.

Coco Fusco: *Your use of Catholic symbolism stands out in part because you are operating in a predominantly Protestant context. An attraction to the sensuality and the carnality that you bring out in your Catholic iconography can develop, since Protestant symbolism looks rather pale by comparison. How would it affect your work to be exhibited in a Catholic context?*

Andres Serrano: I have always felt that my work is religious, not sacrilegious. I would say that there are many individuals in the Church who appreciate it and who do not have a problem with it. The best place for *Piss Christ* is in a church. In fact, I recently had a show in Marseilles in an actual church that also functions as an exhibition space, and the work looked great there. I think if the Vatican is smart, someday they'll collect my work.

CF: *Does your interest in Catholicism have to do more with an attraction to the iconography or is it about wanting to make a social or political comment about what the Church represents?*

AS: Look at my apartment. I am drawn to the symbols of the Church. I like the aesthetics of the Church. I like Church furniture. I like going to Church for aesthetic reasons, rather than spiritual ones. In my work, I explore my own Catholic obsessions. An artist is nothing without his or her obsessions, and I have mine. One of the things that always bothered me was the fundamentalist labeling of my work as "anti-Christian bigotry." As a former Catholic, and as someone who even today is not opposed to being called a Christian, I felt I had every right to use the symbols of the Church and resented being told not to.

CF: *At the same time you have expressed concern about the Church's position on many contemporary issues.*

AS: I am drawn to Christ but I have real problems with the Catholic Church. I don't go out of my way to be critical of the Church in my work, because I think that I make icons worthy of the Church. Oftentimes we love the thing we hate and vice versa. Unfortunately, the Church's position on most contemporary issues makes it hard to take them seriously.

CF: *So you do see yourself carrying on a tradition of religious art?*

AS: Absolutely. I am not a heretic. I like to believe that rather than destroy icons, I make new ones.

CF: *Your most recent portraits of the homeless and the Klan do not appear to have anything to do with Catholicism. Does this represent a break from your past interests, or will you return to them?*

AS: I leave the option open. When I was photographing the Imperial Wizard and saw him put on his green robe, I said to his secretary that it looked like a religious robe, and she said, "To some Klan members, they are." Some people have compared the Klan images to ecclesiastical figures.

CF: *Many critics who have written about you have attempted to situate your work in the context of art that deals with ethnicity. I would say that your work is better understood as a reflection on culture as institution and symbol, and the power invested in certain icons. Do you see interpretations of your work as problematic?*

AS: Any critic can have his or her own interpretation. I have always felt that I am the sum total of my parts. One of the things that I am happy about in my life as an artist is that I am not considered a Hispanic artist. I am just an artist. That is the way that it should be. My work is intensely personal. I don't think that because I am Hispanic I should therefore do Hispanic work. Are cum shots Hispanic? What about close-ups of menstrual pads? Is it Hispanic to photograph the Klan? People have to find ways of explaining the work. Sometimes I don't reach out enough, so they have to fill in the void.

CF: *It is extremely difficult to categorize art by Latinos on the East Coast. The population here is so varied—from the largely middle-class South American emigres, to first and second generation Puerto Ricans, mostly from working-class backgrounds, to Cuban exiles and the newest arrivals, undocumented Mexicans. Little if any of the* *work resembles Chicano art from the Southwest.*

AS: It could be that the New York art world is so cosmopolitan and so international that artists doing this sort of work tend to want to be here rather than on the West Coast. I went to San Francisco last year to give a lecture, a few months after the controversy. The minute I got off the train reporters appeared who wanted to talk to me and all sorts of interviews were set up. People seemed to imply that I was doing something for the race. I was told that no Hispanic artist had gotten this much coverage in over ten years. It was as if they were thanking me. In Boulder, Colorado, I recently gave a presentation to a Chicano class. A student asked me if I would ever want to take pictures of Hispanics, for the race, once again. I said I wasn't sure, but that the best thing I could do for the race, or for any race for that matter, is to do my work.

I usually refer to myself as Hispanic. When I was a kid, we were all Spanish. As we grew older, the terms changed and we became Hispanic. The students I met in Boulder were very politicized and used the term Latino or Chicano. I hadn't realized there existed that separation between those who are bothered by the term Hispanic and those who are not.

CF: *Your approach to issues is consistently indirect, including your stance toward ethnicity, which you suggest could be a partial explanation of a work, but not a complete one. Your work has achieved politically volatile results from what you claim is not an overtly political practice. Many artists are cautious about talking about themselves as political artists because it damages their commercial potential and implies an agitprop stance some take to be too limiting and simplistic. Yet, the conceptual art tradition you intersect with has political implications. What then is the relationship of your work to political issues?*

AS: Being born, especially being born a person of color, is a political act in itself. Everything you do from that point on is political without having to be called political. My work has social implications, it functions in a social arena. In relation to the controversy over *Piss Christ*, I think the work was politicized by forces outside it, and as a result, some people expect to see something recognizably "political" in my work. I am still trying to do my work as I see fit, which I see as coming from a very personal point of view with broader implications.

CF: *Many of the performance artists whose work has been part of the NEA censorship controversy have made art and activist interventions in response to having lost grants. You have not. Your answer to having been taken up in this controversy appears to be, at least in terms of your work, to ignore it. In doing so, you diminish the importance of that judgment. Is this one more indirect move of yours, one more way of stepping around the obvious?*

AS: As far as I am concerned, I wasn't going to let Jesse Helms or any other politician dictate what direction my work should take. If I didn't directly respond to it, it was my way of ignoring them and continuing my own merry way.

CF: *Your most recent exhibition of portraits of Ku Klux Klan members and homeless people seems to take portraits of these groups as an entity, implicitly referring to each other. Whoever views the portraits of these two very different groups of people must momentarily evade a moral judgment, although most art gallery visitors make judgments about these groups of people all the time. In everything I read in which you talk about your encounters with the Klan, you also seemed to avoid making a moral judgment about the people you were taking pictures of. What does it mean to you to throw morality into question in this way?*

AS: The idea of showing the Klan and the homeless pictures together was exciting. I like the tension between the two. They are about extreme poverty and extreme prejudice. I like the way you put it that the average gallery-goer is probably somewhere in the middle, and he has to reconcile his feelings for one group with his feelings for the other. The homeless by themselves could have worked well, people would have liked them, they would have been fine. But then if the Klan pictures had been shown by themselves the first time, it would have been problematic not to have something to balance them.

CF: *I couldn't help wondering about the implications of having an affluent art collector purchase a photograph of the Klan Wizard to hang in his or her living room. Someone who might never associate with a Klan member or admit to being a Klan supporter would end up wanting to consume an image of one. You were bringing them into a relationship with an image of something they might otherwise reject.*

AS: What you just described is exactly what I also imagined in terms of the portraits of the homeless. Collectors would purchase work about people who they would probably never have a relationship with, but are safe for them to admire from a distance. I wondered if there would be any kind of conflict for the collectors. Someone pointed out to me that it wasn't pictures of Klansmen or homeless people that were being collected—they are Serranos, so the subject matter is secondary.

CF: *I don't think that any other postmodern photographer calls on the viewer to engage with subjects as abject or as socially marginalized as yours. Your work demands that the form expand in order to explore its own moral/ethical implications. You can find sublime beauty in these pictures, but they also invoke a sense of horror.*

AS: I am pulling at the form. My intent as an artist is to monumentalize or aestheticize the mundane. But it is also important that I identify with my subjects. The Klan people and the homeless are outcasts. I have always felt like an underdog; I root for the underdog.

CF: *How did you decide to go to Atlanta to photograph the Klan?*

AS: After making the homeless portraits, I still wanted to continue doing portraits. They had to be unusual subjects for me to be interested in them. I thought that masked portraits would be very unusual and immediately thought that the Klan would be a natural. I was in Atlanta giving a lecture. I had four or five names, and I pursued them until I made more contacts and continued from there.

CF: So it started as a formal decision—you weren't thinking about who it was that you were photographing?

AS: I was aware of that dimension as well, and that is why I was attracted to it. Being who I am racially and culturally, it was a challenge. If I had just been a white photographer taking pictures of the Klan it wouldn't have been very interesting for me.

CF: It seems that the way you photograph your subjects changes with these portraits. The images in the Nomads and Klan series evoke a humanist sentiment that none of your previous work does. You seem to be expressing a desire to connect on a subjective level with your subjects. Why did that happen?

AS: One of the things that the controversy made me aware of was that I have always been a loner. There have been times in my life where I have been fairly antisocial. I have never been part of the system. I have never voted in my life. Whenever possible, I operate outside the system. Now, I realize that I can no longer function as a human being in a vacuum. All of a sudden people were reaching out to me—in critical or supportive ways—but in either case I was bombarded by human contact, which was very strange for me. It made me change. I began to allow people to enter my life and work.

In a way, I have become a symbol. But I am just a human being. And it is hard for human beings to be symbols.

CF: So your response to a controversy that made you a public figure was to connect with people more in your work?

AS: One of the things about the controversy was that it actually hurt. It confused me. It caused me a great deal of grief. Maybe I am now trying to reach out to people and in some way connect with them in what I hope is a more positive light. That doesn't mean that I am compromising my work in any way. Like I always say, I like to give people what they want and what they don't want. Besides, I know I can take the heat.

CF: *I don't mean to suggest that you are moving into sentimentalized por-
traiture. I do think that you've chosen your subjects strategically, as
representatives of—*

AS: Of undesirables.

CF: *They are undesirable, but they are also people who in and of themselves are symbols. That seems to connect them with your previous
work, which is so much about iconography and symbol. A homeless
person stands for the homeless, for economic and racial inequities
and for capitalism's lack of morality. A Klan member with a mask
on stands for the entire Klan, and for white supremacy, racism and
the South.*

AS: In dealing with these people, particularly with the Klanspeople, I
realized that they became more powerful as symbols than they
actually were as human beings. I saw them as human beings first,
and then they put on their robes and became symbols. The
homeless too are symbols. I see this as my dilemma as well. In a
way, I have become a symbol. But I am just a human being—and
it is hard for human beings to be symbols.

CF: *They represent two polar opposites of a spectrum of symbols that
have to do with racism. The overwhelming majority of the homeless
people in your photographs and in New York are black, and the Klan
stands for white supremacy. What did you want to express in relationship to race in these pictures?*

AS: I am trying to connect with my own feelings. I am somewhat
ambivalent about most things and sometimes even confused.
I have never been able to fit. I have never been able to see
myself as fitting into one category, and I have never been able
to limit my contact with people to one group of people. I have
always prided myself as someone who got along with people
who didn't get along with each other. I am not talking about
groups of people. I am talking about individuals. I just extended
to a larger arena.

CF: *How did the homeless people deal with you? What were their concerns when you first approached them?*

AS: They were surprised that I would offer them money. After that surprise most accepted the offer. I asked about 50 people. Only two people said no.

CF: *Did any of them come to the show?*

AS: Yes, not to the opening, but several of them went to the show. In fact, the homeless man who opens the door to the Citibank on 14th Street and First Avenue proudly told someone I know, "Oh yes, I have some pictures up at Stux Gallery."

CF: *Your interest in the late-19th-century photographer Edward Curtis and in his portraits of Native Americans is often mentioned. You've said his work influenced the choices you made in taking pictures of the homeless. What is it about his work that led you to take pictures of homeless people?*

AS: His pictures are very heroic. I don't care about the controversy as to whether or not they fabricate a false reality. I like the way the people look, and I get a sense of who they are and I get a sense of their dignity. I think that is really important. Growing up in the '50s, the only Indians I ever saw were on TV, and usually they were savages being massacred by soldiers. Curtis felt he was photographing a vanishing race. I didn't think I was photographing a vanishing race, but rather a class of people who are on the verge of extinction as individuals. The homeless problem will never go away. These people may or may not survive the next winter. Being the faceless and nameless people whom we don't even ordinarily look at made me want to monumentalize them even more.

CF: *Your artwork contains strong statements about institutions like the Catholic Church, and about symbols that relate to politically charged groups such as the Klan and the homeless. At the same time, your use of photography suggests a particular stance toward the medium and its power. What exactly is your relationship to* *photography as a medium?*

AS: I am an artist first and a photographer second. My "medium" is the world of ideas that I seek to present in a visually cohesive fashion. I think of myself as a conceptualist with a camera. In other words, I like to take the pictures in my head that may or may not have anything to do with photography.

My use of the medium—photography—is in some ways traditional. At the same time it is very unconventional. The photography critic Andy Grunberg pointed out that I am not that technical, that I don't care about printing. I feel as though I am anti-photography because I have no interest in the medium except as a means to an end. I am interested only in the final image. At the same time, my role as an artist leads me to want to pursue subjects that generate the tensions we talked about. I think my technique is a comment on my subjects and on photography. I say things, but I say them indirectly. At the same time, I try to make my images as direct as possible.

CF: *Do you think your audiences understand your work?*

AS: Judging from what I have read, people are getting the point—even the politicians.

CF: *But you wouldn't want to reduce the work to its shock value for right-wing politicians?*

AS: No. I think that's the dilemma for them. My work does more than just shock. It also pleases—and that really fucks with their heads. My work has often been spoken of in terms of the sacred and the profane. My feeling is that you can't have one without the other. You need both.

Fall 1991

The Shock of the Real:
An Interview with Karen Finley

By Margot Mifflin

Some people see Karen Finley as one of a long line of "transgres-sive" performance artists, artists such as Paul McCarthy and the Kipper Kids. Others see her as the prototype for a generation of "talk-dirty, nihilist, punk" entertainers like Lydia Lunch and Joe Coleman. Some think she's a feminist, and others accuse her of hurting the feminist movement. In this 1988 interview, New York journalist Margot Mifflin talked to Finley about some of the issues that drive her work. —Eds.

Margot Mifflin: *What's capable of shocking you?*

Karen Finley: Rape and homelessness are the most shocking things to me. Seeing a wealthy city like New York with all this property and abandoned buildings—not taking care of the homeless is shocking. All the sadness that we see in real life is shocking. That's one of my reasons for mirroring this society in my art.

MM: *Do you consider your own work to be shocking?*

KF: No. I see it as a reality, and the only reason it's shocking to people is that they haven't accepted it as a reality. Part of my work is the fact that incest, rape and hostility happen in the best of fami-lies, in the best of countries. As for the people who haven't had those experiences, hopefully my work will make them more sen-sitive to people who have.

MM: *Don't you think people who most need that message would be the least likely to come to your performances?*

KF: I just want to settle something: The audience is really important to me, but the most important thing in my work is a gestalt, catharsis or trance. It isn't my responsibility—not to be a copout—to figure out how people are going to respond to me. That's more your job.

MM: So you're more concerned with expressing your feelings than giving someone something you think they need?

KF: Yes. But I think I have all types of people coming to my performances—do you think otherwise?

MM: I guess anyone who's interested in performance art knows who you are, but that's a limited group of people. A lot of feminist art, for example, preaches to the converted. The uneducated women have no access to it. Likewise your performances: You're talking about helping people with universal traumas like rape and child abuse, but you're presenting yourself in such a way that only club-goers and artists will come see you.

KF: This is really ironic! The artist is always blamed for not marketing the art, which is a really yuppie notion. It isn't my problem that my work won't get on television, or that if it did it would be censored. It's enough for the artist to be doing the art. Throughout history one can see that the work of the radical artist has somehow come into the mainstream. My work may not be accepted for 20, 30, 40 years. I've been doing this for ten years; no one came and saw me five years ago, people are coming to see me now.

> **I still want to show that art is scary, and that large corporations can't buy us, but we still have an effect on culture.**

MM: Have you ever been tempted to compromise in any way?

KF: I don't know what I would need in order to do that—more money? I'm really rather content. I get pleasure out of what I do. I'd rather sling hash and be doing the work I do than get more money for something else. I've had offers to do movie parts—they were too racy for me—and sit-coms.

MM: And you didn't want them?

KF: No, 'cause I think it's important for me to do my work. I still want to show that art is scary, and that large corporations can't buy us, but we still have an effect on culture. Music does that, and I have a great advantage in that I perform live. Women are still keeping up their traditional image in hairstyles, in mannerisms, especially the passivity; I feel it's really important for me to go out and destroy that.

MM: Do you think the subjects you cover will always be shocking?

KF: I hope not. Ten years ago if a woman talked about her menstrual cycle it was considered shocking. Now it's not so bad. There are tampon and condom ads on television. I've really had to keep changing with different issues. One issue that always seems to have shock value is gender. Right now I'm interested in when God became a male, and that we don't question that at all, even in the '80s. That's a gender issue, not a sexual one like showing my pussy on stage, but it's shocking in terms of challenging the values of a system. I've always been interested in challenging systems.

MM: Tell me a little about what you're saying by showing abuse of women in your work.

KF: Something that I think is different in my work from other women who deal with abuse is that a lot of my characters don't remain the victim. There's always some way out. For example, a woman gets raped in the subway and she uses her menstruation as a weapon, something she's been told to consider disgusting, and it saves her. She was abused, but because of her femininity she was saved.

MM: Are most of your concerns gender-related?

KF: Yes. Looking at the art world right now you can see that it's still a small world for women. I feel it's my responsibility to bring up these issues instead of playing some kind of game. Naked bodies aren't shocking to me at all—I used to work in a strip club. In performance I try to present my asshole in an unsexual way. It's many men's fantasies to have a woman bend over and be fucked that way; it's a very sexual position. But when I take over it loses the sexual tension because the sexual tension comes from some-one being degraded by that. I don't make it degrading. When I showed my rear end on stage and smushed these canned yams against it—an act that had a lot of repercussions in the media—I was using the body in an unsexual way. What I proved is that we're supposed to be so goddamn liberated and we aren't. We can't refer to other parts of the body the same way we refer to an ear or an index finger; our orifices are still for penetration or sexual pleasure. We really haven't gone very far beyond the bra-burning of the '60s in terms of sexual liberation.

MM: *How did you first get into performance?*

KF: My father committed suicide when I was 21, which was so fright-ening to me because I'd never considered that possibility; it came out of left field. That was really the trigger for a lot of what I do. I've always done things like faking epileptic seizures in public, or pretending to throw up in a restaurant; it's part of my personality. But because of that incident I have a punch, a motivation behind my work. I've hit bottom. That's really important, because even if you have talent and intellect, you need a motivation to kick it off. That rage can be very healing to people because I think every-one has had some kind of loss, and I connect with them because of mine. It has nothing to do with talent, or class structure. It has to do with life and fate, because even if you're living a good life and you're a good person, you can still fall. But I wouldn't say my father's suicide has been my most shocking experience. My most shocking experience is getting into a taxi on Park Avenue and riding to the Lower East Side and seeing the uneven distribution of wealth—seeing that our government doesn't take care of its poor. Those larger situations, like the AIDS crisis, are more shock-ing than personal problems.

    Reality is always more shocking that art. I think that shock in art is followed by some kind of transformation that happens because of the artist. I mean, you could say that Second Street between Avenues A and B is an artwork, and that's not so. It's not enough just to have the shocking thing, disassociated from everything. The artist frames or mirrors it with brilliance or timeliness. I don't know that there's a clear line between what is an atrocity and what's art, I do know that when Chris Burden shot himself in the arm[1] it was art, but when my father shot himself it wasn't.

MM: What have you found shocking in other people's art?

KF: The most shocking thing I've seen is Richard Kern's and Lydia Lunch's movie *Fingered.* I'm emotional in my work, but I don't act out the abuse. Lydia Lunch does. I had to leave the movie—just thinking about it gets me upset. Also, hearing people laugh when someone is being abused or mutilated—I don't understand it. People laugh at my work and I don't understand it.

MM: What sort of response have you received in Europe?

KF: I was banned in England, and my record can't be sold there. I was to perform at the ICA with Howie Montaug's *No Entiendes* and the Westminster consul told me the funding would be removed from the institution if I did. They have some bizarre laws there about women being nude and talking. Americans are more open to looking at things, I think, and are more vocal and responsive. But the whole thing about the yams in my rear end was something I never expected to be shocking. I thought it was funny. Every city I did it in thought it was shocking, except Chicago, I guess because they have such a tradition of experimental theater there. I really thought the American public was much more sexually liberated than that. I mean, you'd think horrific subjects like real physical abuse would be much more shocking than yams in a woman's rear end.

MM: Let's talk about pornography. You've said that you're trying to strip pornography of its attraction for men, to invert it, as if to condemn it, yet you worked in a strip club and say you like pornography.

KF: Well, pornography should change with the times and I don't think it has enough. It's always been in the hands of men, and, in terms of us growing sexually, that has to grow too. I don't hate men, I just hate what they do! I have a very good relationship with a man. Anyway, as an economic resource every woman has the right to do whatever she wants with her body—prostitution, pornography. I am for pornography, I am against anything that depicts violence towards women. A lot of pornography isn't about sexual pleasure, it's about power.

MM: *Would you ever consider presenting pornography in an appealing way from a feminist perspective? Meaning, introducing a positive alternative to what you're criticizing.*

KF: I don't think I'd be a good person for that because I'm too cynical and have too much of a sense of humor—I would always be inverting it. But I'd be in favor of it. I turned down a writer who wanted to do a *Penthouse* forum on me because that magazine pretends to be an incredibly intelligent magazine. It's pornography, why don't they just say they're pornography? Then Annie Sprinkle wanted to do something on me. I like her a lot, her sense of pornography is fantastic, and I said yes immediately.

MM: *When you use sexual slang are you mocking it?*

KF: I'm repeating street language. I'm showing that language is very important. It's the only weapon you have for your anger once everything else has been taken away.

MM: *It's powerful even though it's bankrupt and clichéd?*

KF: Yes, that's part of the sadness of it.

MM: *What's the most shocking image you've used in a performance?*

KF: Talking about an old woman being fist-fucked in a nursing home, and that she enjoyed it because she hadn't been touched in 50 years.

MM: *So your message in many of these raps is that people are so physically and emotionally starved that even violence becomes pleasurable.*

KF: Yes, and that's where the perversion starts.

MM: *People don't accuse you of condoning what you present?*

KF: Not too much. People seem to understand.

MM: *What are some taboos you have yet to bash?*

KF: God being a man, which I think is really going to destroy a lot of premises. Also, women's biological sexual superiority of multiple orgasms. I'd also like to get into American imperialism, and the fact that Americans aren't first anymore; Japan has beaten us out of a lot, which I think will be good for us.

Notes

1. Artist Chris Burden had a friend shoot him the arm with a rifle, and called it an artwork (*Shoot,* 1971). —Ed.

Spring/Summer 1988

The Artist as Citizen

By Linda Frye Burnham

We have often said that art is essential to the life of the community, and if we're right, then every community ought to have its
own artist: a professional who is called on when the town plan is
being laid or revised, who consults on celebrations and events of all
kinds, as essential to the town as the plumber and the schoolteacher
and the mayor.

As far as we know, only a few artists have ever had this job. In
1986 art historian Moira Roth wrote about one: David Harding, the
Town Artist of Glenrothes, Scotland, from 1968 to1978. Glenrothes
was one of five "new towns" in Scotland run by development corporations. They were to be holistic, homogeneous places for living, work
and leisure. Each of these towns hired an artist for a period of time to
work in varying degrees on the built environment. Harding got his job
by answering an ad for an artist who would work with the architects,
engineers and planners of Glenrothes. The term Town Artist was
coined in 1970 by a friend of Harding's to describe his role. Here
Roth asks him what his job entailed and how it affected the town and
Harding himself.

Harding is a visual artist who, even in art school, sought out collaborations with architects. John Malpede is an artist who traveled a
very different path to serve a radically different community: the
homeless of Skid Row in Los Angeles. Malpede was a New York performance artist with a background in philosophy and street theater
when he visited Los Angeles during the Olympics in 1984. He was so
struck with the drama of the homeless on downtown's Skid Row that
he stayed, got a job with a free law center there, and began putting
up flyers in the neighborhood for a free performance workshop.

Malpede soon gathered a conglomeration of inner-city
denizens—artists, drifters, singers, actors, writers, lovers and fighters
well acquainted with life on the street. They began presenting performances as the Los Angeles Poverty Department (LAPD), and were
soon touring the U.S. and Europe with performance projects, including

LAPD Inspects America, a week (or longer) residency in which LAPD invaded a city and gathered information about homelessness by meeting street people in the places where they gather. Talent shows and workshops were staged in streets, parks, shelters and social-service agencies, and from these local performers were recruited to take part in a performance in a local artspace or theater. The piece is an ever-changing saga that follows LAPD's experiences in this whole process. Almost the opposite of a bleeding-heart liberal approach to depicting life among the unfortunates, LAPD work is street life itself. "You want the cosmetic version," says *LAPD Inspects America*, "or you want the real deal?" Here we include a conversation between Malpede and actress Elia Arce in which the two artists discuss the unique method employed in getting this act together and keeping it on the road.

The Roadside Theater story reveals another way for artists to serve their community and take its story on the road. Their community is Whitesburg, Kentucky, in the coalfields of the Appalachian Mountains, an economically depressed area that in 1969 was suffering high unemployment and devastating exploitation of its resources by multinational corporations. The now-defunct federal Office of Economic Opportunity opened a film and video workshop there for unemployed youth as part of its War on Poverty. Young people were empowered to make their own images and tell their own stories. When the OEO discontinued the program, the community raised money to continue on its own, and it grew into Appalshop, with an arts and education center that includes film and recording companies, a television and radio station, the American Festival Project and Roadside Theater. Here Donna Porterfield, who has worked with Roadside Theater for 20 years, tells the story of how the theater partners with the people of its town and also takes its stories into the wide world.

What should an artist expect when partnering with a community? Most art schools don't prepare artists properly for community-based work, and many have learned some hard lessons on the job. In "The Cutting Edge Is Enormous" we shed some new light on the artist's job by looking at two of the most accomplished community-based artists in the U.S. Choreographer Liz Lerman vastly expands our view of what's innovative and important in dance, and Richard

Owen Geer turns the job of theater director upside-down.

Some artists prefer working with communities inside institutions, and they go there with a wide range of motives. The Imagination Workshop at UCLA's Neuropsychiatric Institute in Los Angeles was founded by an actress who was intrigued by what she perceived as the common ground shared by actors and psychiatric patients. William Cleveland writes here of Margaret Ladd's discoveries about the use of the imagination in a therapeutic setting, and tells some moving stories about the transformative energy of art.

Most performing artists conduct workshops in their areas of expertise. Dancer Blondell Cummings considers her community workshops a part of her own creative process, using them to help her focus on the issues raised in each new piece. She gleans autobio-graphical text and spontaneous movement from her workshops, and sometimes adds them to the text of the new work. Cummings sees this whole exercise, including the performance, as a form of story-telling. Veta Goler interviews her here about the aesthetics and ethics of this process.

Social change is the openly stated goal of some artists working in communities. This is no more true than in the work of Elders Share the Arts, a New York organization nationally recognized for its inter-generational work with elders and children. Theater artist Susan Perl-stein, ESTA's director, claims there is no avoiding social change, anyway, when you live in New York, a city of ceaseless flux that isolates peo-ple, fragments families and separates the old from the young. For decades, ESTA has been binding up rips in the social fabric, working all over the city in senior centers, hospitals, nursing homes, schools and neighborhoods. Here Perlstein shares some of the tools ESTA uses every day.

Pleasure is not one of the benefits that come to mind when you think of working in a prison, but that is what it came to mean to choreographer Leslie Neal when she realized she had bonded with her students at a maximum-security women's prison in Florida. When she wrote this story for us, Neal and three of her dance company members had been going to Broward Correctional once a week for two years. For them it was more than a job; it was a labor of love and personal growth. Her first-person story goes deep to the heart of her commitment to this work.

Arts programs in prisons are some of the most difficult to fund. Why, many ask, should convicted criminals be getting arts programs when the arts have been cut from school curricula all over the country? After 17 years and 50 prison residencies, poet Grady Hillman probably knows as much about arts-in-corrections programs as anyone on the outside. In our interview he talks about some crucial issues: Are these programs necessary? Are they worth money? Do they do any good? Can you prove it?

One of the magnets that draws artists into community work is the desperate need to do something about social problems affecting the places where they live. Southern artists are particularly sensitive to the issue of racism, and some have even made its eradication their life's work as artists. This is particularly true of artists in Alternate ROOTS (Regional Organization of Theatres South), a multiracial organization of more than 200 artists in the Southeast especially committed to making and supporting original art in their communities. *The Selma Project* is a case study of an arts project in the civil-rights city conducted by a ROOTS theater ensemble from Tennessee, The Road Company, that partnered with Selma organizations to bring eight southern artists together to work on healing the wounds of racism. Road Company director Bob Leonard tells the tale.

John O'Neal has been applying his theatrical craft to community issues and activism since the early '60s. He's representative of a large group of artists for whom the concepts of artistic creativity and community involvement were never mutually exclusive, and whose creative energy is invested as much, or more, in the process of developing the work as in the final product. O'Neal and his theater company, Junebug, are part of a large coalition of artists and activists attempting to use the arts to make environmental change in their region. Here educator Mat Schwarzman writes in detail about the meticulous partnering process of The Environmental Justice Project in Louisiana.

Artists experienced in community residencies are often called to work in regions far from home. What tools do they take with them? Atlanta writer Alice Lovelace has been working in schools and communities for decades, but not long ago she began work on a master's degree in conflict resolution; her experience had taught her that conflict resolution is a basic human skill—absolutely necessary for our time—and that poetry can access deeply held values and beliefs about conflict. She wanted to craft a method of teaching students how to use poetry in this way. When she was invited to Oklahoma to work with young girls, she took her new tool-kit with her, including some of the revolutionary theater exercises of Augusto Boal. We asked her to let us in on how things went.

Since the 1950s, Brazilian director Augusto Boal's methods for Theatre of the Oppressed have been working for artists and communities all over the world. Boal, also a political activist in his own country, created his method as a group problem-solving technique, with the aim of liberating people for action towards social change. In our interview, he talks about how his theater differs from traditional theater.

Sensitivity to the community is an important topic in dialogues about public art in the '90s. For most of the 20th century, we have been content to commission monuments and installations—also known as "plop sculpture"—that invade public space without any consideration for the people and the environment surrounding them. In our story from 1996, Los Angeles artist Richard Posner says the journey from the studio to the street demands a change of mind and heart. "The public art administration process," says Posner, "requires the eye of a journalist, the ear of a poet, the hide of an armadillo, the serenity of an airline pilot, and the ability to swim."

Artists who work with nonartists in community settings often articulate their frustration with the way their work is written about and categorized. Even when critics and funders find such work valuable, they tend to separate it from the artist's "real" work. For most artists with whom we have talked, there is no difference between their "community work" and their "own work"—the artwork they do as soloists or with a company of trained professional artists. Here choreographer Stuart Pimsler takes the opportunity to write about his work with doctors, nurses and other caregivers, and finds the thread that binds this work to his own history as an artist.

One thing we've learned over the 20 years of listening and writing about art is that it is at its best when an artist invests his or her own artmaking skills in a community of individuals. When art is allowed to flourish in society, it can help develop communities, address social ills, heal sickness, protect the environment and renew the urban landscape. But art works most effectively when the artist is at the energetic center of the community, not attached prescriptively at its edges.

For our final two essays in this collection we have stories from two artists, each of whom is heavily invested in a community of individuals and deeply concerned about the issues of her community. For Marty Pottenger, that meant making art in the heart of the world she has been a part of for 20 years—the world of manual labor where humans are building the infrastructure of a city. For Aida Mancillas it meant becoming an integral part of the renovation of her own neighborhood, and planning to stay. And for both it also meant writing about the work, sharing what they have learned about art's place in public life. They know their job is not finished until they have told the tale.

We are lucky that they, and all the writers in this book about art and life, understand the importance of the tale.

Town Artist:
An Interview with David Harding

By Moira Roth

*David Harding, born in 1937 in Scotland and trained at Edin-
burgh College of Art, had recently returned from living in Nigeria
when the town of Glenrothes hired him in 1968. Harding worked
as Glenrothes' Town Artist until 1978, when he became a senior
lecturer in the "Art and Design in Social Context" program at the
Dartington College of Arts in Devon. In 1986, he set up a new
course called "Environmental Art" at the Glasgow School of Art.
Moira Roth teaches art history at Mills College in Oakland,
California.   —Eds.*

Moira Roth: *Do you have a sense of how many town artists there are in
England, Ireland, Wales and Scotland?*

David Harding: Yes—not many, because I define the Town Artist very,
very specifically as someone who is employed in a city department of architecture and planning, and involved in the process of
the making of that city. Also, someone who has a long-term and
full-time commitment to it and its community; by that, I mean
three or four years at least. And there aren't many of these
sorts of Town Artists. Mainly what has happened in Britain is that
the social development and recreation sections of city councils
have employed artists. There must be, I think, some 20 or so
towns in the U.K. that employ artists in ways other than for, say,
graphics and exhibitions. These artists are employed mainly to
contribute to social and cultural development.

   It may be that the first example of an artist being involved
in the new towns of Britain was Victor Pasmore in the late
1950s and early 1960s in Peterlee, a town in the north of England. Pasmore was employed as a consultant to work with the
architects on designing the buildings of the town. He would visit
in short bursts and played a very dominant role. From my point

of view, I don't think it was wholly successful work because the houses ended up looking like Pasmore paintings—black and white with the odd spot of color, so that it was said that if people put up colored curtains it would spoil the composition.

In the mid-'60s two other New Towns (this has been specifically a New Town phenomenon) employed artists for some environmental work. So there are one or two precedents.

MR: How did you come to Glenrothes and what was the town like?

DH: At art college in the '50s, I sought out collaborations with architectural students, and from then, I suppose, I have been committed to working with the built environment. When I came back from four years in Nigeria, I worked on my own for a year or so doing a number of urban works. I then wrote to towns in Scotland saying why don't you employ me as your artist. A few months later Glenrothes advertised for an artist "to contribute to the external built environment of the town," one who would work with architects, engineers and planners.

When I went to Glenrothes in 1968, the population of the town was 25,000. The town was planned to revitalize the coal industry in the Fife Region, but the coal mine that was developed for the town actually failed. The town then had to diversify. As time went on, electronics became the main employer; Glenrothes is now known for its electronic technology. The population of the town is now around 40,000, so it has grown by 15,000 since 1968. The visual character of the town was of low-rise, low-density, mainly council [project] housing of no real distinction.

MR: What was the political and social climate of the area like? And your own politics?

DH: It is significant that Fife is a very socialist part of Britain; it returned the first communist member of Parliament and there are streets named Lenin Way, Gargarin Avenue, etc. [laughs]. The Labour Party councilors on the Glenrothes Development Corporation were very much my supporters. I suppose I was going there with a half-formed vision of the artist as artisan. I was a

socialist, but I was also a "nationalist" in the sense of being interested in the preservation of minority cultures, of which my own,
Scottish/Celtic culture is one. The erosion of small cultures is
detrimental to the world. In those terms, I brought these views
to Glenrothes where I was at pains to rediscover and restate
cultural forms from Celtic and Pictish history.

When I came to Glenrothes, I was employed, as it were, as
a civil servant in the town under a contract with retirement at
65. There were doubts about where to place me, and I suggested I should be part of the Planning Department. This was a sen-
sible idea because it meant that I could attend planning meetings
and be involved in early discussions with planners about the
shape of the town. After a couple of years, I feel an historic
decision was made in the town. It was part of the planning briefs
which came out of the planning department to the architects
and engineers. It contained a clause which said that "the artist
should be consulted at every stage of the development." That
was an ideal, of course, but it was something that one could fall
back on if wanting to make a fuss. I decided to live in a housing
project in the town because it was important to experience the
kind of environment one was contributing to. I set up my workshop in the city's Direct Labour yards. Also, after a couple of
years I joined the Builder's Union because I realized that most of
the work was taking place on the building site, and that identifying myself with the men who were working on the building site
was politically very important. I tried to create opportunities for
the building workers to display their, often, latent skills by using
only the materials of the building site, so much so that many of
the works were executed or completed by them.

MR: *What was your pacing in the job over the ten years you were in
Glenrothes?*

DH: Initially, I worked very slowly and at a small scale. I made small
insertions and interventions in the town, meanwhile building up
people's confidence in me and finding out how the town operated and how to finance the work. What one finds is that you

can find these avenues of money when you are in the inside. And so, in that respect, money was never a problem. In fact, the year before I left, one housing architect phoned me up to say that he had 15,000 pounds spared from a contract and could I use it in a residential area which was just being completed. The other thing is that in a situation like this, when one has access to

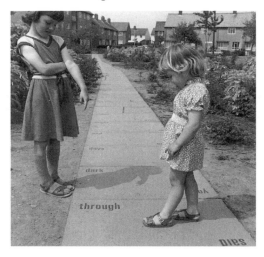

money, one doesn't have to send what one is going to do for approval before one gets the money. Many of the actual works that I proposed didn't have to go beyond myself, the job architect, the engineer and the community.

MR: *All in all, you once said you orchestrated about 250 works during the ten-year span in Glenrothes. Incidentally, what language do you like—orchestrate, direct, inspire, coordinate or what?*

DH: Possibly orchestrate [laughs]. That number of 250 applies to today, as more works were created, after I left, by my replacement and other artists. For the size of the town, that seems a great number of works—they range from the very small (what I term *bijou*), brightly colored mosaics to extremely large works. One might get the impression that surely a saturation point must be reached, but actually, from the experience of Glenrothes, that is not the case. The built environment can soak up as much as we can give it in terms of visual art.

I should stress also that I took on art students who worked with me during the summer; I also took on a number of 16-year-olds who were unemployed. They came and worked almost in an apprenticeship situation with me for two years. One of them painted a mural, which in 1977 was probably the first punk mural in Britain. Incidentally, they were all paid. Then, most importantly, I had one graduate student a year, sometimes two, who would work with me for twelve months in a kind of atelier situation. They were paid a salary by the town. Also, the town was intent not only on developing the visual arts but also other arts as well. One of the things we did was to set aside a cottage in the town where a writer could come and live rent-free. Several writers came: an actor-writer, a filmmaker-writer and three poets, including one who wrote the *Poetry Path*. They often made a direct contribution to the environment of the town: The theater person got involved with the theater events in the town, a film was shot in the town, etc. Another idea which we realized was to develop workshops and houses for crafts-people in old stables in the town.

MR: Can you talk about the impact of all this on the town?

DH: That's difficult because to really deal with that one would need a detailed survey. However, one can pick up hints. For example, peo-ple would write letters to the development corporations, which said, "Why do other parts of Glenrothes have artworks and we don't?", or in the fact that people identified with the works, and would actually look after them and clean them. Most of these housing areas lacked any significant character of their own and the works became an impor-tant part of an otherwise monotonous environment.

For me, the base of art was broadened and democratized with the recognition that there should be cultural democracy...

They became reference points and meeting places. Games have developed around them and, in time, I would hope that one or two of them may stimulate some sort of ritual attachment.

MR: How did your Town Artist role effect you?

DH: It re-emphasized the importance of the context for art. As the job developed, the work became increasingly related to the context and the site. For me, the base of art was broadened and democratized with the recognition that there should be cultural democracy, which means lots of cultures existing side by side.

MR: *Styles too?*

DH: Yes. Of course, some of the things I was doing intuitively and innocently in Glenrothes, I now see as fundamental to public art—in the public-art practice and theory being developed in America and Britain in the mid-1980s. Artists need to work in collaboration with architects and engineers and need to think in terms of urban spaces not as physical spaces only, but as places people live in, and that the social context is as important as the physical context.

MR: *What has the impact of your work been?*

DH: The first thing to stress is that the art world did not realize what was going on in these "Town Artist" situations. When we were working away, deepening the philosophical base for public art, little was known about it. It is in the years since I left Glenrothes that there has been more public interest. A recent development in the U.K. has been the move to create *residencies* for artists to make public artworks, replacing the simple public commission.

I visited Seattle recently and talked with Richard Andrews, the man who has made Seattle world-famous for its public-art program. In his recent essays and lectures, he stresses the point that there is no longer any use whatever simply buying artworks and arbitrarily placing them on sites. The artist has to be there him- or herself in person so that the work can really become "site-specific." In other words, to make the "context half the work."

In terms of Glenrothes as a model, it is not easy to apply the town model in America. In Britain, we have a tradition of government intervention. Many labor councils in Britain are actively involved in financing and supporting the arts in a way that just does not happen in America. So, it may be that the

Glenrothes model would not be of much use here. What may be the element to be learned, however, is that of Glenrothes being yet another example of the importance of site-specific artworks. In Australia, on the other hand, a place rather similar to Britain socially and culturally, a number of towns have created places for artists in much the way I worked myself. I was invited to Australia in 1982 to encourage this. While I was there, I did a great deal of lecturing and consultation. A lot of interest was shown in the concept of the Town Artist.

MR: *Why did you leave Glenrothes?*

DH: I never intended to stay there indefinitely, certainly not until I was aged 65 [laughs]. I felt it was essential that Glenrothes should have a change of artist, and this in fact happened when I left in 1978. I needed also to step back from what I call "the front"—you know, having been for ten years on "the front." Creativity on demand, so to speak. I needed to step back and review the situation and try and deepen the philosophical base of public art and community art. I wondered whether it would be possible to pass on the Glenrothes experience; to develop a way of teaching that would make creating art in a context not the impossibly difficult thing that most art students leaving art school feel it is.

MR: *And what have you found since teaching in Dartington College of Arts?*

DH: I would not claim that I am teaching students to be Town Artists. What I do see the course doing is breaking new ground in terms of art teaching. We are insisting that students look to the "context" and respond to it outside the studio and college. Whether they will do it later on is another matter.

MR: *Are you content with primarily teaching?*

DH: I very much want to continue to make art in the way I made it in Glenrothes. The probem is that there aren't many such opportunities. [Harding moved to Glasgow School of Art, to be a part of the school's Fine Arts degree. The city of Glasgow is presently in the throes of urban regeneration.] I want my course, through my own work and my students, to play a part in this exciting process.

MR: *You mentioned the impact on you of your work in Nigeria, where you were teaching at a college of art in Lafia.*

DH: One of the things that struck me in Nigeria was the very important fact that I could not import European culture to the people I was working with. They were developing their own art, and I certainly wasn't going to import Picasso or Van Gogh to them. Nor was I going to raise Eurocentric perceptions of composition, color, form, organization, proportion, perspective or things like that. So, I simply became an enabler; I organized the opportunities for them to do their own work. Being sensitive to cultural imperialism was a major factor I took from Nigeria to Glenrothes. Also, there was a tradition near where I stayed in Nigeria of modeling mud walls, and we worked together on painting external walls. That element of getting people to actually contribute to the external environment of the place in which they live is the other main thing I brought with me from Nigeria to Glenrothes.

MR: *Do you see your idea of a Town Artist as relating to the Renaissance concept of the artist?*

DH: Yes. There exists a contract drawn up between a client and Ghirlandaio in which there are very detailed specifications about what the artist can do in terms of painting an altarpiece. The contract specifies how much ultramarine paint can be used, the amount of gold leaf and a series of other restrictions. My interest in this is that within those limitations, the artist could create a timeless work of art. Is it possible for artists in the 20th century to work also within certain limitations?

MR: *What other models do you find in art history or political theory?*

DH: I tend not to go back into art history as much as to look at other societies—non-Western societies such as those in Nigeria.

It is almost a cliché now that in those societies the artists were an integral part of society in the sense that they "arted" but also did farming. I suppose it is that integration of art and society that I see more as the model for the kind of thing I was proposing in Glenrothes.

Spring 1986

LAPD, Skid Row & The Real Deal

By John Malpede and Elia Arce

Los Angeles Poverty Department (LAPD) is a performance group that grew out of a 1985 workshop for the homeless of Los Angeles. What makes this group different from other contemporary theaters that incorporate nonartist populations is the method of John Malpede. He brings to this work a patchwork of experience that includes a degree in philosophy, a lot of N.Y. street theater, and some radical late-'70s performance art with Bill Gordh (as Dead Dog and Lonely Horse). When talking about approaching a project as maverick as LAPD, he says, "It's all in how you hold it," and he holds it as lightly as possible, providing minimal direction and tolerating a lot of errant behavior. Elia Arce is a Costa Rican actress and filmmaker. She joined the group in 1986 and became an important performer and workshop leader in the group. This conversation excerpt between Malpede and Arce from June, 1988, begins with a free-form discussion of the importance of diversity in the group's makeup and its method.   —Eds.

Elia Arce: *…countries…and…*

John Malpede: …and ages, too…

EA: *…and ages…exactly, and ages…and ages…that really…*

JM: …and mental states, too…

EA: *…and mental states…*

JM: …it makes it bigger.

EA: *Exactly. And mental states.*

JM: Ya.

EA: *Is like multi. That's what I was saying. Is like multi-disciplinary, multi-racial, multi-cultural. Is just "multi." That's what it is, "MULTI." Multi-everything, which is funny because there is so much to deal with* *that we don't deal with things like color of skin, we deal more with circumstances. Circumstances are what the group have in common—what is shared, not the color of skin. So people just jump in and play those circumstances, regardless of their age, their color, their language.*

JM: Right. That's how it works. We don't sit down and decide whether we want to have multi, multi, multi—we just do it. When we were having those meetings last week about what direction to go and all that, we just had two meetings. And that was good because we didn't decide anything. I don't want to get into the mode where we decide everything at meetings, 'cause then we're stuck with what we decided, which in our case will never work. We couldn't do that anyway. Impossible. It wouldn't work. All our decisions—the real ones—are nuts and bolts, you know, carpenterial decisions. And nuts and bolts means including what comes up as well as what you thought was going to come up. The decisions end up getting made in the workshops with everyone involved, putting themselves in the mix.

EA: *Thinking quickly becomes tripping about the way you would like things to be, and not about the way things actually are.*

JM: There are 15 different opinions about what actually happened in *No Stone for Studs Schwartz:* who the killer was, if Studs knew the killer, if he ever had gambling debts, if Studs had ever seen him before. All that stuff.

EA: *Not being sure what the reality was…*

JM: It's just that everybody in the cast had different opinions about it…

EA: *But also, the people who came to see the show had different opinions.*

JM: Ya. True. But also in different performances the ending—what happened—changed.

EA: *Which changes the whole play around.…Is like juggling, a juggling of the show itself. Because there are all these different things flying up in the air, all the people in the show and their own ideas about it, but sometimes one will fly higher than the other one will...which causes an adjustment.*

JM: And then more adjustments.

EA: *The strength of the group is also that each person gets to grow as an individual, and be part of a group, and grow in a group without having to be the same kind of [person]. Therefore, there is freedom for everybody to grow with their own personal identity. And actually what the group is about is that the stronger and more distinct these identities become, the richer the LAPD becomes. The differences are a plus. It creates a situation in which people who have absolutely nothing in common at all—or who have very opposite positions about life, about politics, about moral issues, about religion, about everything—are working together, doing good work artistically, serving the community and also ourselves as individuals. What's been great about all the imitation we've been doing is that we're mainly imitating ourselves—other people in the group.*

Circumstances are what the group have in common...

JM: Like me imitating Jim in *Studs Schwartz*. In *LAPD Inspects America* it's really gotten out of hand.

EA: *With everybody playing everybody else in the show.*

JM: So it's been an element ever since the beginning.

EA: *Huge! Because you see yourself in other people and you get to see what other people see in you. How they react to you. It makes you aware of how other people are really looking at you; it makes you aware of who you actually are.*

....

EA: *You never tell somebody, "You should do it like this, you should act it like this."*

JM: Well, sometimes.

EA: *But not all the time.*

JM: No, not all the time. It's more like using what's there and putting all the pieces together…

EA: Uh-huh.

JM: …to create a mess.

EA: All these elements are so different from one another. It's like a total rupture of the specialization.

JM: The specialization? In what? Performance? Theater?

EA: I mean, something this country is known for. I don't know if you k ow, but outside of this country one of the things that has always been criticized [about the U.S.] is this obsession [with] specialization. That people here are so specialized that there is only one person who knows how to put on that part of the wheel. So that if that person is not there, then we can't build the car because that person is not there.

JM: Uh-huh.

EA: So in LAPD, the fact that everybody knows the circumstances of the play and that they are willing to and can jump in and fulfill the other people's part makes the group stronger.

JM: Right.

EA: And less individual.

JM: They also change the other person's part. When they jump in and do the part, they do it differently. But also, they save part of what the other person had been doing. So the part gets enriched. People take over other peoples' great lines and save them. Just because they like that line, they use it. They save it.

EA: Uh-huh. So you are like a juggler trying to see how many pots and pans you can get in the air at the same time.

JM: The more the better.

EA: So you are like the balance, you know, like …

JM: Right. That's why Kevin was saying I have a nondirectorial style of directing, or something like that.

EA: Because is like everybody trusts you, they jump. Is like you throw the pan and the pan is trying to do all these weird things in the air, because [it knows] you are going to catch it.

JM: Ya, right. Well mainly, I'm just trying to find a container large enough to justify everything that's going on. I mean, to comprehend all the wildness or whatever that's going on; sort of being able to wrap it in some way.

EA: I was saying the rupture in specialization forces people to learn the other parts. Like in LAPD. But this society pushes for specialization, which pushes for individualism. It's like if that person isn't there, the show can't be done. In LAPD, we're doing the total opposite. We're breaking through that. So then each person is important as an individual because each one has something unique to come along with. And it is great. Everyone has something great to give to the group. But, that doesn't mean that the show is going to stop if that person doesn't show up.

JM: The style we've come up with—where we swap parts, and swap lines, play one anothers' doubles, and nobody really knows who made up what any more—is turning out to be a very communal style. But the reason that came about was because it was impossible to get people to work together. After *South of the Clouds*, I said something in a magazine—that there was only one scene that wasn't a monologue because there were only two people in the show who could interact with the others in the way required for a conventional scene.

EA: Uh-huh.

JM: Which is true. So then the style developed out of giving in to that circumstance. Rather than trying to work toward everyone being able to play conventional scenes, we worked toward developing a layered look where different focuses could coexist at the same time.

EA: So the style came from taking the limitations of the circumstances and making them positive.

JM: Ya. Finding out what the people in this reality knew about better than anyone else. Well, what everyone else knows is how to behave. How to be polite and function in society.

EA: Ya. All these good productive Americans. But, nobody in the country knows what's going on inside their own head.

JM: Skid Row people do. And they don't edit their thoughts.

EA: As Jazz says, "They don't got nothin' but their muther-fuckin' opinions."

JM: I guess that's why so many white people want to quit their lives and join the group. It's why I do. A lot of improvised performance is about the performers' trying to get access to their unconscious.

EA: Is what the LAPD is so great at.

Fall 1988

Appalachia's Roadside Theater: Celebration of a Community's Culture

By Donna Porterfield

Roadside Theater is a nationally known company from Appalachia that has closely examined the art of celebrating the community from which it comes. Here Roadside's Donna Porterfield talks about the beginnings of that work. —Eds.

In 1975, Roadside Theater began at Appalshop, the multimedia organization located in the heart of the coal-mining country of the central Appalachian Mountains. For 25 years, Appalshop has been making documentary film and television, theater, radio and audio recordings on the premise that mountain communities can assume a larger measure of control over their own lives if they can gain control over the definition of their culture, and the tools of cultural transmission. Appalshop works with communities to document and revitalize the arts and traditions that have held them together in the past, to create solutions to the problems that face them today, and to use the performing arts and media as means to affect positive social change.

In 1975, Roadside members, all natives of the coalfields of the central Appalachian region, called on their heritage of storytelling, music and the drama of their indigenous church services to develop a theatrical form and content that made sense to their families and neighbors. The company toured its original productions to enthusiastic audiences in the hollers and coalmining communities around its home—performing in churches, community centers, schools and often in a small revival tent. But in order to finance a growing company, the theater found it necessary to earn income from touring outside the region. It also wanted to offer its own image of mountain people as an alternative to the "hillbilly" stereotype. Roadside found that when it spoke specifically from its own cultural heritage, it also spoke to many people in many places. In the past 16 years, the company has performed its numerous original plays an average of 200 times a year, and toured to 43 states and Europe.

By the early 1980s, Roadside Theater was earning 50 to 60% of its budget from national touring. Most presenters of Roadside's work were colleges and universities or local arts agencies, operating within a national presenting model. This model assumed that culture was something that had to be brought to a community by a presenter. It did not value the community's existing cultural life, nor recognize its diversity. This national, homogenized presenting model naturally excluded the local folk arts and artists, who were often a part of the working-class and economically poor segment of their communities. With the exclusion of this art came exclusion, whether intentional or unintentional, of this audience from the presenter's events. This posed a problem for Roadside, whose artists come from a working-class and economically poor background, and whose artistry springs from the traditional culture of its home. While the company's shows were appreciated by all audiences, when working-class and economically poor people (in any community) were present, the work came fully alive, providing a deeper experience for all audience members.

So Roadside Theater set about developing publicity materials and a producing plan that helped the presenter get out an audience that represented a broad cross section of the community. It worked. Roadside's national performances began playing to enthusiastic, full houses. Most arts presenters were pleased with this new audience, but confused about where these people came from and how to include them in their next season's performance menu. A minority of presenters, thinking this audience lacking in culture, were sure that they should not be a part of their program at all.

This presented another problem for Roadside. How could the company work with presenters to develop a presenting model that included diverse segments of the community in the decision making about programming? And, at the same time, how could the company continue an extensive national tour and still deepen its relationship with its own culture at home, upon which its artistic creativity depended?

The theater began talking to Western and Southern Arts Associates (WASAA), the booking agency with whom Roadside coproduces

its national tours. The idea was to work in partnership with arts presenters, community groups and funders to produce one- and two-
week community cultural residencies that celebrated and perpetuated
the host community's culture, and used that understanding and celebration as a means to address local concerns. It was decided that the
best place to develop and test this model was in Roadside's home
where it could work, over a year's time, in a community and culture
with which the company was intimately familiar. Funding partners for
this new work would be the Folk Arts Program at the National
Endowment for the Arts, the Virginia Commission for the Arts Education Program, the Alternate ROOTS touring subsidy program and the
American Festival Project. While the work was proceeding, WASAA
would follow it closely and begin looking for national presenters interested in this new model.

   In 1990, as part of its pilot program, Roadside conducted a year-
long residency in the small Appalachian coalmining community of
Haysi, Virginia. The county in which Haysi is located has 45% unemployment because it is a one-industry county that has experienced
layoffs due to mechanization in the mines.

   The residency joined the theater with the Appalachian Agency
for Senior Citizens, the Haysi High School drama class, Mountain People and Places (an energetic community history club with 150 members) and the local Baptist church. Each partner brought a particular
concern to the project. As families have had to leave the mountains to
search for jobs, the Agency for Senior Citizens saw that the county's
older people were left behind—becoming isolated and no longer seen
as a community resource and source of pride. The Haysi High School
drama teacher was concerned that her students, faced with bleak economic futures and minds full of images from television, looked upon
their cultural heritage as a disadvantage. This attitude was causing a
rejection of their family and themselves. The history club wanted to
support its local culture by working with the students and promoting
the residency in any way it could. The Baptist church wanted to
encourage an ecumenical spirit among the area's various denomina-
tions. All wanted to rally against the onset of community despair.

   The residency began with performances from Roadside's repertory, and progressed as the company conducted acting, directing, writing and community cultural development workshops with the students; told stories and played music regularly with the seniors; and organized intergenerational conversations about local history and culture. Gradually these activities began to light up the imagination of the community and, by year's end, had sparked numerous informal story and music swaps between the partners; the writing of a delightful, wry play by the high-school drama students

...the residency confirmed the theater's belief in turing to local community cultural resources as a way to build pride and self-reliance, and to engage community problems.

(the first original play in the school's history); and the production of four community festivals celebrating local history and life. One of the festivals, in conjunction with an American Festival Project, included an exchange with Chicano artists from the barrio of San Antonio who were also struggling with similar issues of identity and a similar array of community problems.

The initial festival, a story and music swap that included all the partners, was produced by Roadside. The high-school students, excited by the possibilities such an event offered, decided to produce a second festival themselves. The students contacted the older storytellers and musicians from whom they had learned during the year, secured the Kiwanis Club for an evening, and asked Mountain People and Places to help them get out a crowd. At the festival, the students introduced the storytellers and musicians with anecdotes about the things that had happened that year—about their community, about themselves. The show ended with a performance of the play that the students wrote, and the crowd of over 200 took home a newfound confidence in their young people.

The third festival featured folk artists from the senior citizens centers and was produced by the Agency on Aging, Roadside Theater, and Mountain People and Places. The Kiwanis Club, designed to hold 250 people, was packed with more than 400 folks. Many other people

were listening outside the open windows and doors. The evening
began and ended with gospel singing by the Reverand Hie Mullins and
three generations of his family. The Rev. Mullins began singing at age
eight with his father who taught at Shape Note singing schools
around the central Appalachian mountain area. Also performing was
Clay Taylor—who learned to play the banjo from his father—his son,
Aubra, on fiddle, and his son-in-law, Clayton Belcher, on guitar. They
played old-time, string-band dance music in much the same way it was
played when Clay was a young man, working in the coal mines and
playing for dances and parties in southwest Virginia. Inspired by Clay's
music, an 80-year-old woman jumped up and began flatfooting,
encouraging others to join in her dance. When the music died down,
storyteller Edith Wright told many of her historical remembrances of
life in Dickenson County, as well as her ghost stories and haint tales,
before passing the stage to Betty Deal who sang several mountain
ballads, including "Pretty Polly." Then the older folks asked the high
school class to tell their story, "How Haysi Got Its Name." The evening
ended with all performers on stage singing a final song with the audience. The audience's response to the evening was enthusiastic and
emotional. Many people stayed afterward to swap stories and gathered in small groups singing songs.

The Baptist minister was so affected by the final festival that he
wanted to bring this spirit, and what he called its "cultural content," to
his church. He collaborated with Roadside to create an evening service that emphasized Appalachian gospel music, even though this was
not the music sung by his congregation. Gospel groups from several
indigenous churches joined Roadside that night, ending with an
Appalachian version of "Amazing Grace" that left the audience—representing all the residency partners as well as a broad cross section of
the community—united in the strength of their place and people.

Roadside Theater's residency did not eliminate the economic
problems in Dickenson County, but it did help change individuals' lives
and the way the county regards itself. For Roadside, the residency
confirmed the theater's belief in turning to local community cultural
resources as a way to build pride and self-reliance, and to engage
community problems. The year-long period of the project allowed the

entire county to be affected. The specifics of the theater's new residency methodology were further honed, and a new Roadside play, *Borderline*—which examines the history of the region—was born of the undertaking. Perhaps most importantly for Roadside, the company now has local partners working to help it figure out the next steps in this community-based approach. Haysi volunteers act as resources for other communities in which Roadside is working, and regularly consult about progress in their county.

Since 1990, Roadside has continued to deepen its work at home, and has taken its model on the road nationally. WASAA has worked in partnership with Roadside and national arts presenters to conduct one- and two-week community cultural residencies that involve—as equal partners in the planning, execution and evaluation—various community groups including senior citizen centers, colleges, community centers, churches, literacy programs, libraries, historical societies, environmental groups, tribal councils, schools, ethnic social clubs and arts councils.

This approach raises its own set of questions. What do communities need in order to continue this work on their own on a long term basis? How can people doing community cultural development work across the country strengthen one another? Will the process hold up in all kinds of situations? Will new community and new Roadside plays continue to develop from the work? Will cross-cultural artistic collaborations spring from the national effort? How will this work be funded?

All the answers, of course, are not presently known. But what is clear is that the effort to change our national presenting model to include the celebration and validation of the host community's culture will not come about by the work of one theater company. It will require the collaboration of culturally diverse community groups, students, arts presenters, teachers, funders, artists and producers. It will require bringing diverse segments of a community into the decision-making and planning process with equal voice.

Winter 1993

The Cutting Edge Is Enormous:
Liz Lerman and Richard Owen Geer

By Linda Burnham

Community-based art is changing the very definitions of art, artist and artmaking. Here we get some new points of view from two artists working out there. Choreographer Liz Lerman, director of Liz Lerman Dance Exchange in Washington, D.C., is determined to reorder the priorities laid down for her in art school. Richard Owen Geer had those priorities reordered for him by the citizens of a small town in south Georgia. —Eds.

Something is happening to artists. As more and more of them commit to community projects, their work is raising critical questions about the role of the artist in these projects and about the exact location of the artistic act. Depending on the political bent of the participants, sometimes the artist is restricted to the role of facilitator—apparently submerging his/her own identity, expertise, training and talent into the collaborative action of the group. As art swerves in new directions, the idea of the virtuoso is being challenged.

I have recently participated in intense discussions about the work of two artists now working in community settings: choreographer Liz Lerman and theater director Richard Owen Geer. Originally trained in different disciplines, but also versed in collaborative methods and the history of community-based work, they each wrestle with the question of identity as they strive to contribute to the new wave of thinking in the arts.

Collaboration is the key in this new work. Because one of the primary goals of most community-art projects is to address social questions, artists have found that the most successful strategy is to gather allies outside the art community. Tapping into resources from the fields of social work, health care, the law, community organizing, education and the clergy, they are no longer in the cradle of the art world.

Lerman and her D.C.-based company, The Dance Exchange,

while doing workshops and projects with the elderly and the young, find themselves working with administrators of senior centers and physicians who treat terminally ill children. Geer just spent three years immersed in the social and political web of a small southern town as director of the folk-life play *Swamp Gravy*.

For both artists, the challenges of helping to organize a community project are enormous, and different each time. Sometimes it is even more challenging to find their own roles in the process—roles that may change as the project progresses, and continue to change even after it ends.

Liz Lerman emerges from the stratified and hierarchical world of dance, where virtuosity is the highest ideal, where the choreographer is raised to the level of a god, or at least a master puppeteer.

The Dance Exchange breaks the traditional dance mold every which way. The nine-member touring company ranges in age from 20 to 70, including some who began to dance only in their senior years, and the company repertoire is a product of their work together. In addition, unlike other dance companies, every member of The Dance Exchange is expected to teach.

Lerman, founder and artistic director of the company, is credited as the choreographer of the repertoire, and she sees this as an important contribution ("Dance is for everyone—Liz Lerman too," she says). To the concert stage she brings her technical expertise as a dancer and her artist's eye as the designer of ensemble performance.

But for Lerman, the job of choreography offers more than the opportunity to plot dance, call forth great performances from the company and dazzle the audience in a theater. In her search for personal and artistic growth, collaboration is bountiful. Everyone and everything involved with the work of The Dance Exchange—from structural organization and fundraising, through

"I think there was a time when people danced and the crops grew..."

teaching, performance and critical theory—is a vital part of her work, and she of theirs. Attention to all the ways the company moves through the world *is* the art. This is the aesthetic that underlies the company's mission: "to make dance a real part of people's lives, to make dance matter again."

While in Raleigh, North Carolina, for a recent residency, Dance Exchange company members led workshops with dance students of all ages at North Carolina State University (NCSU), Meredith College, Enloe High School and Arts Together, a "community arts school." They held training sessions for public-school teachers and healthcare providers on integrating dance into their work. Lerman spoke on panels and facilitated a discussion with a group of local collaborators about presenting community art. The dancers even invaded a pediatric-clinic waiting room at a local hospital where they improvised a session of dance for kids. By the end of the week, teens had been recruited from Enloe High to appear in the company's concert at NCSU. All this work is choreography to Liz Lerman.

Dance has become so stripped of its community functions, says Lerman, that dancers are expected to care only about form. It wasn't always this way.

"I think there was a time when people danced and the crops grew," she told an arts conference a while back. "I think they danced and that is how they healed their children. They danced; that is how they prepared for war. Maybe they mainly danced because they could not understand the incomprehensible, and perhaps in a moment of becoming (not interpreting) the sun in a sun dance, they could understand the forces of nature."

Now, she says, if a dancer is interested in the healing aspects of dance, she is told to go into dance therapy. Spirituality? Try liturgical dance. Politics? You want to go to Latin America, they do that there. Work with old people? That's social work. Lerman said:

> Now we have a world of dance specialists. But we've paid a price for this separation, an enormous price. In 15 years at the Dance Exchange, what we've really been about is trying to take these incredible functions of dance and reinterpret them into art. This is something we desperately need right now.

Lerman asserts that teaching dance in a nursing home is just as important as performing at the Kennedy Center. By capitulating to the dance world's hierarchical structures, she says, we lose a great opportunity.

"This hierarchy makes the cutting edge teeny, teeny tiny. Only a certain kind of something can be that. But, you know, when you do *this*," she says, moving her hands from a vertical alignment to the horizontal, "the cutting edge is enormous. There is this extraordinary spectrum of artistic activity that we can live along," stretching her arms as far apart as they will go.

Richard Owen Geer's theories about community performance have been published at length in *High Performance*, but until I traveled to Colquitt, Georgia, one spring weekend, and met his collaborators in *Swamp Gravy*, I didn't have the picture of what it's like to collaborate with a whole town.

In brief, the Chicago-based Geer met Colquitt's Joy Jinks at a workshop in the North in 1991, and together they decided to develop a play in Colquitt around the personal history of the town (pop. 2,000). Three years later, a cast of 70 Colquitt citizens, all nonactors, was playing to sold-out crowds in the town's old cotton warehouse, and *Swamp Gravy* had been officially recognized by the state legislature as Georgia's "folk-life play."

Light years beyond the traditional Southern historical drama, *Swamp Gravy* is a storytelling extravaganza touching on such inflammatory issues as racism and spousal abuse. The play operates on two distinct levels. Performed in historical costume, it contains much material that, in a contemporary frame, might be problematic—politically too sensitive. At historical remove, these tales resonate across time, deeply rooted in the particular character of the town. Still, stories that make entertaining drama to an outsider are the real stuff of local life, and they tug heavily at the heartstrings of the Colquitt native. The night I saw it, a scene remembering the dead brought tears from a man in his 50s sitting near me.

Swamp Gravy is a good example of a work that blurs the definition of ownership. Written by Tennessee playwright Jo Carson from the personal memories of the town, the script is massaged every time it is rehearsed. In transit back and forth from Chicago, Geer was in town for the first and last performances of the eleven-night spring run, and found much of it completely changed by the cast.

In talking with cast members, it is clear that the play belongs to them, not to Carson or Geer. The Colquitt folks are in control of the social and artistic life of the drama. *They* will tour it and *they* will answer requests to assist nearby towns in developing their own plays.

Carson's primary contribution was the organizing of the material and the selecting of language from people's memories. Geer's gift was the imaginative staging that moved the cast through the audience, had them telling stories simultaneously, turned a beauty-parlor scene into a dance, skillfully and delicately showcased racial issues and folded the observer into the history and relationships of the town. ("You never knew when the person next to you would burst out singing," said one audience member.)

The closing cast party was a real love-fest, with members honoring each other in the tenderest of ways. One performer, an outstanding African-American singer, thanked Geer and the entire cast by singing "The Wind Beneath My Wings." Members told me barriers of class and race had been brought down and Colquitt would never be the same. Clearly the show was a success and everything turned out better than anyone could have dreamed.

This, according to Geer, was a miracle. In late 1992, it looked like things were doomed, and the issue revolved around Geer and his role in the proceedings. Ten days before *Swamp Gravy Sketches,* an early production of parts of the piece, Geer did something most actors are used to witnessing: He threw a classic director's tantrum. Only half the cast had turned up for rehearsal and Geer was furious. He flew into a rage, finishing with "the F— word" at top decibels. In the atmosphere surrounding *Swamp Gravy,* which is subtitled *acting together for a better community,* this behavior was clearly unacceptable. Not only was his language offensive, he had betrayed a fundamentally hierarchical attitude.

"I turned around and saw everybody streaming out the doors," says Geer now, still astonished. "They told me they couldn't work with me and three of the men threatened to beat me up if I didn't get out of town!" In desperation, Geer tried apologizing to individuals, but to no avail. Finally, he appealed to the local minister, who called a meeting and explained to the cast that Geer was seeking forgiveness, and they had to give it to him or they couldn't call themselves Christians. After further discussion, they voted to forgive him and go on with the piece. Geer stayed and everyone is more than glad he did, but the *auteur* in him left town for good. This lesson remained with him through every moment of the process, and he says it altered his view of himself and his role as an artist. Far from squelching his ambition, the experience has left him firmly situated in the field of community performance and hungry for more.

Geer and Lerman are only two of the artists who are changing our ideas about the artist—stepping down from the pedestal, getting out of the way, as it were, and allowing us, perhaps, to draw nearer to the vital meaning of the presence of art in life. Both these people bring to their work the training and life experience of professionals, but for them, that was only the beginning of learning. They are letting their work teach them something new about human reality. Or maybe it's something old; something that predates or lies beneath choreography, theater and art itself.

Summer 1994

Between Me and the Giant: Imagination Workshop

by William Cleveland

Art has its own special place in therapeutic settings, far different from that of therapy itself. Here William Cleveland reveals the courageous and relentless energy of Imagination Workshop, a group of actors at work in a neuropsychiatric institute. William Cleveland is a pioneer in his own right of numerous community and institutional art programs, including Artsreach Community Artists, California-Arts-In-Corrections and California State Summer School for the Arts. A longer version of this article first appeared in Cleveland's book Art in Other Places: Artists at Work in America's Community and Social Institutions. *The book, published by Praeger (1992), features case studies of a variety of successful arts programs and projects that have integrated the arts into community and institutional settings.   —Eds.*

I came to the ward as a beast; I came to the play as a real beast. When the play first started, I didn't want to do it. I just wrote down some beastly lines. You said, "Think of a character." I thought of a beast. You said, "Think of two characters." I had two beasts. And I enjoyed the transition. The beast moves to a person of feeling. Sort of what I would like to do here on the ward.

> —A young patient, Richard, commenting on the character
> he created in an Imagination Workshop play[1]

In May of 1984, the Joint Legislative Committee for the Arts of the California State Legislature convened a hearing to gather testimony on the work of artists who had developed programs with support from the California Arts Council's Artists in Social Institutions Program. Margaret Ladd, the founder of Imagination Workshop, began her testimony before the Committee by relaying a message that had been given to her by a young man who was a participant in her drama program at the Neuropsychiatric Institute at UCLA.

Prior to coming to Sacramento to testify, Ladd had asked her class what they wanted her to say to the members of the committee about the work they had been doing. This young man, a catatonic who had never before spoken in class, responded to her question by picking up a hat and saying, "I'll play Jack." Ladd asked him if he had anything he wanted related to the committee. He said, "No," but a short time later while he was doing an improvisation as "Jack," also for the first time, he indicated he did have something he wanted to say. He said, "Please tell them that here we're able to dream." The girl he had been working with then asked, "What are you dreaming of?" And he said, "I dream of a place and a time where love and friendship come between me and the giant."

This young man is one of more than 40,000 seriously mentally disabled patients who have participated in Imagination Workshop classes during the past 25 years. His response to Ladd's question is a small example of what she and the other professional actors who conduct the program's workshops feel is the powerful impact the theater arts can have on the lives of the people they work with. Ladd describes the result as the development of "character muscles."

> By playing characters removed from themselves and creating a repertoire of behaviors, they start to find all kinds of ways to behave. I think it gives people who are too inhibited and fragile to relate to others a second chance. Through their imagination, they feel safer and can give it another try. They develop courage and can then make an effort to relate to therapy. We're a stepping stone.[2]

The placing of these stepping stones has been no easy matter. The presence of Imagination Workshop at the UCLA Neuropsychiatric Institute, Edgemont Hospital, Gramercy Place Homeless Shelter, John Adams Junior High School and other Los Angeles healthcare, mental-health and educational facilities is the result of many years of hard work and sacrifice. As is the case with many community-based arts programs, the impetus for this remarkable program was provided by one person, an artist, who saw a need and responded artistically.

In 1969, Ladd was appearing in an Ionesco play on Broadway.

She and other members of the cast were invited to visit a Massachusetts mental hospital to see a Gertrude Stein play that was being performed by the patients there. As she watched, she began to consider
how she would approach the challenge of working, as an actor, with
patients at the hospital. The idea intrigued her. She was particularly
struck by what she perceived as a common ground shared by the
actors and the patients. She saw that both were dealing quite intensely with the impact and power of their imaginations. Ladd surmised
that while actors use their imaginations in constrictive ways, the
patient is doing quite the opposite. Concluding that the imaginative
discipline inherent in theater work might be of some benefit to the
hospital's patients, she approached officials at Mount Sinai Hospital in
New York with the idea of conducting some drama workshops there.

   Over the next two years, the processes and skills that would
become the bread and butter of Imagination Workshop were ham-
mered out by Ladd and her husband-to-be, writer/director Lyle
Kessler. The more they worked, the greater became their commitment to making "theater discipline" a part of the lives of the mentally
ill. To the surprise of some at the hospital, patients seemed to like it.
Not only that, by all measures their conditions improved as a result of
their participation.

   One example, a woman in her late seventies, had not spoken for
months. Diagnosed as physically impaired, she was among the typically
"hard" cases who were regularly referred to the Workshop. At first,
although she came on a regular basis, her mute status continued. One
day, though, during a script-writing exercise she offered a written
phrase: "Establishing what is there." From that point on she became an
active participant. Ladd adds, "After that she began to communicate
with her therapist; staff were able to reach her. We found that her
silence was caused simply by a deep depression."[3]

   During the early 1970s, the relationship between Imagination
Workshop and the Mount Sinai Hospital flourished. The Workshop's
activities also grew to include a program at the New York State Psychiatric Hospital. There they took on the challenge of working with
severely disturbed patients who were housed in "lock-up" units. The
results, once again, were positive. In 1977, the program was moved to

the Cornell Medical Center at New York Hospital, where it continued until a year later, when Ladd and Kessler moved to their current home in Santa Monica, California.

After the move, with their Hollywood careers taking off—Ladd landing a role in CBS' "Falcon Crest" and Kessler directing films—Imagination Workshop took a short hiatus. But once she got her feet on the ground, Ladd wasted little time beginning again. In 1979, she approached Dr. Louis Jolyon West, the chairman of the UCLA Neuropsychiatric Institute (NPI), with a proposal to establish a new program there at the world's largest university-based clinic. With images of wild-eyed actors running amok among the Institute's patients and staff, Dr. West demurred. After more prodding by Ladd, though, he did agree to contact his New York counterparts for their impressions of the workshop's effectiveness. From them he learned that these were people who had earned their respect, "not flakes or kooks. These guys actually had a well thought-out program, a master plan that had a legitimate theoretical basis. And they were willing to be rigorously scrutinized." With these recommendations in hand, Dr. West gave the go-ahead for the workshop to begin work.

Fifteen years later, in addition to serving patients at the Neuropsychiatric Institute, the Imagination Workshop is providing ongoing programs to twelve other sites in the Los Angeles area. These sites include homeless shelters, schools and veteran's facilities, as well as community and state mental health institutions.

Part-and-parcel of this increased activity has been the ongoing struggle for survival. What began as a simple impulse of curiosity and concern by a single artist has become a complex program. Imagination Workshop, which now touches hundreds of people each year, has even acquired a small bureaucracy of its own. The focus of everybody involved, though, remains on what happens among the actors and participants working in makeshift studios and theaters. Neither Ladd, who serves as an advisor to the program, nor Jonathan Zeichner, the Workshop's artistic director, has lost sight of the simple fact that Imagination Workshop is, in the words of one workshop participant, a place where "the beast moves to a person of feeling."

An Imagination Workshop

Imagination Workshop sees itself as serving two specific groups. The first are the Workshop's participants. This group includes the seriously mentally ill, geriatric patients, homeless veterans, homeless families and youth at risk. The second is the large and often "starving" community of professional theater artists who live in Los Angeles. They feel that bringing these two communities together provides a powerful and effective resource for addressing the needs of the workshop participants, and an opportunity for artists to grow as artists while contributing to their communities.

Every session of the Imagination Workshop is planned beforehand by the three actors who are used for a typical session. These actors are all professionals. Most have extensive backgrounds in live theater, film and television. They have also been trained in the specific theater techniques that have been developed by the company for their work. Although each session is designed for the specific situation the actors will be dealing with on a particular day, they are all structured to include three basic components. Ladd describes a typical workshop:

> Our class size averages around 12 to 15 participants, with an age range which goes from eleven to ninety. With the older patients, we have to be cognizant of any physical limitations they might have. We begin with a physical warm-up. We try to get each participant to relate what they are doing in the warm-up to something imaginary. We might ask them to pretend that they are a plant or an animal or some other element of nature. They get to choose. When they get into being a dandelion, with a strong stem, blowing in the wind, or a cactus deeply rooted in water, their bodies and imaginations are engaged.

The second segment is something the company has dubbed "the passing exercise." In it everybody sits in a circle and shares something with the person next to them. Barbara Weinberg, one-time Imagination Workshop administrative director, says the intent is to begin using the imagination as a means of communication.

This is a quiet time. We ask them to sit in the circle and take the hand of the person next to them and look at them. This in itself is a marvelous achievement for many of them. The idea then is to share a thought. It might be a reminiscence from childhood or a personal sentiment of some sort. It might even be giving the person a gift, like a weekend in Paris or a walk down a stream. It is a nonthreatening way to make personal contact with another person.

After the passing exercise, the company members shift into the main body of the workshop. This segment usually involves one form of improvisation or another. Ladd elaborates:

Here is where we ask them to play a character. Sometimes they choose a character they are already familiar with from another session. Other times we give them a character to play on a slip of paper. This written direction often includes a description of a need which the character might have. In most cases, the patients create characters and situations which are far removed from themselves, usually inspired by fairy tales, myths or history. Because they are so far removed, these improvisations seem to have a liberating effect on them. Many times they will discover alternate ways of dealing with problems or conflicts which they have not been able to solve in their daily lives.

The actors with Imagination Workshop...are very clear...that what they do is not therapy.

When asked about problems in the classroom with disturbed patients, Ladd says the actors rely on their expertise in theater rather than trying to become amateur psychologists.

Whenever we get into what we feel is hot water we try to bring it down by dealing specifically with the character. If someone starts to cry, we might say, 'That's right, that's just the way the character would feel. That's very good. When I'm acting, that's just the way I feel.' Every time it relaxes them.

Our approach involves very little of the probing or pushing of feelings which are prevalent in other more cathartic approaches. It's important for us to keep them thinking within their characters. Then, when the real problems intervene, we have a safer context for them to work them out. Say you've got a guy who chooses to play the Beast in his improvisation with somebody who has been doing Chicken Little. You can imagine some of the conflicts which are liable to start happening. At this point, we might say to Chicken Little, 'Let's stop for a moment. What would Chicken Little like to say about this, what is she feeling?' And then we would do the same for the Beast character. It is very important that we address the character as 'she' or 'he,' and not 'you.' If we ask, 'What are you feeling?' they are most liable to say, 'Wait a minute, that's not me.' They need the safety of the character.

Many of our participants are totally isolated from society, and in particular from any artistic experience. Through the Workshop they make contact with their own artistic potential and are often able to find indirect, artistic passageways out of their painful isolation. As I said before, they feel safe enough to risk trying new forms of expression, including playfulness and humor. These are human qualities which are often left untapped through therapy.

Is Therapy a Dirty Word?

The actors with Imagination Workshop work very closely with the therapeutic staff. They are very clear, though, that what they do is not therapy. Because they are trained as professional actors and not as therapists, Ladd says they are very defensive about being identified with psychodrama or drama therapy. She continues:

In that sense, therapy is a dirty word to us, but only because it is not what we do. We feel that what we do is more effective because we concentrate on what we know best. And that is theater. If we were carpenters and we were requested to come in and teach the patients how to build a house, it would be inappropriate for us to focus on our work as a means to a therapeutic or diagnostic end. As carpenters, or as actors, we will build a house or play with a kind of seriousness and respect for the work itself. We don't get tempted to play a role for which we are not prepared.

On the other hand, we can't deny that we are working with a very special population with very severe problems. We have to know as much as we can about particular patients or the populations in general so that we can know when to ask for help or intervention. If in the course of our work a patient says he is going to jump off a cliff the next day, we don't have the luxury of treating this information as a private work. We have to use our judgment based on common sense.

Studies conducted in 1982 at NPI rated Imagination Workshop as the most beneficial among the 20 or so activities that the patients participate in at the hospital. They also showed that the workshop was more "therapeutically effective" than the use of therapeutic role playing.[4]

Ladd feels the difference can be laid to the fact that when the actors work with the patients "they are acting roles as someone else in an imaginary situation." She says that these very seriously ill patients are far more successful dealing with difficult and painful situations in an indirect manner. When progress is measured within the workshop it is defined more in terms of theater than therapy. According to Ladd, the progress they do see is often "very subtle." For her, the key remains that "the patients relate better, have more eye contact, and more fun, when they are not playing themselves." She continues:

> If, in the course of a workshop, a patient started coming up with something which was therapeutically significant, I wouldn't intervene, even if I had the therapeutic skills to deal with it. If it was disturbing to either the patient or the group I would do something, but otherwise I would leave it alone. The creative process needs time to gestate in the person themselves. We have found that three weeks later—this seems to be the magic amount of time—they will most often bring that issue up in the appropriate place with their therapist. The therapist is often incredulous. But the patient knows the difference between drama therapy and drama. In drama, they are being treated as artists. Drama is a purely integrative process. Therapy is integrative as well but it must dissect before it integrates. It has to make you cognitively aware of the issues. I think the two—drama and therapy—work brilliantly together. I would never want to do the Imagination Workshop without the ability for a therapist to intervene at the appropriate time.

Patton, Merlin, Fairy Godmother, et al.

Because of the high turnover rate for hospitalized patients at NPI and other program sites, Imagination Workshop has been unable to work long enough with these populations to create and present finished plays. The NPI outpatient clinic, though, has offered that opportunity. Outpatients, because of their longer term relationship with the hospital, provide the workshop with a more stable group of participants. The result has been an annual production presented to patients and staff on the NPI stage.

The 1987 production, entitled *The Road to Happiness: We Do It. You See It,* evolved from skits created by the participants in their weekly workshops. Each of the 30 short scenes in the play is written for two characters that have been developed by a patient. The characters portrayed are most often familiar, somewhat archetypal personages borrowed from history, literature, mythology or popular culture. All of the scenes are separate, but tied loosely together by a common theme. The resulting mix of characters, costumes and conversations weaves an extraordinary tapestry of incongruent humor and poignancy.

One such scene involves a meeting between General Patton and the Fairy Godmother. In it Patton threatens the Fairy Godmother with a hand grenade and a court martial. The Fairy Godmother responds by magically transforming Patton into a rapidly changing series of bizarre characters. Among them are Quasimodo, Humphrey Bogart, Tarzan, James Bond, Popeye and, finally, a pacifist.

Preventative Medicine

Back when they were in New York, Ladd and Kessler had had an opportunity to conduct a series of workshops with a group of adolescents who had not responded to traditional treatment. Despite the fact that these twelve patients had been considered "problem" cases, they did very well in the Workshop. Like the many thousands of workshop participants that would follow in the years to come, they wrote and acted in their own plays. Many years later, Ladd was able to follow up and find out what had become of some of these former students. She discovered that two of them had become doctors. Others she found had become artists of one sort or another. She also learned from the "graduates" she talked to that they kept the Workshop play they had written by their beds to see them through the rough spots of their lives—"figuring if they did it once, they could do it again."[5]

Remembering this extraordinary early success, Ladd jumped at the chance to work again with adolescents when the opportunity arose at Edgemont Hospital in early 1988. This new workshop group is made up of young people (9- to 17-year-olds) who have been hospitalized as a result of severe depression. Many have attempted suicide, and have been victims of significant long-term abuse. Unfortunately, they are a part of one of the fastest growing segments of the hospital's population, a trend that is occurring across the country.

Jonathan Zeichner, the Workshop's artistic director, sees the Workshop's growing involvement with young people as providing a new and critical element to the organization's work.

> Our medicine is now operating on three different levels. When we first began we were doing treatment with mental-health patients. As we expanded to other populations, we again found ourselves engaged in remedial work. Now with this younger population, we are really doing preventative medicine.

Weinberg's description of the typical young Imagination Workshop participant is daunting, if not depressing.

> Many of these kids are 12 and 13 years old. They have been victims of gang rapes, incredible abuse at home or sometimes in foster care—you name it, they've been through it. A lot of them have just shut down. They are not participating in this world. When they come into the workshop it seems to give them the avenue they need to just begin to express themselves. Some of them have literally rediscovered their basic communications skills with us.

Zeichner elaborates,

> What we are providing here and all the other places we work is nutrition for the soul. There is an epidemic of malnutrition. At the least, we are giving our participants a sense of community and belonging and safety, a place where they can explore and take risks and yet feel like they are

working with a net. Beyond that we are providing tools and access to their own sources of problem solving, communication and socialization.

It is ironic that many of the professional actors involved with Imagination Workshop feel that some of their best work has been done in workshops with patients in mental hospitals. Ladd feels that the benefits of what their actors do for the most depressed and confused among us should be available to everyone. She considers the absence of opportunities for the active exercise of our individual and collective imaginations in schools and other community institutions to be unhealthy. Her dream is to create an Imagination Workshop Institute that would begin to address this need. Through such an institute, she and her staff would make the techniques and skills developed through 25 years of work available to other artists and other institutional settings. Hopefully, Ladd's dream will become a reality. If it doesn't, it will certainly not be for lack of "character muscles" being exercised by Imagination Workshop artists and more than 40,000 Imagination Workshop participants.

Notes

1 From brochure "Imagination Workshop, a Theater Arts Organization Serving the Mental Health Community."

2 Lyle Kessler, quoted in Kerry Platman, "The Show Goes On for Mentally Ill," *Los Angeles Times*, View, April 19, 1983.

3. Margaret Ladd, quoted in Platman, *ibid.*

4. Ching-piao Chien, MD., and Marcia Schwartz, BA., "Adult Development Group Research Update on Imagination Workshop," preliminary report, UCLA Neuro-psychiatric Institute, February, 1982.

5. Jan Stevens, "Flights of Fancy Reach the Mentally Ill," *Evening Outlook*, Los Angeles, July 1, 1986.

6. "The Road to Happiness," Imagination Workshop, 1987.

Fall 1994

Living with the Doors Open:
An Interview with Blondell Cummings

By Veta Goler

New York dancer/choreographer Blondell Cummings grew up in Harlem where her neighbors "lived with their doors open and you could hear their music." Cummings is still hearing the music of neighborhoods everywhere she goes. Her community workshops provide her with material for her performances. Here she is interviewed about that process by choreographer Veta Goler, who teaches dance at Spelman College. —Eds.

One of Blondell Cummings' most emotionally moving experiences as a choreographer and performer happened in 1983 when she performed her solo *Chicken Soup* on the Dance Black America Program at the Brooklyn Academy of Music. In a videotaped interview with dance scholar Sally Banes, Cummings comes close to tears as she talks about this event.

> Being asked to appear on the Dance Black America Program was flattering. Doing *Chicken Soup* was exciting. The opera house was packed. To do nontraditional dance and have black people say, "I truly understand" was wonderful. I thought, "So this is what it's all about." If I never have another moment like this again, it's been worth all the working.

Cummings was so moved by the warm reception of the black audience because it recognized the connection of *Chicken Soup*—and, by extension, her work—to African-American culture, and it affirmed her as an African-American woman artist, although her unique artistic expression is referential to the black experience in sometimes subtle and oblique ways.

Cummings' choreography and performance style are different from those of some other African-American dance artists in that, for the most part, she does not treat the black experience as isolated from other cultural experiences. Her work is universal as she explores differences and similarities in the lives of diverse peoples. Cummings' choreography clearly expresses her experiences as an African-American woman. However, because her personal growth and development have been achieved through her exposure to the ideas and customs of many nonblack peoples, Cummings has developed a world view in which African-American cultural practices are simply one kind of the many that make up the world.

Cummings was born in South Carolina some 40-odd years ago to sharecropping parents who grew cotton and tobacco, and moved with her family to Harlem before she was a year old. Her childhood appears to have been a blend of strictness and whimsy. Cummings' mother believed in the adage "Spare the rod and spoil the child," the choreographer recalls, so Cummings received the kind of physical discipline that has typically been administered in many black families. Oddly, her punishments gave her a sense of connection to the black community. She remembers yelling and screaming as loudly as she could while being spanked, in the hope that the threat of neighbors' intervention would cause her parents to stop. In fact, neighbors did occasionally check when they heard her screams to make sure that Cummings was not being abused, she says. This taught her that adults in her neighborhood knew much of what happened with her family, as well as with the rest of the community, and Cummings came to accept concern and responsibility for neighbors as an important part of the African-American community.

Her early experiences with music also contributed to the connection she felt to people in her community. In her Harlem neighborhood, Cummings says, "People lived with their doors open and you could hear other people's music. And it wasn't considered intrusive." Just as Cummings learned to appreciate her neighbors' music in her childhood, she later learned to appreciate other peoples' cultures.

Extensive travel has clearly influenced her work in this way. Cummings began traveling by herself in the late 1960s, before she began international dance touring, and before many African Americans traveled outside of North America. She has visited countries in Africa, Europe, Asia, the Caribbean and South America. Travel instilled in Cummings a curiosity about the world and revealed to her similarities

and differences in activities and phenomena common to all peoples—such as eating, migration and death. Consequently, her artistic
expression of African-American customs is within the context of
other peoples' customs.

Cummings describes her dance background as eclectic. She has
studied with virtually all of the major African-American modern-dance
figures of her time. Among those with whom she has worked as a
student or as a dancer are Alvin Ailey, Katherine Dunham, Pearl
Primus, Rod Rodgers, Talley Beatty, Mary Hinkson and Eleo Pomare.
Cummings has also had extensive training in the established white
modern-dance techniques—studying with Alwin Nikolais, at the
Martha Graham school, and taking classes in the techniques of Lester
Horton, Merce Cunningham and Erick Hawkins. She ultimately
became fascinated with idiosyncratic expression and studied with
artists of the experimental Judson Church group of the early 1960s,
including Yvonne Rainer, Steve Paxton and David Gordon. In addition,
she danced with Meredith Monk's company, The House, for ten years.

Cummings is well known for her work as a solo artist, although
she also presents group work under the name Blondelle. Her works
include: *Cycle* and *Flashdance,* which look at menstruation and
menopause, respectively; *Food For Thought,* a series of works exploring
issues relating to food and eating; a number of works dealing with
interpersonal relationships, presented under the titles *Relationships:
Intimate and Not So Intimate, Relationships: Good and Not So Good;* and
Like Family, and *Basic Strategies,* a series of five pieces concerning
money. Her aesthetic—which is multidisciplinary, community-focused
and process-oriented—moves between dance/theater and performance art. She incorporates dance, sign language and other gesture,
text (ranging from oral histories to recipes), props, sets, photographs,
video footage and live and recorded music. She creates work by elicit-
ing the personal experiences of collaborating artists, other performers
and the participants in her workshops.

Workshops figure prominently in her creative process. These
exploratory and participatory gatherings, which she conducts in various communities around the country, center around some of the
phenomena that all people experience—such as family, biological life

cycles, food and money. She leads experiences and exercises designed to elicit from participants diverse responses to questions, issues and situations that she then incorporates into her work. The workshops are not especially for dancers, but are designed to bring together people of various ages, ethnicities and socioeconomic situations to explore cultural differences and similarities.

Cummings also utilizes the oral history interview to acquire autobiographical material for her artistry. She conducts these both within and outside of her workshops and incorporates information from them in numerous ways. She may include portions of the actual interview in a production or may take ideas from the interview and use them as movement or textual catalysts. The spoken text from oral histories completes Cummings' choreography in ways that fulfill her artistic vision. Cummings views her choreographic process as a form of storytelling, as a means of sharing moments with people—not simply of creating dances.

Sharing with people from many different backgrounds and cultures became a way in which I could do research. . .

One of her earliest workshops was based on women's menstrual cycles. Participants in the workshop included women and men from a variety of cultures. They discussed menstruation, sharing their personal conceptions and experiences—one man thought all women's periods occurred simultaneously—as well as cultural myths and taboos related to this important part of women's lives. To Cummings, these workshops, and the performance pieces that develop from them, reveal distinct cultural perspectives. As such, they reflect and perpetuate community. Her sense of community, and her ideas about how her work relates to our changing communities, are revealed in her dialogue.

Veta Goler: How did you come to use community-based workshops so extensively for your choreography?

Blondell Cunmmings: I decided to do workshops because they helped me to focus on those issues that I thought might be important. Initially, when I did the menstrual cycle work, it was from a personal place—my menstrual cycle was an important part of my life. But in order to make it not indulgent, I wanted to give it a broader sense by sharing it with others. So I started talking about doing this piece, and women of all ages started to share their ideas, thoughts, fears, hopes and desires with me. I became the caretaker of that information, and my mission became to present something that was personal and, at the same time, an exploration of the issue on many other levels. Sharing with people from many different backgrounds and cultures became a way in which I could do research, and from that research, choose artistic methods that would best present the material.

VG: *Would you talk more about the workshops—how you choose subject matter and who participates in them?*

BC: Each workshop series is directly related to the project that I'm working on, whether it's food or menopause or family. Although it's not exclusive to the people who are connected to the particular subject matter, it certainly tends to draw people who are.

VG: *So people who come to the workshops are closely related to the subject matter. What kinds of direction do you give them?*

BC: The workshops are also directly related to my interdisciplinary approach to the work. So my work is dealing with movement; photographic imagery; text, such as storytelling, interviews or word associations; music and vocal stuff. Just as my work is a mixture of those things, the workshops will also be a mixture of those things—whether I conduct them myself, and bring all those areas into them, or in collaboration with other artists, who take on certain areas. For instance, in a menstrual cycle piece, we might sit in a circle and just talk about the first time we had our period. Or, if the workshop was on money, we might sit and talk about the first money we ever made. This sharing starts to give people information about each other, but also about the variety of ways there are of handling the very same thing. In the family workshop, we might do movements and put together a family folk dance based on gestures from family members. We might create a chant based on different ways of saying mother and father.

VG: *The creative involvement of your performers, who are sometimes workshop participants, is a distinctive part of your work. How do you utilize their input?*

BC: Basically, when I'm working with other artists, I let them take the lead on how they want to experiment with the idea. I give them the topic and the focus, and a sense of what I'm looking for. With workshops, I work with the material the participants, who are the experts at their particular movement, give me. For instance, someone might give me an excited gesture that a family member does. I might take it up into the air, or put it down on the floor, or turn it around and then give it back to them. So I can take liberties, because that's my job as the artist—to take their information and transform it into an involved kinetic movement phrase that they might not have seen before.

VG: *In addition to providing performance outlets or opportunities to see theatrical work they have helped create, what is the impact of your workshops on the participants?*

BC: I think that the things we do in the exercises are multilevel. The things that are discovered are not just in terms of movement material.

VG: *So there are personal discoveries that people make about themselves and their own lives?*

BC: Exactly. And [they also discover] that their perceptions are much deeper than they realize. Also, I like to think that in the after-sharing, that that automatically brings a sense of community. I had decided as an artist that when I left a situation, I wanted to feel like options were opened up to people, and that there was a possibility of dialogue that maybe didn't exist before—whether it was internal dialogues that people could have with themselves or external dialogues that they could have with other people. That's certainly important with racial things, with the menopause things, with the women's health things. I've hoped that all the subject matter I've chosen, in some form or another, would lead to dialogues like that. I'm getting better at broadening my sense of ways in which people can explore. So now, bringing in people from different areas for panel discussions gives a scholarly look at personal issues. Having the elders on video gives a sense of history. It's important that people feel that what they're doing in itself is history—that they can be affected by it and can affect it, by creating their own sense of history or ritual.

VG: You focus quite a lot on the family. What do you make of the recent emphasis on family in the work of other choreographers?

BC: There is this family thing that's going around. For me, it's just a natural progression of my work. It's not just a project, it's an accumulation of all the things that I've been doing—whether it was about friendships (family can be your friends); whether it was about money (in some cases, you got your first money from doing jobs in your family); or whether it was about food (it was about what your family had in their refrigerator). The family is always kind of the basis, or certainly part of all those projects. So for the last 16 years I've been dealing with family issues; now I'm talking about family as an issue.

VG: Are you saying that all of your work is about family?

BC: That for me seems to be a recurring point of reference—but family in the broad sense, not just your brother. Family in the sense of a focal place where one learns to share a sense of identity; a sense of relating to other things; a sense of interpretation of information. Perhaps eventually, it would be nice to have a Like Family Institute, where people could come and, using art as a basis, work on these kinds of things—either creating a new sense of family, or in bringing their families, do a whole range of activities, using the family and community as a focus.

VG: *How do you feel about the recent popularity of community-based work?*

BC: I think that we artists are naturally community. Just in the act of traveling from place to place, we're taking our works and bringing that experience to a lot of people. And that means that those people who have shared that experience of our work share a point of reference.

VG: *So the artist becomes a point of reference to people who have experienced the work in various places?*

BC: ...which becomes a communal experience. And so in that way, the fact that we travel worldwide, it makes us the ambassadors. It makes us creators of community in that global sense, because of the process in which we work, but also in the act of bringing the work.

VG: *What can you say about the quality of community-based work you see in other choreographers?*

BC: The strongest artists leave people feeling like they have a broad sense of options because of what the artists have shared with them in that community—be it AIDS, like Bill T. Jones; or Liz Lerman dealing with being older; or the women's and family issues that I'm dealing with. They also work with sponsors to create structures that not only allow communities to be active participants in the sharing, but at the same time, set up continuing dialogues after the artists leave. And they have a sense of the globalness that they are creating, because that creates a different kind of consciousness in approaching work and audiences.

VG: *Which artists fall short in dealing with community?*

BC: People who don't understand that doing community work requires responsibility, depending on how deep the subject matter is or how much the community is involved in what the artist is doing. For instance, if I'm going to bring people together to deal with family issues or bring families together to deal with certain issues, I'd better understand that some issues are very emotional and painful. Sometimes people cry! I'd better be clear that when they walk out of the room, if things have been brought up, that I've taken responsibility to make sure that these things are addressed, and taken care of, and that people are supported before they leave the door. You don't want to leave people hanging. We artists can be very powerful. So we have to be responsible to the people we are working with, and be responsible to the audience that we're bringing forth this information to. If you're bringing a subject matter that is very provocative, you make allowances for something to resolve that. I was working with an interracial company and was told that they had some unresolved racial issues. I said to myself, "How can I address this?" So I came in the next day, and said, "I'm going to do a section called *I'm Sorry*." And *I'm Sorry* became a very important part of the piece. Whenever I do family projects there is an *I'm Sorry* section in there. And you get to say I'm sorry about anything you want to say I'm sorry about.

VG: *How does your work translate back to the community?*

BC: Personal investment. People that come to me have a personal investment in what's going on because of the subject matter I'm using. Also the workshops, panel discussions, sharing of personal experiences, personal interviews, storytelling and the act of performing give people options and opportunities to involve themselves with others in the creative process. The creative process is a means of sharing and is a communal act. My work is communal, even when it is solo work. We are all individuals with the ability to connect as groups.

VG: *You've emphasized the community connection of your work, even though you're a self-described loner. How does that work for you?*

BC: When I do solo work, I am acting as the voice of the internal self. But that doesn't exclude the fact that that internal self has a desire to share with other internal selves. And that is part of the aesthetic experience that I hope to present—whether I'm doing a solo, which is dealing with the internal voice and the identity of a self, or a group piece, which brings together many people and many individual selves. To me, both are a kind of community, or an act of community. That's what I'm constantly exploring in my work. I'm trying to open out those options for individuals to define their own identities. I'm also exploring my own options. I'm investigating what that is about—as an artist, as a woman, as an African American, as a dog owner, as a neighbor that lives in my house, on my block, on the Upper East Side. These are all different communities, and they're all a part of who I am. Hopefully, in that act of sharing, people get a sense of community, and get to define community in a way that we haven't defined it before. As we move into the 21st century, our sense of community will be greater than we could possibly imagine, and our ability to grasp that, and rise to that, will directly affect how we connect our past and our future. Because it's not that it's new, it's just far more broadened, complex and expanded. But the issue has always been there. The family will always be there. Whether we have other people carry our kids, or whether we have them in test tubes, the issues will still be the same: Who will take care of the kids; how do people get socialized into the community; how do we nurture people into becoming contributors to society so that we can perpetuate ourselves, address future concerns and go as far as we possibly can go in this hemisphere of the universe? And yet, I think the only way to deal with it on some level is to go back to the very basics, which is what we do in our art and in our lives.

Spring/Summer 1995

We Are All Connected:
Elders Share the Arts

By Susan Perlstein

For almost 20 years, New York's Elders Share the Arts [ESTA] has been creating models for planning and sustaining meaningful connections among generations and between cultures living in the same communities. This article is the first chapter of Generating Community, *a book by ESTA's founding director, theater artist Susan Perlstein, and Jeff Bliss, the intergenerational arts coordinator. It outlines their startlingly creative programs in four culturally transitional neighborhoods—East Harlem, Brooklyn's Northside, Flushing and Flatbush—including groups of deaf children and elders.   —Eds.*

Elders today still remember a time when extended families lived together and shared each other's daily lives. Increasingly, however, elders tend to be isolated from their communities, and especially from children, and come to feel they are no longer useful people: No one cares about what they know and there is no one to listen to their stories. Children, for their part, are cut off from the elders' wisdom and caring.

In ESTA's early days—as we worked with elders to create Living History presentations in nursing homes, senior centers and other settings—we heard many complaints about children. "The kids are ruining our neighborhood," some elders would say. "There's no discipline." "I wouldn't want to be a kid growing up today." It was this isolation of elders from meaningful activities with children—as well as the seniors' real fear of being targeted for ridicule and crime by young people—that inspired us to begin our program of intergenerational workshops. We realized there was a pressing need to reinvent family and community connections.

We started by researching model intergenerational programs. We reviewed current literature in education, psychology, cultural anthropology, social work and the community arts. We contacted national organizations dedicated to the elderly, to the young and to intergenerational or multicultural issues—organizations such as Generations United of the National Council on Aging, and the Center for Intergenerational Learning at Temple University in Philadelphia. We asked them to describe their programs and to refer us to other resources. Locally, we sought information from the New York City Department of Aging and the Board of Education, as well as from other arts and cultural organizations. We also interviewed the seniors in ESTA's Living History program, staff in the senior centers and nursing homes, the young people with whom we had piloted smaller projects, and their teachers.

We discovered three types of intergenerational programs: youth serving seniors, seniors serving youth and mutual or reciprocal programs. Projects in which youth serve seniors include "meals on wheels," "home shopping" and "friendly visitors." Seniors serve youth in mentoring projects, latchkey programs and foster grandparent programs. Mutual or reciprocal programs often involve working together on cultural, environmental or political projects.

Clearly, the reciprocal model fit our goals best. In cultural projects like those offered in this book, young and old learn and practice new skills, cooperate, share experiences, and practice teamwork with decision making and problem solving. Creative expression fosters self-esteem, pride, joy and a sense of accomplishment.

For a few years, we experimented with many different kinds of programs, all based on transforming oral histories into theater, dance, music and writing. Out of this experience we developed the Generating Community program in 1991 as an answer to the concerns of cultures and generations coming into conflict. Seeing that all these different groups had no meeting ground, we conceived of the program as a place for them to talk—not just to complain at one another, but to create and to learn together. Instead of letting the groups face off against each other, in Generating Community we turn everybody's head to face in the same direction, toward a common goal. Creating this turnaround is crucial; it's also tremendously exciting. In the Living History community plays in our programs, the various groups explore their problems, and together find solutions to them. In the process, something new emerges: In our program in Spanish Harlem, for example, participating seniors have become surrogate grandparents for children whose grandparents never left Puerto Rico.

Once we developed our basic objectives, we outlined specific goals for our program and a list of responsibilities for the participating groups. In the beginning, one group needs to assume responsibility for getting the program off the ground. ESTA initiated the projects described here by researching, organizing and fundraising. Ultimately, however, all groups must take responsibility for a project's continuation. Here is a sticky point in partnership development: how to inspire shared ownership of a community project. We compiled a "Partnership Packet," which included a detailed definition and description of both the overall project and the role and responsibilities of each partner. We drew up a two-year contract that would commit the partnership team to figuring out how to sustain the alliance beyond the initial project year.

Creative expression fosters self-esteem, pride, joy and a sense of accomplishment.

We then selected four transitional neighborhoods and called school principals and directors of senior centers to tell them about our idea. If they seemed interested, we asked them to send us letters of interest. In turn, these letters accompanied our requests for funding from national and state organizations and private foundations.

Over the course of the first year, we trained staff members of the groups we worked with, so that after the second year, a different partner became the coordinating group. In one case, the school kept the program going, and in another the community center coordinated.

Generating Community consists of a weekly workshop program that brings seniors in nursing homes, community centers, and senior centers together with youths ranging in age from pre-school to high school. Each program lasts for about 30 sessions. We start out by training the participants in the skills of oral history, in order to produce life histories of both the elders and the youths.

The two groups then work together to turn their stories into theater, storytelling or dance performances, or into murals, paintings, journal writing or poetry. A public presentation of the work—usually as a performance, but sometimes as booklets or other printed formats presented as part of a festival—is the crucial community-building element of the project. The presentation may be staged at the school, the senior center or a central public place—such as a museum, library or theater, or at several of these locations.

The project takes two years to implement fully, and depends on three community groups working together: a senior group, a youth group and an arts group. The senior group may come from a senior center, library, union retirement program, nursing home, volunteer program, adult day-care facility or church. The youth group may come from a school, community center, or scouting or other community youth group. The participating arts group can be a museum, arts council, community artists' organization or settlement house. Any one of these three groups can originate the project by linking up with the two others.

In our programs, elders from the senior group typically come together with the young people in a workshop led by an artist who has been trained in group work. At ESTA, we train the artists ourselves; in many cases artists can be found through community arts groups. Many theater people and dancers have group-work training, so do people trained in creative arts therapy. It is vital, however, that the participating artist have training, as well as experience, in working with groups.

During the program's first year, the artist trains program assistants from the senior and youth groups, who then assume more responsibility for leading the program in its second year. When the second year ends, these trained representatives become central to the groups' ability to continue the program into the future.

This is the basic program model, but many variations are possible. We have found that teachers will often assume the role of the teaching artist and continue the program themselves. In some programs, we had seniors who had been artists. The program gave them training in leading the workshop, and they took over this role when

ESTA's participation concluded.

Our communities face many challenges today. Seniors encounter ageism; youth are adrift; neighborhoods are fragmented. People often keep to their own kind. We have found that Generating Community creates solutions to these problems.

In many urban communities, one ethnic group grows up and moves out and another group moves in—often leaving the poorer, older people living in their neighborhood with people from an unfamiliar culture. Feeling their world shrinking, these elders are likely to further isolate themselves.

This isolation makes it easier for the new young people to see the seniors as "other," and vice versa. Dissatisfied young people can easily target the elders whom they do not know or understand, taking their free-floating anger out on elder victims. Not surprisingly, many older adults fear young people and avoid them.

Our initial approach to ageism is to have young people write poems about what they think of seniors at the beginning of the program, before the groups come together, and then again at the end, after they have spent months working together. In this way, we record the transformation of attitudes that occurs. "Seniors are cranky people," "They don't like us" and "They're dumb" turn into "They're my friends," "We have fun together" and "We can do things together." We find, moreover, that young people and seniors maintain their relationships after the program ends: They walk each other home; the kids bring the seniors groceries; they meet on the street and stop to exchange greetings.

Traditionally, older people functioned as role models for younger generations. Now, the loss of opportunities for relationships with young people has robbed elders of one of life's greatest pleasures. Generating Community gives seniors back the chance to pass on the wisdom and skills acquired in a lifetime of experience; to continue to care for others at a time when they themselves may be the recipients of care; and to learn new skills, remaining creatively engaged in the world.

Young people today are often on their own in a way their parents and grandparents never were. Working parents or guardians may leave them unsupervised; their teachers are often overburdened and lack the time to give them personal attention. Without these traditional support systems, many young people feel unsure of their future.

To discover their interests and direction in life, young people need opportunities to explore ideas, feelings and possible roles in a creative way. They need to develop emotional and social skills, as well as the skills of problem solving, decision making, and planning for the future, which prepare them for adult relationships and jobs, and enhance their sense of self-worth. Finally, they need situations to which they can contribute something real and meaningful, as well as experiences that teach them responsibility and accountability.

Relationships with caring, interested adults are a key factor in helping young people to grow up. Just one person who listens to a young person's opinions, concerns and feelings without judging can create a lifeline to self-respect. This is a traditional role of the grandparent—reassurance and support.

Generating Community creates a setting in which this type of support can be reborn. For example, in the Washington Heights neighborhood of Manhattan, well-known for violence and drug dealing, we brought Dominican teenagers together with frail elderly people. We trained the kids to explore turning points in life, and they interviewed the seniors about their work histories, asking questions about how the elderly people found jobs when they were younger. This process provided the teenagers with role models for solving problems and making decisions in their own lives.

Generational problems are compounded by cultural issues. Like other metropolitan areas in the United States, New York City's remarkable diversity remains a source of both cultural richness and conflict. The "conflicts," however, get most of the attention. With finite public resources and growing populations of disadvantaged young and old, public policy often defines one group—such as "youth at risk"—as "more needy" than another—say, "impoverished elders." This false hierarchy of needs is based on a competitive rather than a cooperative way of thinking. It sets groups in conflict with one another—instead of recognizing that these groups can help each other to solve their mutual needs—and keeps them segregated in daily life.

The lack of a community meeting ground creates a sense of alienation and prejudice between groups that occurs primarily because they don't know each other. For example, in Flushing, Queens, where older Eastern European adults live with many immigrants from the Pacific Rim countries, we assigned the seniors to interview each other about the changes that had occurred in the neighborhood. The interviews were full of remarks like: "The Koreans should go back where they came from—what makes them think they can take over?" But as soon as they got to know real Korean children in the workshop, the seniors realized these kids had the same goals that the seniors' own children once had: to get an education and a job, and to become responsible citizens.

Sol's reaction was to tell his group of children that he would be there to talk to them anytime; he gave them his home phone number. Erna said this was the most important program of her life because she could give the children a real education—and she told them of her escape from Nazi Germany. The appreciation the seniors received from the children as they shared their life experiences was a wonderful surprise.

Generating Community's vehicle for dispelling age and cultural stereotypes is the process of creating an intergenerational presentation. The program offers many young people their first real friendship with an older person. One fifth grader said: "I thought they wouldn't be interested. I really can talk to Sol, and he gave me his phone number." A teacher remarked, "One caring person encouraging a child can make all the difference in that child's life. ESTA helps make those personal connections."

On a practical level, seniors feel safer walking home when they are greeted on the way by children they know. On a deeper level, they feel needed, useful and creative. "I like being with the children," said Mary. "I feel younger, and they help keep me spry." Fanny said, "Children tell you the truth about what is happening now. I like listening to them." Another senior admitted, "I didn't expect to get so much. We really care about each other and had a great time making the play."

Generating Community exemplifies lifelong learning. In sharing stories, both seniors and youth learn about the past and the present. They get to play out roles that give them a deeper understanding of the stages of life. For seniors, the process reawakens a sense of what it was like to be children, and shows them what children are like today. Young people tend to be isolated from elders; the program connects them to the human story.

Finally, Generating Community demonstrates how culture builds community. At our community presentations, the audience sees itself reflected in the Living History play, or mural, or writings by young and old. "That's me they're talking about!" they exclaim. "I like this because it's about my life and what I care about." "I like how they spoke. It's honest and about real life!"

One parent credited the program for the fact that her child behaved more respectfully at home. She said that the oral-history interviews brought her family closer together, and added that she was proud to see her daughter on stage. Another parent remarked, "Every time I walk into the school and see the Community Tree mural, I'm reminded that we are all connected."

Spring/Summer 1995

Miles from Nowhere: Teaching Dance in Prison

By Leslie Neal

Dancing Inside Out—Movement Workshops for Incarcerated Women *was established in 1994 by Leslie Neal Dance at Broward Correctional Institution in South Florida. Part of a ground-breaking program of the Florida Department of Corrections' Arts Bridge Project, the work deepened the artists' commitment to social action and their belief that movement and performance can be a positive force for change in their community. The dancers would come to be astonished at how much change it would make in their own personal lives.   —Eds.*

Every week I take the same journey. I travel north past farm-lands and zinc fields, toll booths and baby palm trees, industrial cranes and great blue herons, and ticky-tacky subdivisions that all look the same and share swampy Everglades backyards. It's desolate and pro-gressive all at once. A constantly changing, razed landscape that is dis-tinctly South Florida.

The end of my journey begins as I turn east onto a dreary, no-name road off old Highway 27. I pass the Broward County Landfill with its massive incinerator glowering at the top of the only hill around. It's big, bronze and square—nightmarish—always burning. I call it the Gates of Hell.

Strange metaphoric images aren't unusual along this one-way street. I see eagles, owls and osprey lined up on black wires. Once a walking catfish crossed the road. Occasionally, the sight of turtles sun-ning on the yellow line causes me to stop the car and move them to the safety of the edge. Once a red rolling feather blew by. The air is always filled with the alien call of black crows mixed with mourning doves and sporadic splashes of fish in the lily ponds.

For some, this road is the end of the road. It leads you directly to the pink awnings and silver razor wire of Broward Correctional Institution.

Once a week I go to prison.

The need to do this came on me suddenly, with certainty. One morning two years ago, I woke up and said to myself, "I'm going to work in prison." Six months later, I was sitting face-to-face with 25 female inmates trying to act as if I knew what I was doing while explaining my intentions to share creative movement and dance with them once a week. I got in quickly. I didn't know how long I was in for. Unlike the women inside, I went into prison without knowing when I would get out. Now, almost two years later, I still want to go there. I may be one of the few people in the world who waits for hours outside trying to get in. I keep finding new answers to the question of why I go each week.

Broward Correctional houses an estimated 650 inmates and is the only maximum-security prison for women in Florida. I looked up "prison" in the dictionary and was surprised by the simplistic definition: "a place of confinement or restraint." To me it is much more than that.

The majority of women in prison are victims of extreme violence and sexual abuse. They have histories of addiction to drugs and alcohol. We have a lot in common.

To reach the entrance to the compound I follow a narrow sidewalk contained within a chain link fence. Since my tour of Death Row, I always look toward the thin rectangular windows up ahead and know I'm being watched by the dark eyes that I saw that day, staring from the dark cells off that horrible pink hallway.

Chilling air blasts as soon as I walk through the glass doors of the reception area. They keep the climate-controlled temperature very low. Prison always feels cold. Indifferent. Freezing.

Keep cool. Think cool. Stay cool.

Here's where the waiting begins. I used to be able to stand at a window behind the control booth and view the prison yard. It felt voyeuristic, unreal, removed—like watching a movie. Pacing, freezing, waiting to be cleared and escorted through the compound.

That sound. Rolling heavy door. Sliding and locking down. Standing in that tiny space. Waiting for the opposite door to snap up and roll back. Walking through that threshold. Clanging lock slams shut behind me. Separating one world from another.

Now each Monday I wait at the new "sally port" while they remodel the reception area. It looks like a huge new warehouse with industrial garage doors on either end. The buses pull in here with new

> ## I was sitting face-to-face with 25 female inmates trying to act as if I knew what I was doing...

arrivals, as well as those in transport. This arrangement is much more secure—meaning less chance of escape. Lining the walls are the compressed cardboard boxes that are handed to the newcomers to store their personal belongings: jewelry, clothes, keys, photographs, money, credit cards, make-up, etc. *Just like in the movies.* They are given the option to deliver their belongings over to family members, or have them held until their transfer or release. The length of their sentences often determines their decision.

This new sally port was built by taxpayers' dollars and inmate labor. Male convicts. I would see them each week, counted down and hanging around in the yard. Working out. Waiting for the bus. One step away from the chain gang. To kill time during breaks, they built a set of weights out of cement blocks. Each week as I passed by the restricted construction area I was reminded of The Flintstones.

Having done this project for almost two years now, I'm no longer a stranger. The correctional officers who have been there awhile know me. They usually make some joke about dancing. It seems as though the staff has finally accepted my weekly appearances. They are much friendlier. The Sergeant even sang me "happy birthday" this year. Maybe it's because I've been consistent each week, and I haven't presented any problems. But still, occasionally a new officer is on duty and the standing memo to approve my entry is misplaced, or the whole prison is in lock-down, and I can't get in at all.

"ATTENTION ON THE COMPOUND. ATTENTION IN THE DORMITORIES. RECALL. ALL INMATES REPORT TO THEIR ASSIGNED STATIONS."

I follow the sidewalk circling a grassy mall surrounded by pink buildings. There are a few trees, lots of shrubs and planted pink impatiens. My first few walks through this compound felt surprisingly familiar. Communal. Reminded me of the women's college I attended. Familiar—the confinement, the discipline. The women like birds in a cage.

Once during this weekly journey I was surprised to see a bevy of ducks waddling through the green. This became the immediate topic of conversation in the workshop. Visiting ducks are not unusual, however they are "removed" fairly quickly.

"ATTENTION ON THE COMPOUND. ATTENTION IN THE DORMITORIES. CEASE FEEDING THE DUCKS. INMATES CAUGHT FEEDING THE DUCKS WILL BE SENT TO LOCK-UP. CEASE FEEDING THE DUCKS."

Depending on the time, there's a variety of activity inside. Before the workshop, the place is fairly quiet. Most of the women are working or in class, except for the ground crew and the women pushing the food carts from the kitchen to the dining hall. The dining hall is purposely located away from the kitchen. The kitchen contains weapons.

I'm escorted to a large, windowless, pink room where the inmates are waiting on blue mats, neatly arranged in a circle. They are very good at waiting. They are always happy to see me and often cheer when I pass through the door. This makes me feel welcomed and appreciated. They applaud the fact that I come every week and managed once again to get in. I bring with me the sounds, smells and stories of the free world. Tammy once said that I come more often than their families. As a group, they have allowed themselves to trust me, and I trust them. Since learning about Isadora Duncan, they now call themselves the Lesliehorribles, a take-off on the Isadorables.

They wear funny-looking dresses. Horrible uniforms that snap down the front. Drab colors of blue and mustard yellow. They remind me of the smocks women wear in a beauty salon to keep their clothes from staining. As time progressed, we gained approval to wear more comfortable attire for the workshop. Now, most change into T-shirts and shorts right there by the pool table in that inevitable, surreptitious way women undress and dress themselves among other women.

In this pink room we share of ourselves differently than in any other space and time in our daily lives. We share our movement, our little girls, our children and our mothers, our pain and our laughter. We play, explore, create, draw, tease, cry and make dances together. We never go outside and outside never comes in. We are dancing inside out, within those pink prison walls.

"ATTENTION ON THE COMPOUND. ATTENTION IN THE DORMITORIES. COUNT TIME. ALL OFFICERS CONDUCT THEIR COUNT."

Normally Officer Swanson is there in Recreation/Wellness. She's okay. But when there's a male officer assigned to that post, the energy is distant and reserved. Doing this kind of work often means "shooting from the hip." Unlike the correctional officers, I am not armed. I protect myself by listening, observing and checking in. I have learned to trust my intuition and the faces of the women who come every week, without fail, to the workshop.

Most of the time, once I arrive in our special space, I forget that I'm in prison. It could be a workshop for women anywhere. I have even learned to accept the constant loudspeakers and the ongoing interruptions. I'm so accustomed to "count time" that the correctional officers sometimes count me in with the group.

"You do what? You teach dance in prison? Do you really think you are doing any good? You hang out with murderers? Do you mean to tell me that I can't afford to send my daughter to dance class, and you're teaching dance to criminals? Why can't you be an accountant like your sister? What did they do? Are you scared? Why would you want to do a thing like that?"

Some days as a group they're anxious and frustrated. This is usually caused by some event on the compound. One Sunday they had to sit on their beds for six hours while two inmates were hunted down, found "trapping" in a "cut" above the dining hall. Sex in prison. That's another story.

Once Rhonda came in very agitated because the apparel area

was raided and the women who work there were searched, hand-cuffed and marched through the compound to jail over a pair of miss-ing scissors, which were later found in the room.

"Where's Toni? Sent to Lock-up. Please don't give me a D.R. Come on, Officer, I didn't mean it . Please don't send me to Lock-Up. Please don't send me there. Don't send me to jail. 30 days? What'd she do? She kicked Officer Jones in the butt. Why? Cuz she was pissed. You know Toni's got a mean temper."

Mary was visibly shaken after meeting with her three children, who come only once a year from Indiana. The youngest one was three years old when she came in, now she's sixteen. She got two good Polaroids, though, that the corrections officer in Visitation takes and allows the inmates to keep. A nice family portrait.

They miss their kids the most. Each week we pass the cowry shell and recite our heritage. We speak our names, the names of our mothers, the names of our grandmothers and great-grandmothers, and the names of our children.

"Mother of Tamika, Daughter of Gayle, Granddaughter of Rose and Lilly, Mother of John and Tiffany, Mother of Josef, Mother of Maria and Carlos, Grandmother of five beautiful girls."

Annie's husband writes every day. Sometimes she shares the pic-tures he sends of home. Land, forests, small house on a field. She's becoming more beautiful every day. I don't know if it is just my per-ception, but she has blossomed. She used to be so plain and quiet. Painfully shy. She says this workshop has helped her overcome her fear of being in front of people and she recently sang with the gospel choir in the chapel. She was the only white woman in the group.

Celia's mom just died. She hadn't spoken to her for many years. She hadn't spoken to anyone in her family since she went inside 20 years ago. She did get to say good-bye, but for weeks she refused to call the name of her mother in the group circle.

There's a lot of death inside. Santa Claus died this year. Really. The woman who played Santa Claus at the Christmas Jubilee. She was beautiful—mahogany-skinned, with white sparkling eyes. Oh, the whites of their eyes. Once an inmate died in her bunk and wasn't discovered until morning. Walking through the compound you can spot the ones with AIDS, and the elderly on walkers. They have very little time left to serve. Life in prison is very contained. Small events are big. Big events become symbolic.

Suzie's doing really well in class. She's slowly overcoming her fear of dancing. This year she actually enjoyed performing in the shows we present for the other inmates and staff. Once during class, she remembered a bad experience with some guy in a dance studio, when she was young and practicing alone. Besides, she was a stripper, only able to dance after six or so shots of Jack Daniels. Now she's in recovery and facing demons straight on.

Often when they dance their stories, they dance out abuse. They dance out pleading and falling and crawling and shrinking. And sobbing. And Genie always does a split. Lately, they've been dancing out anger. It's also allowed. They say it helps them to release that particular emotion in a way they've never done before.

Louise is a prolific journal-keeper. She draws and writes all the time. She's beautiful and tall and when she dances she lengthens out to her full, powerful self. Celia, the sultry daughter of a Southern Baptist preacher, is deep and mysterious, moody and strong in spirit. And Joy ("what a pistol, smart as a whip" her father used to say), with lovely long fingernails and that contagious smile. Stubborn. Joy's been in prison since she was seventeen. Now she's thirty-six. She didn't do it. I miss her. Her appeal was coming up and she was hoping to get out, start over, and teach dancing back home. Her appeal was denied, and she was transferred to another prison in the middle of the night. We never got to say good-bye.

I thought prison was a place that did not change, and the people did not leave. "Hey, you finally found a captive audience," my friends tease me. In a way it's true. All my life people have left. Now I leave them. Perhaps I thought I had finally found a place that would stay the same.

Why do I go to prison once a week? I go because I feel safer there, with them, than I do outside. I go because now they expect me to come. I go because I believe in the change that we have all experienced with each other. I go because I miss them. I go because they heal me. I go because they are hungry to learn. I go because I really love them. I go because I am a woman, and in them I see parts of me.

Leaving is the hardest part. If something happens, I never know when I'll see them again. The walk back through the compound is always hesitant and I watch their walls go back up as they leave the safety of our time together.

"Good-bye! See ya next week! Take care! Drive safely! Wish I could be in traffic! Can you bring that shell next week? You know the one when you hold it to your ear, you can hear the ocean? O.K. Bye. Love ya. So long."

And then I'm outside, walking back to my car. They remain inside. I am leaving. The air is humid and warm. The mosquitoes are biting. The owls fly overhead. The sun is setting—beautiful turquoise, orange, red and yellow. The wind carries the haunting sounds of black crows mixed with mourning doves and splashes of fish in the lily ponds. Is this freedom? In the distance I hear a train and then the sound of my car alarm beeping me into solitude as I remotely hit the switch and climb into the silence of driving home.

Spring 1996

Maintaining Humanity:
An Interview with Grady Hillman
about Arts-in-Corrections

By Steven Durland

*Grady Hillman is a poet and writer who first became involved
with "arts-in-corrections" when he did a creative-writing residency
in the Texas prison system in 1981. Since then he has worked in
more than 50 correctional facilities in Florida, California, Massachusetts, Colorado, Idaho, Oklahoma, Texas, Peru and Ireland,
and has become a nationally recognized correctional arts
programmer. In 1991, he cofounded the Southwest Correctional
Arts Network. In this interview he comes up with some cold,
hard statistics in defense of arts programs in prisons.   —Eds.*

Steven Durland: *Times are tough. How do you justify arts-in-prisons
programs?*

Grady Hillman: There's always that argument: "Why should we support these programs? This is taxpayer money and we could be
spending that money on other programs. These guys in prison
need to be punished."

But California, Oklahoma and Massachusetts have come up
with documentation that shows that when you bring an arts
program into an adult correctional setting it reduces the incident
rate—everything from stealing steaks from the commons area
to stabbing other inmates—by 60 to 90%. You can document
this readily because there's a high degree of surveillance and
observation. Those programs were able to really document the
radical rate of personal transformation within the institution.

California quantified that on a cost basis and found that
arts programs in prisons not only paid for themselves, but provided significant savings for the institutions at the same time.
There was one study of four arts programs in the state that
were funded to the tune of $125,000. Some independent pro-

fessors from UC Santa Barbara were able to quantify the incident rate reduction and found that the institution actually saved $225,000 through the effects of the programs.

So you go in saying that [an arts program] makes your correctional facility more manageable, it reduces the rate of violence inside the institution, and it cuts down on guard overtime hours. It cuts down on work time and cuts down on many different aspects of prison administration. It is actually saving you, the taxpayer, a lot of money.

I can say this having worked in the area for 14 years. I've now worked in 50 adult and juvenile correctional facilities, in half a dozen states and three countries, and there's nothing that works better than the arts at that kind of in-house transformation.

The third area of accountability is in recidivism rates. California did a seven-year recidivist rate study and found a dramatic drop in the recidivist rate of these inmates [who had participated in arts programs] after they left prison, compared to the general prison population. These people did not commit crimes when they got back into the free world. Something really profound had happened to them in the prison setting that transformed their behavior. So you can also make the argument that you're reducing crime on the outside by bringing these programs in.

When a guy comes up to me and says, "Why should I be paying for music lessons for some convict when I can't afford it for my own kids," I say, it just makes the world a little safer for your kids. Yes, your kids should have art lessons. Everyone should have art lessons. But these programs pay for themselves and they represent a significant benefit to the community at large. These people come back out. Ninety-five percent of the people who go into prison come back out. And how do you want them to come back out? Do you want them to be bitter and angry and hostile? Or do you want something in place that maintains their humanity and keeps the human side alive? This is the most compelling argument.

SD: *Yet, more and more what we're hearing in public and political debates is, "Stop coddling prisoners. Take away their TVs and their rec rooms." Is it getting harder to sell these programs?*

GH: Yes and no. I think it's getting more difficult to sell adult programs. There is that attitude that you want people to do hard time. I think it's a lot easier to place programs for juvenile offenders, because there's a compelling economic argument there, too. Once you send someone to prison, you're going to spend $20-40,000 per year just maintaining that person behind bars.

There's this old joke that we could send [a convict] to Harvard, buy a car and get them a nice apartment and it would be cheaper than sending them to prison. And that's the truth.

Right now there's this struggle going on for the hearts and minds of the public. In Texas, there's this multibillion-dollar bond proposal for new prison construction and, suddenly, people are realizing that this will cut down their ability to finance education, highways and public utilities. Those areas are beginning to suffer because you're spending so much of your state budget on prison construction. Texas is going to have the largest prison system in the world in a year or so. We're talking about something like 150-160,000 inmates behind bars. We're spending $20-30,000 a year to keep them in there. It's not on TVs and rec rooms, it's on highly sophisticated security systems and guards.

Getting construction projects out of legislators has become a pastime in most states. And what's the easiest construction project you could possibly get? That would be a prison construction project. Because they're away from the public eye, and it's basically concrete and steel. They're highly lucrative projects. So there's a huge economic incentive in the construction industry for more prison construction. So you're establishing a huge industry: the prison industry.

I think the public is saying we need to stop doing this. If you turn one kid around with an arts program—maybe getting him involved for six months, he pulls his life together, gets his high-school diploma and goes on and doesn't wind up in prison—then you might have saved the public a quarter-million or a half-million dollars over the life of that kid.

SD: *It sounds like what you've got is more than an argument for art in prisons, but for art in the schools.*

GH: Yes. Definitely. When we were working in the Harris County juvenile probation department, I was working with these artists and they were reporting back to me. They kept saying, "These programs are great. The kids are eating it up. But why didn't they get it in school? Why didn't they have this opportunity before?" If they'd had this opportunity then they probably wouldn't have wound up in this setting. They just found school to be boring and not challenging and not interesting; tedious and with nothing that allowed for any kind of expressive medium. They had very powerful forces working in their lives and they needed something to turn to that would give them a way to get a handle on their lives.

> **The one thing I got out of my prison experience is the power of poetry.**

In the correctional facility, they start getting a handle on their lives through the arts. They have to face up to who they are, and where they've been and who the people are in their lives; the tragedies and the stories. And suddenly they transcend. They get on top of it. Had that happened in the schools, many of them wouldn't have turned that way.

The unfortunate thing is that you're seeing schools in budget processes that cut the arts. The first thing that gets cut in a high-school budget is the band. [But] those are the programs they need to retain students. There's just a lot of contradictions inherent in the educational system, and in the American attitude toward education and what the arts can do to integrate all of those things together to make a healthier community. The blatant truth is that art needs to be in the school curriculum. Some sort of cultural tie-in has to be there for all youth. Otherwise, they're just going to become alienated and they're going to turn on society. That just seems so obvious. And yet you don't see school boards and probation departments making that connection.

SD: *What are the benefits for the artists doing this kind of work?*

GH: All of the artists I've talked to who go into this kind of setting say they've learned as much or more than the folks they work with. Certainly when you're conducting a creative writing workshop in a maximum security prison, you're gaining insight into cultural settings and milieus and conflicts and tragedies and images that you just don't have access to on the outside. Our lives, our experiences, provide our material. And by sitting with a bunch of writers and listening to their stories, you learn a lot.

The other thing that's real interesting is that prison culture is a distinct culture. It's a little bit like visiting a foreign country and living there for a while. Time has an entirely different meaning in prison. Trust, intimacy. The constructions of identity were highly sophisticated. You learn about both the potential and the tragedy of the human condition. And that's the stuff of art.

The one thing I got out of my prison experience is the power of poetry. Working in the free world—writing poems, going the artist path, publishing in magazines, talking to other artists—was about craft more than anything else. And then I started working with inmates, for whom the creation of a poem was the most important thing in their life. To get it right. They taught me the power of language and the power of poetry. So I came out of the prison experience a much stronger writer, a much more careful writer. They gave me that. They showed me how powerful a thing I'd latched onto, that I was working with something that was dangerous and explosive and intense and wonderful and magical, and that was good for me. They showed me how powerful poetry could be.

SD: *There are activists who spend a great deal of time exposing the abuses of the criminal justice and corrections systems in this country. Do you ever find yourself feeling like your arts-in-corrections activities make you complicit with a bad system?*

GH: No. Generally when artists go into a correctional facility they don't work for the correctional facility; they're under a contract, usually with some arts agency. It's not like you give hell legitimacy. It's there. It's hell. You didn't create it. You're not complicit. You're going inside. You're sharing with inmates what it is you do.

You don't see a lot of solidarity in prisons. It's such an uncomfortable setting that most people just want to do their time and get out. Some live lives there and become players—politicians or con artists—or they just become institutionalized. But most people want to get out with as much of themselves as they still have. They tend not to trust. So the artist who tries to get something started—who says, "You need to stand up for your rights, you need to do this, you need to do that"—gets expelled. Not by the guards, he gets expelled by the inmates.

They realize that this person is not going to be able to help them. What they want that person there for is to teach them how to paint or how to write poems and, maybe, to serve as a bridge to the outside world in some manner. To give them some shred of dignity or humanity in a really negative setting. To create an oasis. Not to get riled up and be challenged by oppression, but a place to relax.

The guys who came to my workshops, for a little while they weren't convicts anymore, they were just people. They'd always joke about who was going to get the beer and pizza next time. And that was what they wanted. They wanted that sort of pub-gathering feel, where we could sit around and share stories and be human beings with one another. "We're not going to overthrow the system. We're doing time. We love you because you come here and for a little while we're not convicts anymore because you respect us. You talk to us like human beings instead of animals. And you let us talk to each other, and teach us how to talk to one another so that we don't dehumanize one another." That's what the artist does. It's a matter of personal integrity—not a matter of political integrity.

SD: *What kind of artist does this work? What are the necessary skills? It's*

*not the sort thing you take a class on in school, and I'd guess that
not everyone is cut out for this kind of work.*

GH: You're right. Art therapists have their role to play in society and
art teachers have their role to play. But the model that I promote, the model that I think is the best, is the professional artist
and the artist-mentor relationship. The master artist. When I
look for an artist to come into a correctional setting, I generally
look for someone who's good and has proved themselves in the
free world. As visual artists, they've had exhibitions, as a writer
they've published books. You're providing somebody to this population who, by their own standards, is real. They see you as a
model. What they want from you is to show them what you do.
They want somebody who will give them feedback on what
they do. They want a professional standard. They want to know
how good they are. And they want to know what they need to
do to get better.

People in prison write. They write a lot. People are working on screenplays, novels, all sorts of different projects. They're
pretty accomplished. They need somebody who can give them a
professional eye.

The second thing in a prison program is that you want
someone who's open to the inmates. Who doesn't think they're
Neanderthals and doesn't come in afraid that they're going to
say something wrong and get stabbed. Or, on the other hand,
they come in and say, "These people are all victims. I'm going to
nurture them and take care of them." A paternalistic attitude
that people are babies—they don't like that either.

What you want is somebody who can go into a prison
setting and look at them as human beings. They've made some
tragic mistakes. A lot of artists want to know what they did. I
don't. I never want to know what kind of crimes they committed. I don't want to be put in a position of my own moral values
judging them. That's not my role. They've been judged, they've
been convicted. I'm just there to share, and give them my per-
ception and feedback and criticism so they can make adjust-

ments in their work; so their work can develop and they can become better writers.

I tend to stay away from art therapists and art teachers, because they come in with a curriculum. I don't like people to come in with a curriculum. I like people to come in with technique and experience with art. That's what works the best.

Spring 1996

The Selma Project:
Understanding, the Struggle
for Community

By Bob Leonard

*One of the most perplexing and monumental social-change pro-
jects an artist can undertake is to heal the wounds of racism.
Here Bob Leonard, director of the Tennessee theater ensemble
The Road Company, talks about a large arts project in Selma,
Alabama, bringing a wide range of artists and community partners to the task. It took all of their arts and organizing skills and
every ounce of partnering energy they could muster.   —Eds.*

People in Selma, Alabama, are doing something about improving
race relations within their town and they are using the arts to do it.
This is cause for praise, and opportunity to reflect on the difficulties
of divesting ourselves of the legacies of our cultural and social history.
Understanding, the Struggle for Community, an artistic residency that
brought eight artists to Selma for two weeks in March, 1994, revealed
a lot about the successes and struggles going on in this historic
Southern town.

At first, I resisted the invitation extended to The Road Company,
the Tennessee-based traveling theater company where I work as co-
artistic director. Buddy Palmer, then the executive director of the
Selma/Dallas County Council for the Arts (SDCCA), had asked the
company to come to Selma for an arts residency that would demonstrate how the arts can aid in healing the wounds of racism. The project seemed overwhelmingly ambitious and the out-of-town theater
company less than sufficient for the task. But I did not know Buddy
very well. He is quietly resolute and very brave. While he is far from
insensitive, accepting "no" must come with a thorough understanding
of "why not." Over several conversations, Buddy convinced me that
the project was being carefully designed for Selma and with Selmians. I
found myself compelled by his care and his realistic approaches. He

meant to do tangible work and he was asking people to help. He had been planning this residency nearly two years before it happened.

We agreed to a partnership between the SDCCA and The Road Company for planning, developing, casting and executing the project. In July, 1993, seven months before the project would take place, Buddy and I spent several days meeting people in Selma who had expressed an affinity for the project and an interest in participating. Buddy had developed the list over the previous months. It was an extraordinary series of meetings.

Like everywhere else in the United States, Selma has suffered a long history of racism. Unlike anywhere else, Selma is the site of the march that led the country to the passage of the Voting Rights Act of 1965. The march arose from the protests and demonstrations of the Student Non-Violent Coordinating Committee (SNCC) and the Southern Christian Leadership Council (SCLC) that broke loose in Selma. For that brief period of time in 1965, the heat was on and the frightened eyes of the nation were focused on this little town. Then, as quickly as they had arrived, the national leadership and national attention left Selma. Something of national significance had been birthed in the town, but the town itself was left greatly bewildered and little changed. For some, particularly within the African-American community, there was increased hope that change might be coming. For others, fear of the same. The 30 years that have followed have tempered both the hope and the fear. Change—the kind of change that reshapes social practice and political power—takes a lot of time.

Some Things Don't Change

When I arrived in Selma I was astonished to find that the mayor, who was elected on a "moderate" segregationist ticket in November of 1964 on the eve of SCLC's decision to target Selma, was still the mayor of Selma in July of 1993. Joe Smitherman had been mayor of Selma every day for nearly 30 years (except for a two-year self-imposed respite when he didn't run for office). Mayor Smitherman has accomplished this extraordinary term of office by going with the flow and keeping things normal—evidence of a careful and strict adherence to the rule of "the more things change, the more they stay the same." It is a complicated history in a complicated town, administered by a smart man.

It became apparent that one of the keys to his success, in the face of a radical increase in black voters following the Voting Rights legislation and its enforcement, was the appointment of African Americans to committees, councils, boards and other such positions of authority and power. Deftly if blatantly, these appointments were always just short of a majority. The mayor gained voter loyalty with no forfeit of power. In issues concerning race and African-American community building, the committees, councils, boards, etc., were effectively reduced in size to the number of the majority white vote. This situation exploded in 1989-90, when the school board fired its first African-American superintendent in a racially-split vote. The town erupted. The schools were closed. While the schools were quickly brought back in session and the town resumed normal life, nearly every white student in the junior and senior high schools fled to local "private" schools—a demographic reality that exists today. Selma High is 98% African American while the general population statistics put African Americans at 58%.

Partnering at the Grassroots

This was my surface view when Buddy and I began our meetings. The people we met revealed a deep layer of commitment to change that is disciplined, determined, skilled and permanent. We met with Frank Hardy, an award-winning boxer and visual artist in his late thirties, who runs a training program for young people in boxing, painting and dance. He had begun the program entirely on his own, without funding or public support. Called the Selma Youth Development Center (SYDC), Frank's program is housed in an unused school building. The SYDC maintains the facility and raises money for any improvements, even though the building is owned by the Selma School Board. The SYDC is producing competitive boxers who have gained placement on U.S. amateur teams. At the same time, Frank teaches painting everyday and heads up the dance program. Frank says, "The arts play a very important role in the development of a child. They allow a child to develop as an individual. Sometimes a child does not fit into the realm that society sets for you. The arts gives you a way to make your own place." Frank bore witness to the fact that the arts had saved him. "When I was a kid I got into a lot of trouble. I found myself through boxing and painting. Then my life changed. I've come back to Selma to run a program I needed when I was a kid."

Funding for SYDC deserves a special story, a tribute to one Selma business responding to a Selma need. Frank is employed by a local corporation, Tri-Tech Services, Inc., makers of airline ground-support equipment. This business was so impressed with the program that Frank had initiated in his own spare time that they reassigned him from the assembly line to be the director of SYDC. One of the corporate partners, Calvin Bowie, said that they think this is the way business and private individuals should do things. "We're proud of SYDC. It is very beneficial to Selma. We can't provide everything the program needs but we can provide this." Calvin, in response to my questions, said, "We don't do this for publicity. In fact, publicity is the wrong way. People could get the idea that Tri-Tech is taking care of SYDC and no one else needs to, which is way wrong. The programs at SYDC need broad community support." In addition to Tri-Tech, three local churches and a few private individuals keep a thin line of cash supporting SYDC. However meager in program support, SYDC is rich beyond imagination in human and community power.

We met with Meria Carstarphen, a junior high-school teacher of Spanish and Photography in her twenties, who has taken on the prodigious task of renovating an old and unused high school building into an arts center that will serve children and adults, black and white. Meria's dream is a center where people of Selma can make art of all kinds for their own creative expression. Meria made it clear that she has the vision and the personal capacity to see this ambitious vision become real. She also made it clear that, if our residency project could bring a poet into her photography classroom, she could promise a vibrant and creative partnership that she would strongly support.

Like Meria, Frank was immediately willing and anxious to participate in the arts residency that Buddy and I were proposing. He too was able to provide a clear picture of what kind of arts residency might benefit his program. He wanted dancers and choreographers who could nourish SYDC's dance program. He offered use of his facility as a principal site for the residency. Frank also offered a valuable partnership, a partner who had a deep understanding of how community grows through people helping each other.

Organizing from an Arts Base

Frank's knowledge did not come from some vague inspiration or some mystical source. I learned that Frank and many others in Selma had benefited from a strong education in this approach, with a long local history. When he was in his late teens, Frank had been involved with Black Belt Arts and Cultural Center (B'BACC), an arts-based organizing program in Selma that had begun in the early '70s. B'BACC, the brainchild of an activist lawyer named Rose Sanders, was founded on the use of storytelling, music and African dance to provide African-American children strong positive self-image development, personal discipline, community pride and vision beyond the limitations of the social framework dominant in Selma. It worked. Not only in Frank's case but in person after person we met, including the executive director of the Brown YMCA, as well as a social worker who teaches parenting classes to preteens in the housing projects and writes plays for children to perform in housing-project community centers.

B'BACC, still a strong program itself in Selma, has also spawned the National Voting Rights Museum, run by JoAnne Bland and Sam Williams, both alumni of B'BACC. The museum honors Selma's heritage in the history of the Civil Rights Movement with a specific and particular focus on the hundreds of otherwise unnoticed and barely-remembered people in and around Selma who actually were the protesters, the demonstrators, the marchers and the citizens involved with the struggle. The museum, housed downtown on the banks of the river in sight of the famous bridge where the march met the armed forces of segregation, is more than a repository of memorabilia. It is a facility for art and education. Sorely underfunded, it exists through the dedicated hard work of people in Selma who keep the faith in community-building. Here, again, Buddy and I met with people who knew the difference between a cosmetic program of "nice" art and a valuable program of creative power. We were put right on the spot.

Real Goals to Meet Real Needs

A couple of white, liberal guys with some grant money could certainly make an arts program happen in Selma, but when it was over what would it mean to Selma? Would the visiting artists depart after the final performances, taking their fees and leaving pleasant memories, or would the residency provide anything of permanent value in Selma? What would be different in Selma after the residency was done?

Buddy and I had to go way beyond the generic do-good impulse to aid in healing the wounds of racism. Obviously, to begin with, the people of Selma were struggling with that task all by themselves—for better or for worse—and a half-dozen outside artists would not/could not do much one way or another in that regard. We could, however, begin to build a residency that was designed for the real needs of the people and programs that were working in Selma. To do that, we had to bring artists who could complement and augment the work that was already going on. This realization made casting the residency team much more manageable. It was clear, for example, that we had to bring dancers in as part of the residency team. We also had to bring storytellers and musicians. In addition, we began to know exactly the kind of artists we were looking for, not simply in terms of artistic disciplines but also in terms of the community work happening in Selma. We could cast artists whose training and/or experience coincided with the project goals that had become clear as Buddy and I finished the series of meetings in July.

We worked up a very complete goals statement. We were successful in accomplishing these goals because they were practical and achievable. The first order of need was to use the residency to help Selma artists and cultural workers to recognize each other as a mutually cooperative group, reducing the sense of isolation within Selma that each group of workers expressed as we met them. During and following the residency, several artists and arts groups began coming together for weekly lunches to get to know each other better, and to find out how they might serve one another's needs. These groups recognized that they all shared a common interest in building healthy communities and reducing the adversity of economic and racial boundaries. This group of Selma cultural workers continued to meet regularly after the residency was finished.

We agreed that we would use the residency to attempt to find new resources that could aid the efforts of the Selma artists and cultural workers who partnered with the project. We contained this goal within the frame that one new donor, or one new volunteer, would be the kind of new resource that we were hoping to uncover—rather than some unrealistic hope to "answer the survival needs" of the groups. At the final performance of the residency, a trained dancer, who had returned to Selma after her education, came forward as a volunteer interested in helping SYDC's

> **A couple of white, liberal guys with some grant money could certainly make an arts program happen in Selma, but when it was over what would it mean to Selma?**

dance program. Residency artists opened doors to funding sources that have expressed interest in the kind of programs operating in Selma. A Selma writer, working on his first playscript, developed an ongoing artistic relationship with a residency artist who continues to help him in the struggle of rewrites and edits.

We intended that the residency would produce tangible products that could "live on" after completion of the residency: i.e., photo essays, videotaped documentation of performances by Selma artists, desktop publication of writings created in workshops, etc. A photo essay created by Meria Carstarphen's junior high-school class while working with a residency poet is the property of the class and continues to be used for a number of community purposes. Collections of poems written by students in poetry workshops are being published in a cooperative venture between the project and a local community college. These publications will be distributed to the participants and will also be on hand in the schools for demonstration and fundraising purposes. Alabama Public Television videotaped the project and aired the resulting program in June of 1994. This videotape and other video and photographic documentation have been compiled by the Arts Council to serve in conceptualizing and developing new projects in Selma.

We agreed to provide training time for artistic leaders in Selma designed to share the administrative as well as artistic skills of the resident artists, and targeted to the needs of Selma activities. This was accomplished on a one-on-one basis, as the need was identified. The residency artists have made themselves available for continued relationship with their Selma partners. In addition to the one-on-one approach, a county-wide teacher workshop was conducted as a mentoring session, presented by a local college.

We identified the need to centerpiece a final performance that would celebrate the people and artists of Selma, using the resident artists to shape the celebration and to complement it with their own performances. This performance featured new dances choreographed by the resident artists and danced by Selma youth. This way the dances remained in Selma after the residency. New songs, written by workshop participants about their personal experiences growing up and living in Selma, were composed and arranged by residency musicians and performed by the Selma youth who had written them. The photographic essay—a slide show of student photographs intercut with poetry written by the same photographers—was compiled by a residency poet and presented as part of the final performance. Praise Poems, written by students in workshops, were performed by those same students. A small play, portraying a family's struggle to find money for shoes, was written and performed by the young people of SYDC. Performances by the residency artists were interspersed throughout the evening.

This event was presented at the 300-seat Selma Performing Arts Center to a standing-room-only crowd, racially and economically mixed. Tears and laughter filled the evening as the audience responded to the varied expressions of life as it is felt and lived right there at home. It was a repeated refrain that this event was a long-awaited first for Selma.

We had agreed that the project would present the Arts Council itself serving as a resource and facilitating agency for the whole community across racial boundaries and class distinctions. The Arts Council coordinated extensive workshops throughout the school system, working with teachers and principals at all grade levels to bring the right artists into classrooms where the arts could serve the ongoing curriculum. Workshops were also arranged in senior centers, in a home for battered women and in other community centers. Again, the workshops were carefully designed to bring the artists into working partnerships with the participants. These workshops were covered by the local paper and public TV, highlighting the importance of the process of the residency that allowed for creative activity in a broad social spectrum, facilitated by the residency artists.

Building a Committed Artistic Team

The artists that were brought together for this residency were a very special group of people. They represented a wide variety of artistic disciplines and personal life experiences, yet they shared a common commitment to progressive social and political change through the artistic event of person-to-person expression of truth and love. Adora Dupree, from Johnson City, Tennessee, is a storyteller, writer and actress. She works as a solo artist and performs with Carpetbag Theater of Knoxville and The Road Company. Alice Lovelace, from Atlanta, Georgia, is a poet and community organizer. She has run a number of community-arts organizations in Atlanta and works extensively in schools throughout Georgia. Joyce Williams and Jacques Howard, also from Atlanta, are a singing duo called Joyce and Jacques. Since they met in the choir at Spelman College, they have been writing and singing their own songs for audiences throughout the Southeast. Willie Jordan, a graduate student in directing at Virginia Tech, Blacksburg, Virginia, is an accomplished theater artist who has taught theater in high schools throughout North Carolina, helping scores of students attain state and regional awards. Toya Lewis, a dancer with the world-traveled African American Dance Ensemble from Durham, North Carolina, and Beverly Botsford, a drummer who also works with the AADE, completed the team.

In January of 1994, two months before the residency, this team met in Selma for a long weekend to plan and schedule the residency activities. The artistic team, along with Buddy and myself, met with some 25 people from Selma who were committed to building partnerships to make this residency work. Frank Hardy was there, JoAnne

Bland and Sam Williams from the museum, a dozen teachers from the public schools and several other folks who had become involved over the months of preparation. An amazingly-motivated group, with enough time to identify needs and consider creative solutions, these people created the base for our residency.

We used the meeting time to introduce the artists to their potential partners in a workshop format. We identified our understanding of our mutual goals. We negotiated those goals so that all involved agreed and shared in the vision of the project. Finally, we identified partnerships, getting artists together with programs for mutual benefit. This was a crucial and very creative time. It resulted in a strong base of personal involvement on all sides as well as a working plan of activities. We had built an enormous energy and a structure to put it to use. We also found the name for the residency, *Understanding, the Struggle for Community*. After that, it became a logistics effort of some size, but the success of the project was safely in the hands of the participants. It was a joy. The results were assured by the care and realistic approach that Buddy had initiated and infused at every step along the way.

The residency is complete and the out-of-town artists are off to other projects. Selma is still Selma. But some very important little things have changed the way things are. Frank is working with Adora. Meria has found helpers in her effort to fund the renovation of the old school into a cross-cultural arts center. Young writers have written about what it feels like to live in Selma, and they have a book to give to people who are interested in reading what they have to say. Young dancers have a new dance and a new way of understanding their own lives through their dance. The school system has the documentation in hand to substantiate the development of more projects. The Arts Council is an experienced and recognized force for change across cultural and social barriers. This makes no guarantee about the future but it establishes progressive change in the present, right now. This is the work of the arts in communities.

Spring/Summer 1995

Drawing the Line at Place:
The Environmental Justice Project

By Mat Schwarzman

Artists are working with environmentalists and residents to make a political change in Louisiana, where toxic waste is devastating communities along the Mississippi River. Mat Schwarzman of the Institute for Urban Arts in Oakland, California, writes about what it's like for seven arts groups and eight community organizations to collaborate in The Environmental Justice Project (EJP). Taking part at the time of this article were the following New Orleans organizations: Chakula Cha Jua Theater Company, Christian Unity Baptist Church, Guardians of the Flame, Gulf Coast Tenant Association, Junebug Productions, New Orleans Youth Action Corps, Nkombo, People's Institute for Survival and Beyond, Tambourine and Fan, Twomby Center and the Welfare Rights Organization. They were joined by Carpetbag Theater Company (Knoxville, Tenn.), Roadside Theater (Whitesburg, Ky.) Robbie McCauley & Company (New York), Urban Bush Women (New York) and the American Festival Project, a nationwide coalition of community-based theater groups based at Appalshop in Whitesburg.

—Eds.

It was during the Spring of 1989. I don't remember clearly where in New Orleans we were when it happened, maybe Maspero's Slave Exchange. Maybe we saw one of those Mammy dolls beckoning the wary tourists. It might have been right after we'd heard the idea about buying one of the old plantations on River Road to make a museum that really shows what life was like in the "good old days." I really don't remember where we were, but I do remember that Jawole Zollar, the visionary leader of the Urban Bush Women, said, "Somebody ought to do something about purging the demons of slavery here in New Orleans." —John O'Neal

The 90-mile long River Road that runs along the Mississippi

River from New Orleans to Baton Rouge has been dubbed "Cancer Alley" by environmentalists and many of the residents. In addition to a group of predominately low-income African-American communities, it is home to a concentration of more than 130 major petrochemical plants, grain elevators, medical waste incinerators, solid waste landfills and other industrial operations that account for the bulk of toxic chemical releases in Louisiana. Residents face enormously high rates of cancer, miscarriages, birth defects and other health problems. The population of Cancer Alley is reported to have the highest rate of cancer in the nation.

Soon after his discussion with Jawole Zollar, John O'Neal was invited by Pat Bryant, of Gulf Coast Tenants Association, to an organizing meeting with people living on River Road. O'Neal learned that the map of Cancer Alley is a perfect template for the map of the old Mississippi River plantation system. While the nature of the bondage might have changed, he realized that this form of "environmental racism" was just a new face on an old problem.

So begins the story of the Environmental Justice Project, a multi-year, multidisciplinary, multiracial community-arts project being planned for 1998 by Junebug Productions, an African-American, community-based theater ensemble in New Orleans founded and directed by John O'Neal. "Environmental racism is the modern demon of slavery that Jawole had been talking about," says EJP Project Director Roxy Wright. "Junebug realized that our job as artists was to help these people struggling to exorcise this demon through environmental justice."

The Environmental Justice Project has grown from these initial conversations to encompass the work of seven community-based performing arts groups, eight community-based organizations mobilizing their memberships around issues of environmental justice, and a national network, with combined constituencies totaling in the thousands. While the project is still very much in formation, EJP participants have already met an important challenge facing cultural and political activists today: working together.

A Project About Process

The structure of the Environmental Justice Project is complex and multifaceted, illustrating the multiple goals of the project's creators. It is built around a cluster of partnerships between community-based theater groups and community-based organizing groups. Participants believe that the collaborating organizations, unaccustomed as many of them are to working with each other, have a lot to contribute and benefit from being part of the EJP.

The most visible product of these collaborations will be a festival of new theater works scheduled for 1998 in and around New Orleans. The organizing groups will provide stories and critical feedback to the theater groups. The theater groups will create and perform the new works and continue performing them on tour after the festival is completed.

Through the process of creating and producing these premieres, the work of all the participants will be advanced. They will develop their ability to collaborate with and draw sustenance from one another as an ongoing network of cultural and political organizations. They will increase their audience/constituency base through the crossover and synergy produced by the collaboration. Ultimately, says Ron Chisom of the People's Institute, one of the EJP collaborators, the idea is

> to try to get the cultural groups, along with the organizing groups, to see how we can begin to work together. The organizers need to know more about the cultural dynamics in their work. The cultural groups need to learn about the difference between just doing a 'community-based project' and how to participate in long-term organizing work.

More specifically, the role of the theater artists is, in Roxy Wright's mind, to provide their organizing partners with the opportunity to have their stories portrayed publicly and proudly, in a fashion that wouldn't be possible otherwise. "Each of these organizing groups has a wealth of stories," said Wright, "but nobody gets to know them, inside or certainly outside the organization. That's what we can make happen." In addition, Junebug and the other theater groups will be able to pass on some of the collective cultural techniques they have created, such as the "Story Circle" exercise, which the organizing groups can use to enhance their membership's unity and self-awareness. "I have seen it time and time again," says Adella Gautier, Junebug's

Associate Artistic Director. "When people have the chance to witness their collective stories, they get energized, more critical, and more powerful as a group."

Since these beginnings, EJP participants have worked together in planning meetings, conducted story-telling sessions and theater workshops, and organized public cultural events, including a Juneteenth picnic and local performances by some of the participating theater groups. Donald Harrison, Jr., a jazz composer in residence with Junebug Theater, also composed an original piece entitled "Don't Drink the Water" that Gulf Coast Tenant's Association is using in its organizing efforts. The culminating festival in 1998 will include performances, visual arts exhibits, community education projects and a special training institute for artists, administrators and community activists. It has already been a long time coming, says O'Neal, but it has been worth it. "We've tapped into something larger than either Jawole or I as individuals could have possibly imagined."

Taking the Longer View

There is another place to begin the story of the Environmental Justice Project—the Civil Rights Movements of the 1960s. At that time, O'Neal was a part of the Free Southern Theater, a New Orleans-based group allied with the Student Non-Violent Coordinating Committee (SNCC), one of the most important and radical African-American-led organizing groups. The Free Southern Theater began in 1963 and was conceived as a "theater for those who have no theater." It supported the work of SNCC by bringing church and other activist groups together, recruiting students for SNCC's freedom schools, and providing a more entertaining form of political education.

During this period, the arts and organizing were inextricably linked. Ted Quant of the Twomey Center for Peace Through Justice, another of the EJP organizing groups, remembers:

> In the Civil Rights Movement we sang a song [by Cordell Reagon] that
> went: "I'm here from New Orleans and you're here from Alabama and
> we're all here together in a Selma County Jail." That lyric and the experi-
> ence of people singing it together connected everybody to a higher level

of commitment and understanding of our collective consciousness than would have been possible otherwise.

Quant believes that "in every revolution, there have been cultural workers. They are the ones who create the cultural and spiritual connection that people are willing to fight and die for."

O'Neal, Quant, Wright, Chisom and Bryant knew each other during this period, and while they never worked together in the field, they developed a deep respect for one another's work. Their relationship forms a vital core to the Environmental Justice Project.

Begun in 1981, Junebug Productions became the successor to the Free Southern Theater, and in many people's eyes, the theatrical legacy of the Civil Rights Movement itself. And yet its work has been different in some important ways. Rather than focusing on New Orleans and the South, Junebug has toured nationally, working in a wide range of rural, urban and suburban communities. This has meant that the relationship between Junebug and the communities they work within has had to be greatly shortened, often lasting less than a week. And while Junebug has continued to create theater about people in struggle and to connect with grassroots communities through residency activities, they have done less and less of the direct-action type of social-change theater that Free Southern Theater was known for. Instead of having community-organizing groups as sponsors and partners, most have been schools, colleges, cultural centers and other types of social-service agencies. These organizations have tended to be oriented more around community development than political enfranchisement, and have validated marginalized cultures rather than agitating for change.

While O'Neal continues to believe this is vital work, it has also begun to feel too safe: "As with many social-change institutions today, our work became more about survival and less about fulfilling our mission." The EJP partnerships, because of their greater focus on direct action, has been a way for Junebug to reconnect, not only with its roots in New Orleans, but also its origins as an organization.

Dudley Cocke, director of Roadside Theater in Whitesburg, Kentucky, and another of the EJP collaborators, calls this "drawing the line at place." "One of the biggest problems in our work [at Roadside] is the lack of context," Cocke says. "Too frequently, there's nowhere for people to go with what they experience or learn in our performances. Even if we generate all the positive energy and righteous anger in the world, what happens if there's no organization to follow through?" He sees this as part of a larger dynamic in our society's "drop-in culture": "As grassroots theater artists, we have a body of ideas, relationships and symbols that we can offer as catalysts for social-change movements. They can't just be disconnected from their roots and served up like fast food." EJP represents the next logical step in community-arts work, according to Cocke, and EJP could turn out to be an invaluable opportunity to explore the issues and create new models for partnerships.

In this sense, EJP is enabling Junebug to "draw its line" differently in two ways: first, by grounding itself more firmly within the fabric of New Orleans communities, and second, by resituating itself and the participating theater groups at a different place within the community, aligned with grassroots organizing efforts directed at systemic social change.

"We Do It By Doing It"

The Environmental Justice Project collaboration has served as a fundamental challenge to many participants' assumptions about their own work and the work of their EJP partners. The connection between theater and organizing is a difficult one for many activists on both sides of the equation. The community organizing groups, no less than the community-based theaters, have had to do serious analysis and soul-searching in order to make sense of their involvement. Ron Chisom of the People's Institute says,

> The project is clear to me one day, and then not so clear the next. When I get it, it's crystal clear, but if I am away from it for even a few days, it's like I have to start all over again." After 30 years as an organizer, Chisom admits this is a little unnerving, but believes the confusion points to the radicalness of what EJP proposes: "We took something on that was big, and it turned out to be bigger than we thought.

Many organizers and artists, it seems, hold very different—and frequently judgmental—notions about one another. EJP participants learned about this from tensions that grew between Junebug and Gulf Coast Tenants Association staff. Roxy Wright of Junebug Productions remembers that she and Junebug's Managing Director, MK Wegmann, "began to sense some hostile undercurrents. We had been very careful not to approach the organizing groups with the old attitude—'we're artists, and we're here to teach you'—but it became clear that that's just the attitude Gulf Coast thought we had."

Ted Quant and Bernardette Mills of the Twomey Center were brought in to help mediate the situation. They had each group—the staff of Junebug and the staff of Gulf Coast—draw a collective picture of what they each imagined their relationship to be, from the other's perspective. "The picture showed that the grassroots organizers believed that the artists and the organizers were two separate groups," said Ted Quant. "From the standpoint of the organizers, the artists were an elitist, separatist group in an ivory tower who were not interested in getting their hands dirty. From the standpoint of the artists, the organizers had no respect or understanding for what they bring, and instead wanted to turn them into organizers."

While Quant understands each group's position, he has come to believe organizers "cannot be disappointed with where people are, because that's real. You've got to work with it, no matter how 'correct' you may be." Conversely, he also believes "the artist's attitude cannot be: 'my work has value, and if you don't see it, fuck you.'" Quant says the artists

> have to be able to stand firm, with integrity and awareness of what they bring to the table, and make no apologies for it. At the same time, artists also have to listen to the organizers and acknowledge that they do have to get down and dirty. The truth of the art will only be reflected through the experience of the artist, so they have to be there to get it.

Pat Bryant, of Gulf Coast Tenants Association, agrees. He knows personally the power of the arts to affect social change:

> During the Civil Rights Movement, I would stay up all night and work with other people to change the lyrics to popular songs. There isn't anything

that fucks up a target like a gospel choir singing about him using words from a popular song. Killed one guy, J.C. Lawrence, that way. He was a vicious, racist slumlord, and I swear that that song gave him a heart attack.

At the same time, Bryant is concerned about the whole notion of artists going "into" communities. "People—especially African Americans—have been taught to rely on outside experts, as opposed to people in their community. We try to make it clear to people that they have the power to deal with their own oppression. We need people to come, write songs, make t-shirts, do plays, etc., but we don't need any 'artists.' We need workers. They must participate as regular people." It can't just be in the form of a temporary residency, Bryant believes. "It has to have an organic relationship to the work of the struggle."

When EJP community partners have become directly exposed to and involved with their artist partners, a lot of the mystification and tension has been cleared up. When Jennifer Cumerbatch, executive director of the New Orleans Youth Action Corps, first heard about the EJP she thought "the project sounded like it could be beneficial, and it was related to our interest in the environment, but I can't say I thought it was very important."

"For the first year of EJP, it was difficult to stay connected," Cumerbatch told me. "We had an opportunity to be in the audience of a theater performance, we had a chance to travel to Tennessee where Carpetbag Theater [their artist partner] is located, but these things were not directly relevant to what the organization was trying to do." All of that changed when Carpetbag visited the New Orleans Youth Action Corps in October 1995. "Carpetbag's visit was great. Our Corps members loved the exercises, and Carpetbag learned a lot about our organization and how we might work together." The two groups are now considering creating a short play for Youth Corps members to perform in the schools on environmental themes, and Cumerbatch feels more invested now that these possibilities have appeared.

MK Wegmann sees this kind of hands-on cultural contact between collaborating arts and organizing groups as a key factor in determining the effectiveness of the partnerships. "We can't underestimate how strange the notion is for people that the arts are a catalyst for social change. Programs—direct interaction with the staff and members of these organizations—are the best way to get things to 'click.' While planning is important, we do it by doing it, not by talking about it." Because Junebug is an arts organization, "we have to do it from the place of art. The community organizations are going to have to do it from the place where they are. Us trying to be them, or trying to get them to be us, won't work."

The culture of the organizations themselves may be another important factor in determining which organizing groups are most receptive to cultural/political partnerships. One of the most enthusiastic of the community organizing partners has been the Christian Unity Baptist Church. This action-oriented church is already utilizing art and culture more than any of the other EJP community organizing groups. Their membership regularly participates in creating plays, songs and visual arts projects that deal with issues in their community, and brings the diverse poor, working-class and middle-class African-American groups within the church together. They have a number of talented parishioners who teach and model for the others. Rev. Audrey Johnson, assistant to the pastor Rev. Dwight Webster and the church's EJP liaison, says "we have yet to find a tool as powerful as the arts to get people in our church thinking. People are so accustomed to being told by television what they are and are not capable of. Making art themselves helps show people—poor people, especially—just how creative and powerful they can be."

> **"We can't underestimate how strange the notion is for people that the arts are a catalyst for social change."**

When asked why she thought her organization was so involved in the arts when the others weren't, Rev. Johnson said it is because—thanks to their pastor—the church has become steeped in its African and African-American tradition and history: "His leadership," she said, "has led the congregation to a rich awareness of the power and potential of the arts and culture to make a difference in the community." More generally, she referred to the story of King Jehosephat in the New Testament, and the direction from God for the "righteous to overwhelm their enemies through song," to demonstrate the extent to which the church as an institution is steeped in art and cultural tradition. "You have to be able to take the long view," she said, "in order to see the value of using art and culture to organize people. This is not something we're doing for today. This is something our grandchildren will benefit from."

Without a creative, multigenerational view, Rev. Johnson believes, it may be hard for community organizations in crisis to see the value of changing society over the long haul: "Social change is about doing things we haven't done before. It's about taking risks. If you have never seen the other side, your circumstances will always appear normal and inevitable, and they will never change."

Many of us allow ourselves to be painted into such small boxes, Rev. Johnson believes, "and art and creativity makes us jump out of the box. If we don't see that struggle itself as important," she concludes, "there is little for artists and organizers to even talk about."

"Jumping Out of the Box"

Ted Quant of the Twomey Center believes that "to consciously reassert the role of the arts at a moment when we are being smashed by the right wing, and to bring forward our truth in a creative, expressive way that objective analysis doesn't, seems to be an extremely important project." Both artists and organizers will need to expand their notions about their own work, as well as their partners', in order for this to be possible. It may be difficult, but as the Environmental Justice Project suggests, it can also be immensely rewarding and powerful. "In my wildest dreams," Quant concludes, "I imagine the proverbial organizing discussion of the future: 'OK, now that we've talked about tactics, strategy and analysis, where does the cultural side come in?' Cultural workers will be invited to the table at the very beginning, and they will know how to plug in and do their work."

While community arts are still struggling for recognition in the scheme of things, community artists are finding their efforts more widely understood and validated than they have been in quite awhile.

Even as the resources for our work continue to shrink, there has been a relative proliferation of community-arts funding and policy initiatives, writings, conferences and exhibitions, all of which at least begins to suggest our maturation as a movement.[1] It seems incumbent upon us to begin comparing notes, clarifying our approaches and building upon one another's work. The Environmental Justice Project is a bold effort to draw and redraw the lines of our understanding of the issues and opportunities we all face, and we should all eagerly await its fruition.

Notes

1. Kesler, Grant. "Aesthetic Evangelists: Conversion and Empowerment in Contemporary Community Art." *Afterimage* magazine, January 1995. Rochester, NY: Visual Studies Workshop. Pages 5-11.

Summer 1996

We All Are Theater:
An Interview with Augusto Boal

By Douglas L. Paterson and Mark Weinberg

The following is an excerpt from an interview with Augusto Boal at the University of Nebraska at Omaha during his residency there March 18-26, 1996, and the Second Annual Pedagogy of the Oppressed Conference, March 21-23. Boal conducted workshops and "jokered" two Forum Theatre performances, one with conference participants and another with Omaha residents concerned with a recent incident of police violence. He is interviewed by Douglas L. Paterson, teacher at UNO and founder of the Center for the Theatre of the Oppressed, Omaha, and Mark Weinberg, teacher at the University of Wisconsin Center, Rock County, and author of Challenging the Hierarchy: Collective Theater in the United States. *The article opens with an introduction to Boal by Paterson, originally published on the* World Wide Web *in* Webster's World of Cultural Democracy. *—Eds.*

Brazilian theater director Augusto Boal developed The Theatre of the Oppressed (TO) during the 1950s and 1960s. In an effort to transform theater from the "monologue" of traditional performance into a "dialogue" between audience and stage, Boal experimented with many kinds of interactive theater. His explorations were based on the assumption that dialogue is the common, healthy dynamic between all humans, that all human beings desire and are capable of dialogue, and that when a dialogue becomes a monologue, oppression ensues. Theater then becomes an extraordinary tool for transforming monologue into dialogue. "While some people make theater," says Boal, "we all are theater."

From his work Boal evolved various forms of theater workshops and performances that aimed to meet the needs of all people for interaction, dialogue, critical thinking, action and fun. While the performance modes of Forum Theatre, Image Theatre, Cop-In-The-Head and the vast array of the Rainbow of Desire are designed to bring the audience into active relationship with the performed event, the workshops are virtually a training ground for action, not only in these performance forms, but for action in life.

The "typical" Theatre of the Oppressed workshop comprises three kinds of activity. The first is background *information* on TO and the various exercises provided by the workshop facilitator (or "difficultator," as Boal prefers to describe it). Such information begins the workshop, but is also interspersed throughout the games and exercises. Moreover, the group is brought together periodically to discuss responses to games and to ask questions of the various processes.

The second kind of activity is the *games*. These are invariably highly physical interactions designed to challenge us to truly listen to what we are hearing, feel what we are touching, and see what we are looking at. The "arsenal" of the Theatre of the Oppressed is extensive, with more than 200 games and exercises listed in Boal's *Games for Actors and Non-Actors* alone. Several years ago, Boal's Center for the Theatre of the Oppressed in Paris (CTO-Paris) proceeded methodically through all the TO activities; the inventory took two years to cover. Ultimately, these games serve to heighten our senses and demechanize the body, to get us out of habitual behavior, as a prelude to moving beyond habitual thinking and interacting. We also become actively engaged with other participants, developing relationships and trust, and having a very good time.

Finally, the third area of activity involves the *structured exercises*. Although there is a kind of gray area at times when one might call an activity a game or an exercise, the exercises are formulated so as to infuse a given structure with genuine content.

These activities are designed to highlight a particular area of TO practice such as Image Theatre, Forum Theatre, Rainbow of Desire, etc. Thus we are invited not only to imagine new possibilities and solutions, but to actively participate in them, Forum style. Group problem solving, highly interactive imagining, physical involvement, trust and fun combine to create vigorous interpersonal dynamics. As a result, we learn that we are, if not the source of our difficulties, at least the reason for their maintenance. More importantly, we are clearly the source of our mutual liberations.

—Douglas L. Paterson

Douglas Paterson and Mark Weinberg: *Your approach to theater, it seems, offers one of the most profound critiques of, at least, the Western approach to drama. You write that it divides a people into those few who do and those many who watch, and that this becomes a model for the ruling structure where there are few in power who do, and many who watch the action of history. And that through a process of catharsis, people watch something, are concerned for the well-being and stability of the state, and then are persuaded through some kind of purging not to do anything; to accept things as they are and not to take action. We have been intrigued by how, at least in the United States, people in established critical circles have not come after you. Has there been, do you think, much of a critique—a real critique—of TO and your work anywhere?*

Augusto Boal: Well look, it is the critique by silence. [TO is] absolutely ignored by the press. The press [have] criticized by silence. They say: That's not theater; if the spectator also uses theater then theater no longer exists for them [the critics]. Never comes a notice in the press to say we are going to have a festival…not one critique appears. They rarely—when they know it is TO—they rarely come. So there is a criticism by silence, by not acknowledging the existence of something which is there. They are publishing books on TO all over the world. But all these books are by practitioners, people who do it and then they tell their experience—which I find is wonderful—but not a single book tried to analyze what's happening with TO in the world.

P&W: *I think one of the really important things that needs to happen to expand the practice is a rigorous, critical examination of the process. As you're saying, it needs that, as part of the dialogue. So, as a way of beginning that, we've put together some questions that we'd like to pose to you. The first question is about making stereotypes on the stage. Perhaps in the structures of Forum Theatre,*

*maybe Cop-in-the-Head and Rainbow of Desire as well, it's easy to
use stereotypes. We are invited in TO to represent our antagonist,
our oppressor, or those who aligned with us, in either/or ways—the
good guys and the bad guys. Is there a way to really negotiate in
discussion between stereotypes and what is probably a more complex reality? How do we get away from using stereotypes as a way
of thinking about issues?*

AB: I think that in the Forum Theatre or in the techniques of Rainbow
of Desire we can start by stereotype, but the theatrical discussion will go as far as the participants are capable of going. There
is not a recipe to make people see more deeply than the
stereotype. But there is a method [in] which you can start with
a stereotype and then you go deeper. The presentation of the
model, inevitably it is a stereotype. For instance, yesterday we
were doing that presentation there at the church, and then the
presentation of the scene—it was a stereotype. People…are
playing dominos or cards or drinking beer, and someone comes
and says, "You have to mobilize yourself, get out of here and let's
do a manifest and participate." Particularly, I was impressed by
the boy who said, "Why should I? The more I read about, the
more I know about how things are happening in this country,
the more I think there is no solution." And then I felt some people that are inactive, they're not inactive because they are like
that. It's because you have so much information—by the media,
by the press, by the television, by friends—that it's horrible
what's happening. But that's the way it is. There's some sort of
fatality that makes people accept it; people who are not fatalists,
they become fatalists. I was very much impressed. That's not a
stereotype. A stereotype is to show someone [who says], "Oh
no. I don't care about that." The person who says, "I don't care
about that," in reality cares about that, but is discouraged—is
afraid. So I believe that stereotype is a part of the picture, but
depending on the people gathered to discuss the theme, the
problem, we can go beyond stereotype…We develop techniques, but the important thing is who is going to use that tech-

nique and how strong is the desire to find something by the people? If you have a strong desire, if you have not given up and you still believe, things can be changed.

P&W: *In other words, it is from the stereotype that the spectactors and audience learn about the situation. They really have to discover what it is about, what they've done that might be a stereotype. It's up to them to discover that, rather than for you—as Joker or academic or critic to point that out from the start. That needs to be discovered by the group.*

AB: By the theatrical process. And sometimes what happens happens because there's a stereotyped model, or it's a stereotyped story, but sometimes it's a stereotyped character. I always remember, when they talk about stereotypes, a discovery from the work I did in Chile. It was with someone who was fighting against Pinochet, [who] was known to be almost a hero among the workers in the fight against Pinochet, who had been tortured to hell. But when he made the play about his own family, he discovered that in his own family he was behaving like Pinochet towards his wife and towards his children—especially the daughters. So he discovered he had a stereotyped behavior of "father." He was not being a father that was fighting Pinochet that had such a wife and such daughters and sons. He was not behaving like himself. Every time…someone [came] who wanted to date one of his daughters, his reaction was not of the person who's fighting tyranny. His behavior was tyrannical behavior. "You had to be back at this hour, you had to do this, you had to do that." He reproduced in his home a stereotyped behavior of fathers having to protect their daughters, and having to impose upon their wives a certain form of behavior of work and all that.

P&W: *If I am making an image or if I'm involved in Forum Theatre, someone could say that it's too easy for me to separate my own personal experience from the social context to which it belongs. I make my image of oppression only from my point of view. And the criticism might be made, then, that I can believe my image somehow is true* *in the larger sense because it's true for me. Does the spectator audience reconnect the individual to the social?*

AB: It depends also on what is the structure. For instance, you have the structure of the worker that is going to talk to the boss because he needs more pay or better conditions of work. So all the other workers that belong to the same factory, the same [work] place, they are going to identify [with] the situation and there is [no] doubt for them that they are oppressed. And then they are going to fight against the boss because the boss wants more profits and gives less conditions of good work, of comfortable work, of human work. But in those cases it is very clear to someone you are going to strike. It's very easy.

But the complication begins when the relation between one and the other one cannot fall in well-established categories.

---

what I believe is that in the normal theater, there is a paralysis...

For instance, in all relations—men and women, emotional relations—sometimes both feel oppressed by the other. And then I can present a play in which I feel I am oppressed by the woman, and then by doing the play in forum, I can discover that maybe I am [the] oppressor more than I am oppressed. Not only in forum. The other day, we did the screen image[1] and one of the boys at the end, he was really very moved. He said, "Look, I was showing how I was oppressed and I was surprised that everyone took the position of the other one. And then finally, I understood that maybe I am [the] oppressor of the other one, and that's why the other one oppressed me." Sometimes the situation is not socially very clear, very concrete and [yet is] very stereotyped, very ritualized. And it is also the question of feeling, the question of emotion—it is very difficult to say who is oppressing who, because the other one can be oppressed too. So that's why those techniques were developed in which you don't really try to find the oppressor or the oppressed, but you try to understand the situation between one person and another.

P&W: *Is it possible that the techniques of TO limit possibilities, so that the theatrical representations of realities and ideal outcomes become similar from situation to situation? The techniques of image or rainbow might be leading us to a narrow range of possibilities that are, in effect, constructed in advance by the very techniques themselves. We end up universalizing the particular when it may be the techniques that make for a predictable outcome and process.*

AB: I believe that when you have a forum, for instance, there are many, many alternatives that are predictable, and [that] are stereotypes. Replacements[2] are also stereotyped. For instance, the idea [that] you go alone there or you go with other people. [It's] predictable that after one moment or another, some spectactor will say, "Oh, I'm not going alone there. I'm going to take other people with me." That's predictable and it happens very often. But the fact that it's predictable does not mean that it's not true, that it does not reveal that most of the time we try to solve our own problems alone. And then, if it's predictable, [it's] still good that someone is going to say that we can go together, not go alone.

At the same time, what I believe is the most important effect of Forum Theatre is not the solutions that it can find at the end, but the process of thinking. Because what I believe is that in the normal theater, there is a paralysis: the spectator paralyzes his power of action and he is suffering the empathy of the character and, for some time, he's only answering. He is only doing what the actor does, only feeling what the actor feels, the character feels. And what is important for me is not exactly the solution that we found, [but] the process of criticizing, observing and trying to find solutions. Even if we don't find any solution at the end of Forum Theatre, I say, "OK, it's good. We did not find that solution, but we looked for it." And sometimes I think if you find a *predictable* solution at the end, it's not as good as [when] you don't find any, but you have been thinking about it. What changes is the attitude of the spectator, of not being only consumer, but someone who questions.

I like very much the game I have been using lately about the leader—the designated—leader in which you have to find out who is the leader, and in reality there is no leader. And then the people find out I gave a wrong instruction, and I was deceiving them. I like very much that because I want them to have confidence in me, but not blind confidence. And so this game says, "Whatever I say, don't take it absolutely. Analyze, think if what I'm saying is good or not, if you agree or not." And then I think that TO as a whole should always be that. Always think, "Is that true? Do you agree?" It's to provoke thoughts and to provoke actions and to provoke invention. Whatever we invent, whatever thoughts we have, whatever actions we take, the most important [thing] is to have this as a [starting point]—to be dynamized and not to be like the character of yesterday who said, "The more I read about that, the more I see that I am powerless. I don't want to do anything. I'm going to do dominos." And TO says the opposite. You can do lots of other things. What? Let's try to find out. We don't bring the message. We bring the methods, not the message.

P&W: What is your response to the theater that we have on Broadway and in our universities and in our regional theaters here in the United States and certainly down in Rio—the performance of standard plays? You're not against that, I know, but is it your sense that we need a whole companion area of theater that is community-based interactive?

AB: That's what I think. I think that, for instance, in France people are used to having teachers of theater in schools but they teach only Moliere, Racine, Marivaux, Corneille. They reproduce inside the school the same plays that they see outside of the school. And I think that it should be the opposite. The school should learn the language of the theater, not finished production, but the language. And TO is the language of the theater and not necessarily the final product. And I think that it's good for everyone. For instance, the Schauspielhaus in Germany, sometimes they produce theater like they produce sausage. Every year they have to do a German classic, they have to do a boulevard, they have to do I don't know what. And then every year it's the same. It's repetitive. If they could also have a place in which they would do Forum, I am sure that it would revitalize the theater that they do. I am sure that if we are going to do *Hamlet* with Rainbow of Desire techniques,[3] I think it's going to revitalize also their acting in Shakespeare, when they do Shakespeare in the normal way. It makes acting more vital. So what I think we should not do is to exclude the learning of the language and go to the final production. That's what's being done now.

I have been told that Omaha is one of the more violent cities in the country. Dialogue between the people here would only help to understand why it is so violent and [why you can not] stop violence, because you cannot stop violence, but [you can] make it less than what exists. I'm quite sure that social TO can be important, not only statically showing another form of doing theater, but using this other form of doing theater to make life more bearable. For instance like in Brazil now, sometimes it's unbearable…

P&W: *We've talked this week about hope in the face of violence. In Brazil, in the United States, around the world, the free market is becoming the only moral order. In the face of all this is your theater, which implies a kind of future, a kind of hope. Do you have hope?*

AB: Yes. I think there are some words that…should always be connected, because if not, it can become only religious words and not socially workable words. One is hope. Because what hope should we have if not the hope of our desire? And what desire should we have if not the desire to change our society toward something that can be better for all of us. So sometimes, I hear people talking about hope. I see very much in Brazil, miserable people [told], "You have to hope." And I say, why should they hope if they know that if they don't fight, if they don't have the desire to fight, nothing is going to happen? To have the hope, blind hope that one day something is going to happen. To have the blind hope that someday God's going to help you. The blind hope I think is even worse than no hope.

But [when] I do believe in hope is when you have a strong desire. If I believe that here, the people here, they have the strong desire to end or to make less the extraordinary racial violence that exists, then people have the right to have hope. I think that to have hope is a right that we have if we have desire. If we don't have desire, we don't have the right to have hope.

And which desire can you have? Desire here in Omaha. The desire to be richer than Mr. Warren Buffet. That's a desire, infantile desire. You cannot have that; that's not a legitimate desire. But desire that no one in Omaha should die because it's too cold, or should die because they are hungry, or die because there are gangs that shoot one another. This desire is legitimate. And we would develop that desire and then we have the right to have hope. Hope is a right, it's not something you should have by all means. If your desire is active, then you have the right to have hope. But to stay at home and say, "I hope that this is going to happen"—to have hope that you are going to win in the lottery—that's not legitimate, that hope. To have the hope that the government is going to do all good things for the people, that's not legitimate.

Notes

1. A technique used to help participants see how their image of another person influences conflict. For more information about Boal's techniques, see *Playing Boal* (bibliography).
2. When a spectactor comes on stage to replace the protagonist during a Forum Theatre performance.
3. Boal has been invited to Stratford, England, to work with the Royal Shakespeare Company on *Hamlet*.

Summer 1996

Resolving Conflicts:
A Poet's Residency in Tulsa

by Alice Lovelace

During March, 1996, poet Alice Lovelace was invited to spend one week in Tulsa, Oklahoma, to participate in a year-long series of events highlighting women's lives through the arts and humanities. Events were sponsored by a coalition of Tulsa cultural and social organizations and coordinated by Planned Parenthood of Eastern Oklahoma and Western Arkansas, Inc. Her goals were "to celebrate the private and communal life; to question societal values regarding women; to provoke critical thinking around deeply rooted social issues and conflicts."   —Eds.

The Beginning

Georgia Williams:

I attended the Community Arts Revival in Durham, N.C., sponsored by Alternate ROOTS. Alice read her poems "Freakin' Out," "Tomahawk Poem," "A Daughter of Trial (A Sister of Tribulation)." I remember thinking that she could burn poetry into your psyche and I wanted to share her with my community. I have worked as a community arts coordinator for nearly 20 years, and developed good instincts for placing artists with audiences appropriate for their needs and the needs of our community.

There is an excellent core of artists within my own community who need work, so it is important that I have a darn good reason to bring in an artist from outside our region. Knowing Alice's background in arts-in-education and performance, our agency worked with Planned Parenthood, Resonance Listening & Growth For Women and Theatre North to design an introductory one-week residency that would allow us not only to become familiar with her teaching style but to showcase her poetry.

Alice Lovelace:

It was during the 1993 Community Arts Revival that I met Georgia Williams. We shared a meal and talked about the need for community-based residencies that serve the social and emotional needs of a diverse community. Several months later, I gladly accepted Georgia's invitation to visit Tulsa. When she told me my sponsoring partner was Planned Parenthood, I knew Georgia understood how important it was to me that my residency and performance combine the arts and education. I was eager to use this opportunity to bring together my ongoing studies in narrative performance and my unfolding knowledge in the analysis of conflict and the practice of resolution.

Narrative Performance and Conflict Resolution

People often ask me why a poet would decide to get a master's degree in conflict resolution. The first few times I was asked this question, I stuttered, searching for words to convey the connections. But in my heart, I knew this was a natural match. For the past three years I had worked with schools and community organizations to design poetry/narrative-based, conflict-resolution programs for elementary students and incarcerated youth.

My goal: teach them to utilize narrative poetry to access deeply held values and beliefs about conflict, subtle and overt. To explore the possibilities of resolution. But while the institutions gave a lot of lip service to conflict resolution, their concerns were to make the youth more manageable and their jobs easier.

Between the time I agreed to this residency and the day of my departure, the world changed. The images of tortured steel and twisted bodies simmered fresh. As I packed, I recalled the faces of the Oklahoma City tragedy; I remembered my cynicism giving way to tears as rescuers lifted the bodies of children trapped in their daycare center.

The United States spends more tax dollars on munitions than on all social-service programs combined. We are a nation armed for war, yet we are a people uneasy with the idea of being involved in a conflict. The word connotes something wild and out of control. Our choice of responses has not changed since the cave days: fight or flee! Too often violence has become the response of choice, even for our children.

Calling for reconciliation between white and black Americans during a recent visit to Texas, President Clinton blamed the O.J. Simpson trial for exposing the racial gulf that divides Americans by race and class. Those who honor the legacy of the peace and justice movements know that the wounds of intolerance and disparity are old wounds open for all to see; the problem is, few care to examine them.

We need to learn new skills and ways of bridging the social conflicts that separate us. We have yet to assume individual responsibility for the state of our union. To foster understanding, we must keep open the lines of communications.

Clinton was correct when he asserted that "blacks and whites see the world in vastly different ways." (*Atlanta Journal/Constitution*, 10/17/95). The tragedy is, while blacks are educated to see the world as whites do, few whites take the time or effort to see the other side of the story. And we all need to cease thinking of Native Americans in the past tense or as museum artifacts. The bombing of the Federal Building in Oklahoma City was a wake-up call.

Angry white men are poor white men just like angry black men are poor black men. And while I do not believe we are headed for a race war, I do believe we are building up for a cross-cultural confrontation based on class.

So What Happened?

Despite flight delays and a missed connecting flight, I finally arrive in Tulsa, three hours late. This means Georgia has to drive me directly to my first site, Apache Manor, a secured and gated public housing complex. Apache Manor is clean, the streets appear lifeless—no pets or children. No people sitting on the stoop, no one walking. A guard checks our identification (Georgia vouches for me) and we drive to the apartment where Planned Parenthood operates the "It's Your Future" program:

> This is an innovative educational program designed for teenagers in areas
> of the city where teen pregnancy rates are the highest. It is a holistic
> approach…which provides the teens with a place where they can go after
> school, as well as a variety of planned activities that expand their horizons

and give them hope for the future.

"Tell us about you," the girls inquire, and I remind myself that a residency begins with the first word uttered:

> *We birth the babies.*
> *We birth the men folk too.*
> *All the joy in life,*
> *We bring to you.*
> *Wild Womyn,*
> *Come Follow.*

I choose this poem because we have only two sessions planned and a lot to talk about.

On the drive to my hotel, Georgia fills me in on the local history and issues, and offers insight on life in Tulsa. Being part of the great movement west, Tulsa continues to hold fast to its image as solitary pioneer struggling against the elements: the rugged individual who neither wants nor seeks help.

My recollection of my stay comes back in fragments. The second day I visit Holland Hall, a private Episcopalian school; my hostess is Ruth Brelsford. For 8 a.m. chapel I deliver a lecture-demo for high-school students. This is the kind of school where emotion-based response is drilled out. All intellect and no emotion. I talk to them about why I write, what I write and what performance means to me. Georgia tells me about one restrained young man seated in front of her who turned to his buddies during chapel reading and confessed, "I just want to get up and dance!"

Journal Entry 3/21/96: I came down from my room in the hotel to find a conference on Native American education. This reminds me of an article where the writer referred to Native Americans as "super Citizens," implying that they get more than they are due. I take a 40-minute walk around downtown Tulsa at 11 a.m. I nod and say hello, but the only person who speaks to me says, "Hey, nice coat."

Following the intergenerational workshop at Osage Hills Apartment Community, I beg for a home-cooked meal. Georgia takes me to Wanda J's. We drive through the remains of a once prosperous community, now vacant lots, unregulated dumps and a sparse display of small businesses. This is the African-American side of Tulsa. It is obvious that for generations there has been no investment, no development. This community has been sucked dry and exposed, like a dust bowl. But the food at Wanda J's is heaven and home.

My thoughts turn to a letter I read in the local free paper, *Urban Tulsa*. A man wrote, "Civil human contact, if it occurs at all, has dwindled to a few locations—work, stores and social circles." I ask Georgia if this is true. "It's true," she answers, "it's true."

At the Write Place, I am greeted by a room filled with a diverse group of writers. We begin. I share with them my ideas about the role of poet as performer and the power of the human voice. They ask what I require. Flexibility in space, audience and script. What do I strive for? Minimal separation between me and the audience. I ask them to tell me what they think, to tell me stories, urge them to speak. I press for a dialogue.

In all of my work this dialogue is essential. This asking is my way of seeking permission to involve myself in my audiences' affairs, an essential part of the ritual leading up to the performance.

Next is a workshop at Resonance, a volunteer-based nonprofit organization dedicated to providing programs of support for women of all ages who are experiencing change or adversity, or wish to realize their full potential. My audience is composed of social-service providers from several agencies. More talk about the performer as a mediator of social conflict. I share with them what I have come to know and understand about the work of Augusto Boal and his process of Theatre of the Oppressed (TO).

Every day, like those faithful circuit riders of the old west, Georgia delivers me to my post. Along the way, we collect audience and interest. I listen for local issues and perspectives, listening mostly for the unsaid. From several people, black and white, I hear whispers of "Little Africa." Bits and pieces about a mass lynching and an affluent black community wiped out during a white riot in 1921. I hear scars deep and silencing; the unspoken message I receive loud and clear: harmony above all.

I ask Georgia if she knows any local drummers who might be willing to join me. It is essential that someone from this community stand with me. She refers me to Askia Toure. On Saturday, we meet at the Living Arts Gallery and sort of rehearse. I begin reading a poem and he comes in with a beat on his djimba. We settle on four or five tunes. He will rehearse the other drummers, which include his wife, Carmen, and another couple, Jason and Borah. I am off to find incense and objects for the altar.

Narrative Performance as a Social Conciliation

Conciliation, as an alternative dispute-resolution strategy, provides a forum for disputing parties to deal with emotion and values perceived as barriers to forward movement, personal or social. Like the mediator in conciliation, as a narrative performer I have the power to carry the message—this power exists as long as the audience is together and they want to possess it. I act as a facilitator of issues, separating the people from the problem. Through the saying, I probe deep feelings and thoughts. My obligation is to honor the audience and respect the limits of their emotional/social situation.

I accept the responsibility to facilitate a process (performance) to improve the emotional health of disputants (audience). Combining the theory and practice of narrative performance and conflict resolution in a process of community artmaking allows the parties (audience) to hear the difficult. It encourages the discovery of common territory, and aspires to transform conflict into energy, to conceive of and strive for social change.

Marie MacLean, author of *Narrative as Performance,* believes narrative is, "...how we organize our verbal thinking...essential to how we develop memory, communicate ideas and learn. Narrative performance...involves an intimate relationship which, like all such relationships, is at once a co-operation and a contest, an exercise in harmony and a mutual display of power."

West Africans and Native Americans have high regard for the story and the teller as a source of magic. Michelle LaBaron Duryea, associate professor of conflict analysis and resolution at George Mason University, understands why these cultures value stories: "Stories communicate values, beliefs, hopes, fears and dreams of a people in a way that engenders respect and understanding in the listener. They are vehicles that touch not only the intellect but the spirit. They move us beyond the rational 'yes' towards getting to the more fundamental 'heart.'"

Reflections on the Performance

In the beginning was the word
and the word was power
the word was protection

Georgia:

The culminating event, Saturday night's performance at Living Arts, filled the room with youth from private schools and housing communities, and adults from several areas of the community. Standing room only. This was the first time, that I know of, that our community was so enthusiastic about attending a poetry event.

Alice challenged them to find a way to honor anger and understand that it doesn't mean danger or violence is evident, only that something is out of sync. As a white female, I know that my people suppress our anger. Anger suppressed turns into denial because you learn to fear the expression of anger. We think nothing of expecting others to suppress their anger to maintain harmony. Following the performance, people shared conversation and food. It was a time to meet new people, to cross a few bridges.

Alice:

My work is rooted in ritual and myth. I pay homage to the past and ask permission from those present to proceed. Narrative performance predates the advent of literature and drama. The theoretical and aesthetic root of my work is narrative performance. Narrative is performance married in the body of the performer (sayer), the text (saying) and the audience (hearer). Narrative depends on the relationship between context—what is capable and what is expected—and the requirement that it engage an audience in a dialogue.

The ability to maintain "textual authority" and the audience's acceptance of my guidance depends on constant feedback. Eye contact and silent cues lets them know that I am actively listening for their input. Identifying the fringes—pulling all towards center—creating a place for the difficult to be heard. Success, according to MacLean, depends on "the power of the text over the players involved."

The challenge is to use the energy generated by anger, first to address issues that incite anger, to seize the thoughts that trigger the anger and to challenge the thoughts in an effort to deflate and redirect the anger. As the sayer, I mitigate the conflict the audience feels because the message is sent in ways that allow people to hear what is being said. Together we begin the process of evaluation and reflection. I hope this will encourage qualitative critical thinking about our situation, turning conflict into energy to create social change.

I strive to create segments that reflect the greater whole. My role as the sayer parallels the roles assigned to the Joker in Boal's process of Theatre of the Oppressed and the Third Party Intervener in conflict resolution.

Askia Toure, lead drummer:

Ritual paved the way for Alice to touch those folks. In many ways it became more than a performance—a conversation and dialogue. She got that permission—like a preacher gets his amen in church. Permission to go deeper, let's talk about this. She made the audience aware of some issues that I know people in Tulsa have never thought about. What was said is often not said in Tulsa—but often felt. That was the gift of [her] saying.

Harriet Harris, who was in the audience that night:

I went willingly into Alice's life through her poetry that eloquently expressed her love, pain, fears, hopes, dreams, and what it feels like to be a revolutionary woman.... Her poems are contributing in all ways—socially, culturally, politically and intellectually...[they] transcend race, religion and political affiliation.

What Next?

Georgia:

Even though we are a deeply troubled society, our future is being redefined by people of capacity and conscience—like Alice. She allowed me to achieve my goal as a community coordinator, to redefine what the spirit of community is about. My community wants her to return.

The workshop with service providers from Planned Parenthood, Resonance, Call Rape and Theatre North inspired the staff at Resonance to work to develop a way to use intervention theater/TO techniques. This would include working with women who are participating in a post-release program that helps

I act as a facilitator of issues, separating the people from the problem.

them determine a positive future. The idea is to bring Alice back to work with our community artists and social-service providers on the philosophy and practice of intervention theater. We were inspired by Alice's skills as a facilitator of social transformation and as a mentor. And, of course, another public performance.

The Last Word

Alice:

I am a narrative performer, giving voice to the sayings, feelings, images and sounds of my people. Together, narrator and audience, we make art. Creation and reflection. Tradition demands that I honor the past. My pledge is to sustain and pass on the cultural evolution representative of a community of people and a community of spirit. I assist in the maintenance of a free society by providing a crucial social intervention, mediating conflicts of class, race and religion.

> *I am the metaphor, crossed with time,*
> *defying traditional dimensions.*
> *Bridging the tri-continental cultural*
> *divides of this, my nation, to nourish*
> *the emotional intellect of my audience.*

Summer 1996

Professional Jaywalker:
Richard Posner on Crossing
from the Studio to Public Art

By Douglas Eby

*Richard Posner has received commissions for major large-scale
works at science museums, federal buildings, urban parks, universities, hospitals and numerous private locations. Here he talks to
Los Angeles-based writer Douglas Eby about public art that is as
important for what it does as for what it is.   —Eds.*

"Public and studio art practices are different disciplines—for
me," claims Richard Posner, a Los Angeles-based visual artist. "The
public-art arena forces an artist to learn how to become an aesthetic
samurai— someone who is visually literate, streetwise and fluent in
both interdisciplinary communication and cross-cultural understanding.
Public-art practice is a process that embraces both 'the public' and
'the art' as equal sides of the same equation."

Richard Posner knows whereof he speaks: a Fulbright Scholar,
and recipient of McKnight, Jerome, and Pollock-Krasner Foundation
Fellowships, Posner has received public commissions for major large-
scale works at science museums, federal buildings, urban parks, universities, hospitals and numerous private locations. His studio work is also
in the permanent collections of The Metropolitan Museum of Art, the
Victoria and Albert Museum, The Smithsonian, The American Embassy
in Stockholm and in numerous private collections. Posner says,

> The completed [public-art] work, shaped by discussion and debate, is as
> important for what it does as for what it is. A Socratic question-and-
> answer process among all members of a design team forms the search for
> the right questions to ask of a particular place, at a specific time, that
> addresses the people who will use it.

Posner notes these critical questions may include:

Does the site currently exist? If so, how is it used? If not, what kinds of intentional and unintentional activities do you foresee happening there? How do you want to feel when you approach, enter and exit the space? Will there be first-time as well as repeat users? Is the location a 'verb'—a kinetic interactive space—or a 'noun'—static and discrete? What is the history of the area? Are there future development plans? What are the daytime and nighttime site conditions? What effect does seasonal, as well as indoor and outdoor temperature, have on the location? What is the acoustic and tactile landscape? Is there pedestrian and vehicular access? What role, if any, does the 'borrowed landscape' play in shaping the project? And, last but not least: what are our budgetary and schedule parameters? How can each of our skills as a visual artist, architect, engineer, landscape architect, etc., be of service?

Posner says he finds that the "ability to navigate the currents and eddies of the public-art administrative process requires the eye of a journalist, the ear of a poet, the hide of an armadillo, the serenity of an airline pilot and the ability to swim." These characteristics, along with a dozen other survival skills, come in handy when, as artist David Ireland and I once listed, any of the following happen:

> **"The public art administrative process requires the eye of a journalist, the ear of a poet, the hide of an armadillo, the serenity of an airline pilot, and the ability to swim."**

1) The wrong artist is selected for the project
2) The client doesn't like the artist or proposal
3) The administrator or client retires from the project
4) The artist, client or fabricator goes broke
5) The project takes three to five years to complete
6) The collaboration is poorly conceived
7) A disagreement between artist, architect and administrator puts the kibosh on the project
8) The project is put on hold or stopped
9) The artist ends up having to economically subsidize the project

10) The administrator urges the artist to be "more considerate" of the project budget.
11) The necessity to be on the road a lot takes its toll.

"Studio-art practice, on the other hand, is an entirely different animal," Posner says. He observes that graduates of academic studio-art programs

> are trained to make statements, more than to ask questions. This should come as no surprise, since most college and university studio-art faculty have little or no experience in doing community-based art. Students learn gallery-world language—its customs and mating rituals, all the trappings of connoisseurship that manifest themselves in statements like, 'This is who I am. This is what I do.' Public comment is neither invited nor welcome. Although ill-prepared for the rigors of Socratic inquiry (and inquisition) that are inherent in public-art practice, each year fresh cadres of unemployed—and unemployable—MFAs struggle to wean themselves from the academic teat and 'do public art.'

Posner notes that some artists are able to make the transition from the studio to the public-art world, including himself:

> I happen to find sustenance and nourishment in both. I suppose this is because professional jay-walking is an occupational necessity for the type of work I do—other occupational requirements are being impervious to insult or rejection. I need the freedom to travel between disciplines, and not worry about critics who act like self-appointed cops of the beat, writing jay-walking tickets for crossing between the lines.

> Ironically, Thomas Jefferson, the patron saint of professional jay-walkers, would be hard pressed to have his designs for Monticello or the University of Virginia realized today with public funds. The reduction, and in many cases elimination, of federal, state and city art budgets have coincided with a national epidemic of 'content-phobia.' Jefferson would find his dictum that 'design activity and political thought are indivisible' is anathema in much of today's art world.

Posner recalls,

For two decades, I realized numerous percent-for-art projects that examined the relationship between American institutions and the people they serve. The very qualities of Jeffersonian "design activity and political thought" these projects were praised for have now fallen in disfavor. As an art consultant recently told me, "Your work is too public, it attracts too many people—including the homeless, aliens and undesirables." An arts administrator, in response to a courthouse proposal that incorporated a three-dimensional representation of the letters T-R-U-T-H, informed me that "The truth is incompatible with the mission of our County Regional Justice Center." Another consultant confided, "Your work is too FM. We want something more AM." I thanked her for providing new insight into the expression "substance abuse."

My current projects are a hybrid of what I once viewed as separate studio and public activities. The first, *Hope Diamond* (*High Performance,* Summer, 1993), was realized in 1992, and I am now preparing the *LIVE NOT ON EVIL Anti-Fascist Theme Park* for exhibition and travel. In both instances, the actual models and drawings in themselves are less important as 'artwork' than as a 'stage set'—an empty vessel, to be filled by public interaction and discourse.

Fall 1996

Toward a New Folk Dance:
Caregivers and Other Partners

By Stuart Pimsler

Noted choreographer Stuart Pimsler and his partner Suzanne Costello devote a major amount of their energy to "Caring for the Caregiver," their workshops and collaborations with healthcare professionals, designed to offer a creative outlet for the stress and complex emotional issues often encountered by doctors, nurses, medical students, hospice staff, social workers, therapists, counselors and administrative personnel. Their company now includes many of these caregivers, who create new work, rehearse and tour regularly with the professionals. We asked Pimsler to write about his work and what draws it all together into what may be viewed as a new dance form.   —Eds.

I made my official debut as an adult choreographer in a sleepy New England town on an extremely hot summer's day. I separated the tiny but enthusiastic audience from the performing area by seating them on the opposite side of a tall chain-link fence. The work was performed in silence but for the ambient noise, which included the slapping of my sneakers on the clay tennis court. I was a graduate student at Connecticut College presenting my first dance/theater work, titled *Net Game*. I enjoyed the gladiator-like feeling suggested by the caged setting, which transformed an unexpected place into a temporary theater. As art, *Net Game* was a modest offering, garnering mixed reviews. One of my esteemed instructors voiced his disappointment at the lack of "breath phrasing." (At the time, his criticism was particularly confusing for me since I spent most of my time in *Net Game* running all over the court until I was gasping for air.)

Twenty years later, I can only speculate whether my passion was enough to balance the naïveté of my first dance. However, I am convinced that my tennis-court dance did foreshadow many of the aesthetic concerns that I have continued to refine throughout my career.

My interest in familiar, ordinary and predictable locations and their potential for being transformed has since been realized in a variety of works by my company, Stuart Pimsler Dance & Theater (SPDT). In *McKinley's Carnation* (1992)—a site-specific performance work on the grounds of Ohio's capitol building—a cast of 54 individuals, ages 7-86, including third graders, body builders and senior citizens, distilled idiosyncratic historic facts about the Ohio Statehouse. *Rest/Stop* (1994) transported audiences on school buses to five different outdoor locations in Gainesville, Florida. Ticket holders and random onlookers observed performances along a nature walk, at a rest stop, inside two rooms of the Florida Motel and its adjacent swimming pool, on the verandah of a retirement home and at a man-made beach in a vast parking lot. An intergenerational cast of 35 individuals offered commentary about "travel over a lifetime." An empty, sandblasted public swimming pool in Allentown, Pennsylvania, was the site of *Out Of Our Hands* (1995), a work for four dancers and four nurses. All of these works have stirred new ways of looking at locales that have often been taken for granted, forgotten or even unknown. These site-specific performance works have extended the experience of creating and performing outside of the theater into the actual communities of their origins.

> ## Creating...in community settings...has often felt like a new kind of folk dance.

The counterpart to my investigations of art staged in real places has been a fascination with real people and the spectacle of the everyday. My partner Suzanne Costello and I created *Glory Portraits,* our first full-length work in 1981. Its premise set the American family against the nationalistic politics of the nuclear age. At that time, Suzanne and I had been living together and working together for two years, sharing our space with other artists in a downtown New York City loft. Our extended family was our loftmates and company members. In *Glory Portraits,* Suzanne and I became instant parents by incorporating three dolls in the work. (Suzanne and I have since had a daughter, Sophia Cecile, who is four years old.) At the personal layer of meaning, *Glory Portraits* was about Suzanne and me, two artists as a contemporary couple struggling with our own personal politics. In the final scene, ten couples of varying descriptions left their audience seats and danced with the six SPDT company members.

Real life and real people were again focal points in our next full-length work, *House/Home* (1985). Highly personal and driven by child-hood memories, *House/Home* also included a cast of community per-formers joined with our company ensemble. Each company member ballroom-danced slowly with a community performer who undressed his/her partner. In the work's final tableau, the company became live nude sculptures resting on their knees atop five tables (where five tele-visions had been), watched from chairs by the community performers.

The desire and need to make art connected to the stuff of real life, with real people, has continued to drive our work. Creating away from traditional stages, in community settings or on stage with commu-nity performers has often felt like a new kind of folk dance—a type of social dance with a movement vocabulary that is redefined for each project and often created by the participants. The style of this work often has an awkwardness as well as a generous, emotional abandon and a simple, human elegance. It allows participants to connect in deeply intimate ways. Creating performance work with community performers extends the experience of art outside of the theater into people's lives. It offers people an opportunity to make art for which, like the doing of most activities, there can be no substitute. Working with communities has given us the chance to extend our aesthetic belief that everyday life can be a rich source of creative expression.

Recently, the community of healthcare providers has been a par-ticular population of real people with whom we have formed an extraordinary connection. During the past five years, Suzanne and I have worked throughout the U.S. and abroad with doctors, nurses, therapists, hospice staff and other caregivers. Our "Caring for the Caregiver" program includes movement/expression workshops and commissioned performance works that provide caregivers with cre-ative outlets for the emotional stresses encountered in their work. These workshops begin with discussions reflecting the issues—such as loss and grief—that participants confront in their work. In the work-shops, caregivers explore through movement and voice, memories and stories, the concepts of support, trust and release. For individuals who confront loss daily, being held by a colleague or telling a patient's story can be a powerful experience.

In retrospect, there was an extremely poetic connection for our introduction to the healthcare community. During a southern tour in 1992, Suzanne and I, with our company, were asked to present a series of residency activities as sponsored by our cohosts, The University of Florida and Florida Arts Celebration. One of our activities included a workshop for physical, recreational and occupational therapists at the university's Shands Hospital. The workshop atmosphere was extremely charged, and, as the residency week progressed, we continued to meet with more caregivers from the Gainesville community. Simultaneously, we were touring what has become a signature work for our company, *Swimming To Cecile* (1988). This work, dedicated to my mother, who was killed in a car accident when I was 15 years old, is a personal meditation on living with loss. The subject matter of *Cecile* was all-too-familiar territory for those caregivers attending our performance at the end of the residency. Our work, with its embrace of real-life matters, brought us to this intersection with the emotional availability and knowledge of the caregiver. This experience led us to subsequent projects with the caregiver community in Gainesville and the establishment of an Arts in Medicine Program at Shands Hospital. It marked the beginning of a new relationship for us with the caregiving community throughout the U.S.

We continue to broaden our making of work with the healthcare community, which includes performance works created with and performed by caregivers. Last season's *Still Life With Rose* (1996) was performed by twelve Columbus caregivers and inspired by their personal histories. *Still Life* focused on their relationships with their patients as well as their rage, fear, pain and hopes about their workplace. Our company has subsequently expanded to include this dedicated group of twelve caregivers who rehearse weekly, usually at the end of their daily shifts. There is an emotional power in their directness and commitment. Audiences continue to comment that they are deeply moved by their simple elegance. *Still Life* was presented as the closing work during our 1996 home season and will be toured this season, including a National Performance Network residency in Tucson, Arizona.

For our dance/theater works, caregivers have been ideal partners, as they are eager to express the emotional complexities precipitated by their work and their workplace. In collaborating with caregivers, at home and on tour, we have been deeply affected by their personal wisdom and strength. The caregivers' influence is also evident in two recent SPDT stage works. *Saba* (1994) pairs four audience members with four company members and is in memory of our friend who died of AIDS the year before the birth of our daughter. In *Schvitz* (1996), I talk and dance with my deceased grandfather, father and uncle in a steam room as we bemoan the twisted pleasure and tradition of sweating. This persistent desire to make art connected to an emotional underbelly has been encouraged and confirmed through our relationship with caregivers. One healthcare provider described our work this way: "You ask us to seek out movement that comes from inside, that comes from an experience or that comes from something known. When you ask people to do that, you don't get a trickle, you get a torrent."

Out Of This World/The Life After Life Project is our newest collaboration with the national healthcare community. *Out Of This World* will be presented in New York City, Pittsburgh, Tucson and Columbus over the next two years. It will join healthcare providers in each city with other community participants to create and perform a new work inspired by a collective vision of afterlife. This new project begins at the place where last season's *Still Life With Rose* ended—exploring the caregivers' personal belief systems and coping strategies for surviving daily losses. Our early rehearsals have included vivid portrayals of near-death experiences and descriptions of the other world. Caregivers/performers have talked about their visions for getting to "the other side" as: "riding on a big yellow bus," "like going down to the basement as a kid, looking over my shoulder," "holding my breath five times," "in slow motion," and "alone." Some of the participating caregivers have countered these prosaic projections of afterlife by firmly stating that "dead is dead."

As our new project promises to look through potential windows to the other world(s), our partnering with caregivers feels ever more strongly connected to *this* world. Our new folk dance continues in and with communities—making art where it lives.

Winter 1996

CWT#3: Making *City Water Tunnel #3*

By Marty Pottenger

*Marty Pottenger is an artist, carpenter and contractor with
more than 20 years of experience in performance art and the
construction business. Her New York City multimedia project
City Water Tunnel #3 tells the story of the planning, building
and financing of the largest non-defense public-works project
in the Western Hemisphere. Created in collaboration with the
people and organizations who are building this five-billion-dollar
tunnel project, Pottenger's artwork includes an Obie-winning solo
theatrical production, gallery exhibitions, performance and video
installation at the tunnel worksites, weekend fairs, story-swapping
circles and water-tunnel-related activities for young people. City
Water Tunnel #3 arose from the stories of the people building
the tunnel. As storyteller, interlocutor, reporter and guide, Pottenger wove together interviews with tunnel workers and her own
distilled narrative, adding images, video, graphs, tunnel objects and
ambient-sound recordings mixed with an original score by Steve
Elson. High Performance asked Marty Pottenger to reveal the
process of City Water Tunnel #3 in all its grandeur, complexity
and intimacy. The italicized sections are from the script.   —Eds.*

The water man from Phoenix said: "You have to recognize we're a
closed system—the earth is a closed system—three-fourths of it is covered with water. Only a small percentage of that is drinkable…the rest
brackish. The challenge is universal. Consequently, it being a closed system,
we're drinking the same water that Napoleon drank. We're drinking the
same water that Archimedes drank. We're drinking the same water that
Galileo drank. So you just have to recognize that, put it into that context,
and realize you can only do so much with it." It rained tonight as Galileo's
tears boiled hot in my Maxwell House. Usually I hate instant, but this
tasted different, richer, more…rebellious. Insistent instant. It had never
crossed my mind that I could be sipping the sweat and salt from the
Inquisition's nastiness over 300 years ago.

Leaning back, I smell France and Marie Antoinette's cake. I take another sip, blowing first to cool, steam rising, curling back in on itself, whooshing the warm brown liquid around in my mouth, savoring images of Joan, the Maid of Orleans, dawn, head bowed, her newly metaled knee down on the ground, resting in the dew that covers the battlefield, her forehead wet with holy water. Of Melissa Etheridge in the pouring rain on stage in Texas, rain on her face, sweat on her upper lip. Of my grandmother Marjorie, now dead for 21 years. Her tiny Chicago countertop kitchen, the drops of water collecting on the wall next to the stove water boiling our three-minute eggs as the black-and-white TV fills with pictures of women in Vietnam, stretched out in rice paddies…not sleeping.

Most of the coffee's in me now, down and inside the parts and passages that make up me. Where does the black of coffee go? I think of the East River, the Atlantic Ocean, my eighth-grade cloud charts, of Phyllis Schlafly and Gloria S., of mothers whose water breaks too far from help…holding the cup, its curve a circle…of all my nieces—Jacquelyn, Madeleine, Lydia, Jessica and Beckia. The last of the liquid cool now, I drink, letting the possibilities of past, present and future swim, float, dive and pool together, as if time were just a part of it and water…was the heart.

The performance had just ended when a young woman from the first row walked up to me, said, "I'm John Cunningham's daughter," and put her arms around me for a cry. A week later, her mother Pat came with her best friend from childhood, bringing with them a photo album filled with pictures of the same daughter's birth, and a photo of John laughing, looking very much alive—leaning against a rail, arms flung round his daughter and his wife, with an ocean stretching out behind them. John was killed on the job four months back, bringing to 22 the number of people killed working on the third water tunnel since 1970. The performance was dedicated to him.

After the performance the three of us—Pat, who had divorced John and remarried years ago, her friend Toby, and a friend of mine—sat together for almost two hours listening to "John" stories, sharing the photos one by one. John who left school in Ireland when he was 12 to work the farm after his father died, oldest of eight; John who worked for 18 years as a miner in NYC, going to night school at Fordham to get a master's in economics and political history; John who got his parish priest in Ireland to write Fordham that the school John attended had burned down with all its records, so they'd just have to accept his word that John graduated from high school; John who 20 years ago ran against Local 147's union-backed slate on safety issues, lost and went to work for the Bureau of Land and Mines as a safety inspector for 20 years; John who had just retired (20-year pension) from BLM and decided to finish out the two years left to 20 in Local 147 to get the tunnel worker's pension plus full benefits for silicosis (black-lung disease); John who died four months into that last two years at 19B, falling off the top of the Mole where he was changing a lightbulb overhead; John who "loved mining," a "good man," "safety conscious," "loved to laugh," "kept to himself" and "who never told much about his job" to his family.

Pat thanked me for showing her more about John and his work than she had known, telling me that last Saturday her second husband was at his synagogue with the rabbi, who had just seen a performance of *City Water Tunnel #3*. It was Rosh Hashanah, the Jewish New Year, which includes a ritual called Tashlik where one's sins are thrown into a body of water. In her sermon, she spoke about what the show had meant to her, about work, meaningful work, about people figuring out how to stick together. As the rabbi encouraged people to go see the performance, Pat's husband jumped up and said, "Hey, that show is about my wife's ex-husband's job." Which is how Pat heard about the performance.

The Tunnel and Its Tales

New York City's third water tunnel—64 miles long, 800 feet down, 24 feet in diameter—is bringing water to nine million people. The tunnel is being built by more than 1,000 people, most of them pink- and white-collar workers living in the most diverse population in the world. I have been gathering their stories. Their diversity is reflected in hundreds of interviews with tunnel workers (Local 147), operating engineers (Locals 14 and 15), city and state politicians, general contracting companies, upstate and watershed farmers, financial analysts, bond traders and buyers, insurers, and employees of the Department of Environmental Protection (DEP), material supply companies and more.

Working both in the world of construction and the world of art, I've learned something about these stories of humor, challenge, struggle, mistakes and triumph: Amidst the differences and segregation in any group of workers, lifelong friendships are forged as people build relationships while they are building something big.

The size of the tunnel and the scope of its labor allow us to consider the connections and the fragility of our relationships to each other and to the planet. It powerfully reveals the ability of people in our society to work together, to continue to cross lines of race, gender and class to accomplish tremendous goals. Joining the power and vision of art with the power and vision of the people who are making the tunnel a reality offers all of us the opportunity to consider the connections they have among themselves, and to glimpse the tremendous impact that their individual and collective labor has on the world around them.

Sugar Story

Roosevelt Island Valve Chamber, 170 feet down, pouring the east wall of the Main Chamber, huge mother fuc—oh—excuse me—concrete form. Bottom kicks out 'cause of the weight. Whole form—which is there to get the concrete to hold a shape until it dries—pulls away, concrete slumps down, 20 elephants worth, big elephants. Contractor has a shit fit, sends two guys to the only supermarket on Roosevelt Island, buying out all the sugar the store had—I still remember them racing back to the job with shopping carts filled with boxes, bags of sugar, all the men dumping it into the mix, shoveling with one hand, tearing open cartons with the other, throwing sugar everywhere. Sugar keeps concrete from setting. Keeps the load "live" longer, so the concrete can get scooped up and thrown out before it hardens, which would mean days and weeks of teeth-rattling, cost-overrunning, job-delaying jackhammering. Granulated, powdered, white, brown, confectioner's…sweetest job I ever worked on.

Planning: The Steep Side of the Learning Curve

CWT#3, like any big job, started with planning. Months of time were needed to explore possibilities and build relationships in a way I'd never had the chance to before. The initial planning work—30 hours of taping interviews, transcribing, videotaping, attending the four-day American Water Works Association's National Conference, touring the Department of Environmental Protection offices, union halls, construction sites, valve chambers, water filtration plants, reservoirs, contacting museum designers and staff—was greater than entire performances I'd done start to finish. My partners included foundations, arts organizations, performance presenters, government agencies, unions, artists and tunnel workers. They participated in the creation of *CWT#3* through art surveys, artist residencies, workshops, joint public activities and meetings.

To give some idea of what it means to get as far as I did during this planning process, here are some of the rocky shoals *CWT#3* had to steer through:

a) Obtaining and maintaining from a minimum of three parties (involving at least 15 individuals) ongoing permission for access to the various sites and offices.

b) Juggling suspicions and concerns as to where *CWT#3's primary* loyalty lay—the DEP commissioner, employees or management, the general contractor, the union members, the union's officers or one union over another union?

c) Was I a tabloid or TV reporter trying to get a quick'n'easy, dirty story? or…

d) A woman activist trying to get into one of the trade unions or simply trying to bust someone for something? or…

e) A secret OSHA safety inspector ready to pounce and file a huge lawsuit? or…

f) A spy from the other general contractor working on the tunnel trying to snap photos of the one-of-a-kind $450,000 jumbo drill, which could cause the general contractor who designed and paid for it to lose out on the next $220-million-dollar contract? or…

g) A klutz who was going to trip over a pump hose and fall down a 700-foot shaft, making headlines in tomorrow's *New York Post*?

These are all very real, possible and serious concerns for each party involved. I found navigating all this challenging, but also fun.

Underneath a few tons of the accumulated debris that is now part of any big project in the late 20th century are really great people who are eager to talk about themselves and their jobs and to share what they know, and excited to work with an artist making a project about something they care a lot about. The time spent in audience development became a chance to build trust among us.

Part of that process included editing a cassette of a few collected stories and giving those out to individuals I wanted to work with, each time transforming slightly suspicious, always busy and overworked individuals into eager, excited advocates for the art project and for getting the word out to others. I was able to collect photos that workers had taken themselves, integrate them into *CWT#3*, and return high-quality reproductions back to the individuals in new forms—slides, color Xeroxes, prints, photo CD's—to everyone's excitement.

Extending the traditional intent of audience demographic surveys (a requirement of the Arts Partners grant from the Lila Wallace-Reader's Digest Fund), questions put attention on the role of art in each respondent's life, asking them to recall an arts event that really moved them, as well as one that they didn't like, and why. These and a few more questions—like "Did you take any art classes in school or on your own?"—were meant to call to mind their past and present relationship to art as *something they themselves did at one time* rather than *something that other people do somewhere far from here*. My goal there was to offer the individual a chance to locate him- or herself early on as an art maker (current or former).

Most personally and artistically satisfying was to work with this tunnel-construction community over the six months of the planning process. Time after time, people offered me the name of someone who's "a great storyteller—oh—he'll tell you stories." One resident engineer, after he listened to my demo tape, told me about making his own ambient-sound recordings. ("You've got some great sounds there. My sounds aren't as good. You sure did a nice job.") Engineers gave me rides from one site to another; timekeepers handed out my surveys to their own staff; receptionists got permission from their supervisors to talk with me; technicians took me on tours of the quality-assurance laboratory; department heads hooked me up with now-retired workers who mentored them when they were starting out; elected town supervisors had me over to dinner with their families; retired upstate sandhogs suggested I come back for a weekend and have a "roundtable on the watershed issues" with them. Even those in the bureaucracy around the project did so much more than they do for any newspaper, college student or tourist. The idea of helping an artist was one that interested everyone, even if it took a little time. My challenge was to keep my learning curve short enough so I didn't get in folks' way as they tried to juggle their own lives and jobs building Tunnel #3.

White Oats—from Mike, Chief Engineer, Tunnel #3

Once we were down in a tunnel—must've been up at High-bridge—and we couldn't get this leak to stop. Water was coming in pretty good: underground stream, we get them all the time. We tried everything, stuffing it with oakum, caulk, concrete. After a bit, whatever we put in would come right out with a rush of clean water right behind it. Finally we got some oatmeal, good old-fashioned oatmeal, and stuck that in there. Oatmeal swelled up and gave us just enough time to fill it in with a chemical grout. Water stopped and we finished, packed up and left. About a year later we had to come back to check on something. As we walked to where the leak had been, there was something growing all along the floor of the tunnel, two, three feet high. The chemical grout we had used was nitrogen based, so the nitrogen had fertilized the oatmeal and since there wasn't any sun, this was 700 feet down, the oats came out albino. White Oats.

To Make Art about Someone Else Is an Opportunity to Make Art with Someone Else

My research and experience told me that human beings who work on a project as big as the third water tunnel—which is bringing a resource as critical and poetic as water, and involves activity as human and dangerous as construction work—would make art about it. It's human nature. Work itself can have an integrity, separate from the surrounding institutions and companies. From the beginning, I wanted to make sure that openings were created that allowed the art being made by the tunnel's working people to have voice and visibility.

Only scratching the surface with *CWT#3*, I was able, with lots of help, to locate the photographs of three people who work on the third water tunnel: a concrete inspector's intimate black-and-white portraits of the sandhogs and DEP people; a resident engineer's formal, stunning color photographs of the construction and equipment; and an insurance company safety inspector's lyrical color photos of the construction work and the people doing it. All of these were part of an exhibit in the galleries of the two theaters that showed the performance. And much more: photos, cartoons, de/re-constructed "official" DEP memos, scratched memo-poems and jokes, graffiti—most of it now buried under thousands of tons of concrete—work totems/mementos (rocks, test borings, boots worn every day for a five-year Valve Chamber job) and the stories, told and retold. They exist as poignant and powerful examples of the role art simply plays in each of our lives. The second gallery installation had boots, hard hats, work gloves—all very muddy and some still wet—delivered by Paddy: "What do ya want this junk for, Marty?" And Ed: "Wait 'til Chipper finds out we gave you his hat."

The performance project also included people's art through my retelling of their stories—the particular events that they had made into "stories"; the humor and perspective in their art in the telling of them; the poetry in their descriptions. Not included, but out there, are several short stories, books, partial books—autobiographies, detective adventure tales, fiction, humor (some published)—that different sandhogs, concrete inspectors, resident engineers, and operating engineers are writing about their work; homemade and semi-professional videotape documentation (some scored to popular music) of the work; and much, much more. For a weekend fair we set up a video monitor and played some of these tapes continuously.

Long, wonderful audience discussions after each performance at Dance Theater Workshop included any of the tunnel-working people in the audience, often bringing in their wives, husbands, fiancees and children. People got to meet them for themselves, ask questions, hear each other talk about what they love about the work, what they hate. The people working on the tunnel were shocked time and time again at how interested what they called "regular people" were in the water-tunnel work. Most nights the discussion ended with a solid burst of impromptu applause for those tunnel workers present. The audience also got to participate and watch the relationships that the sandhogs and I had built with each other. Me, a lesbian carpenter/performance artist, and them, members of the only construction union that has successfully kept women out of the union entirely. Lots of teasing went back and forth, allowing each of us to express our affection, exasperation and pride in what *CWT#3* and the third tunnel had become.

Stuie—Sandhog retired after 34 years

It's been a custom among us sandhogs for at least the last 100 years—farther back than that, I can't remember—to see that every man was doing his fair share down in the hole. The best way we come up with is to paint his boot white. If he's sleeping—taking a little nap, sometimes things get a little slow down there if they're fixing something or waiting for something—we paint his boots white while he's asleep. Then we get to say, "Guess you was sleeping there, weren't you?"

Where Can the Audience Be in Charge?

The video installation, with a 40-minute video directed and edited by Mary Ellen Strom, allows some of the stories to be recorded by the storytellers themselves, even as it documents the participants involved in a public-works project of this magnitude. People who have worked on the third water tunnel for 10, 20, 30 years got to "meet" each other on the videotape, which traveled as a video installation to the various construction sites and DEP headquarters in Queens. This video and installation offered a chance for the people working on the tunnel, and their coworkers in the DEP offices, to have a completely self-determined relationship to the art being offered, and it used video, a more familiar medium than live performance. The installation was designed as a five-foot-high pipe that could be viewed from either end. The videotape would play if you placed your hand on top of a tin hand-shape mounted on a Plexiglas circle. The videotape would stop if you took your hand away. The idea was that someone could watch a few minutes or 40 minutes, on their way to the bathroom or during lunch hour. Stories they heard from the video sparked conversations with coworkers, sparked stories of their own, sparked further exploration into *CWT#3*. The video installation traveled to the worksites in the weeks leading up to the performances, offering people a first-hand opportunity to become familiar with the project and consider coming to the live theater performance.

On-site, lunch-hour performances were scheduled to come in between the video-installation site visits and the theatrical performance. Challenges forced scheduling them after the first run, which allowed word-of-mouth. The performances on the construction sites were scheduled in the hoghouses (above-ground trailers with showers, lockers, washers and dryers). The DEP lunchtime performances were in a conference room at Lefrak City, the workplace of more than 3,000 DEP employees from hundreds of departments. Construction performances were full houses. Lefrak City performances—an audience who we knew already went to some theater—were poorly attended. Even coworkers going out between the first and second performance of a day, and telling their coworkers that it was the best thing they had ever seen, had little impact. Interesting.

My working understanding is that the reasons for this are three-fold. First off, it's related to the hopelessness, sense of exploitation and alienation that individuals who work for large corporations/city agencies feel about their jobs and their employers (DEP had canceled some annual employee events in the last few years due to lack of interest). Secondly, the lunchtime performances were advertised primarily through interoffice e-mail, a medium some people feel fascinated by and other people feel overwhelmed by. Also, e-mail, while one excellent way to advertise, squarely places the "identity" of the performances as DEP domain. That is very appropriate, as DEP was one of our art partners, but I think PR that spoke directly to the employees—banners by the elevators, flyers at nearby shops and restaurants, notices in union newsletters—would have made a significant difference.

The last place to look when thinking about the low attendance—four performances averaging about 65% capacity—is the tremendous emotional risk that going to live performance brings up for most people (including those of us who do it). On this last reason:

I have noticed that being at a "bad" performance feels horrible in a way nothing else does. It can feel like you are personally being tortured. When a live performance is good, it has the potential to truly transform one forever. To create a memory that will be treasured, drawn on like water from a well forever—that is humbling. But when it is "bad" (define for yourself), it is close to unbearable in ways that movies, TV and music just don't seem to engender. I have learned a lot about the role of an audience and audience member from doing *CWT#3*. My respect and appreciation has deepened. It is a gift to us, the art-makers, that they come and bring their most vulnerable, intelligent, open selves.

Natasha—DEP

Marty Marty, don't take my picture, oh no, no, no, don't take it now, I don't look so good. No, no, why you want a picture of me. I not pretty. I'm too old. Get the pretty girls. Go take pictures of the pretty young girls. They pretty, young, not me.

My job. In Russia, I am aircraft engineer. Here [gesturing], all us women, from Russia, from Ukraine, from Poland. We meet here. We like each other. We become friends. We all engineers in our own countries. Mechanical, Physical, Civil, [gesturing to self] Aircraft…I think perhaps the hardest. Here we are all Associate Engineering Technicians. We help our engineers. We coordinate and keep track of information. We love our engineers. Good boys! Good boys our engineers! For my job I keep track of everything that happens. For this project—City Water Tunnel #3. All written information comes to me. Anything written, it comes to me. Contracts, Change Orders, subcontractor's memos, letters, post-its. If it's written and has to do with third water tunnel—it comes to me and I keep track. Not on computer, but in Log. I write down everything, give number and file it. We have to know everything, record everything. We need to know what problem we have and how we solve problem. Did we solve problem? Not just for us, but for the future. For five years, ten years, twenty—five hundred years from now. We need to know. It's very important. Do not forget. I come from country with Chernobyl. I think of them sometimes—five hundred years.

You look so good Marty. So pretty. You look good, like artist, all

dressed in black. For your job, you look lovely! I too try to dress profession-
ally, for professional job. You like? Marty. You are so pretty. You look so
good! Marty...you...should...wear...lipstick! You no like lipstick?

Called to Account: Policies, Ethics, Morals

   Natasha, a Russian engineer with the Department of Environmental
Protection, had become a friend over the three years I was researching
and working on CWT#3. Natasha. I went to talk with her about my plan
to have her and her words in the show as one of my characters. "Why
you want to do me Marty? Why me? Do
somebody else. My accent...it's too big.
Don't make fun of me! All those peo-
ple...why you want to make fun of me?
You my friend." I knew, even without
names, her coworkers would affectionately
recognize her from the character, and
returning to the workplace "do" the char-
acter—thick, lovely Russian accent and all.
I knew that without a context (the entire
performance and its base of love and
respect) she would find it humiliating. My request/offer to perform the
character for her repeatedly met no response.

To make art with communities, new rules have to be made, rules that require and rely on trust, integrity and honesty.

   Accountability in Community Performance Work. Making the
long trip out to where she worked several times before the perfor-
mance so we could talk in person. So the discussions would happen
on her turf. That any pull on my part to gloss over the effects of what
I did on her life and relationships at work would have to "answer to
her" in person. To not be so sure of my intentions that I silence her
real voice, picking and choosing only the "parts" of her that I want to
make use of. Editing the stories from interviews with a stern careful
eye toward the impacts on the people.

   I went to Natasha's boss Mike Greenberg, the chief engineer for the
third tunnel, for ideas and help. He was a key supporter of the art project
CWT#3. He suggested I meet with Natasha's husband, also an engineer
at the DEP, and offered to come with me. The two of us set off and spent
the better part of an hour trying to convince him that he would love the

show, that Natasha must see it, that the chief engineer would buy them tickets and go with them himself. We got nowhere.

Spending the time, as long as it takes, on each project to address issues of accountability. Setting up a formal "policy" (for myself) of respect for the people I'm working with. There were days when I failed as much as I succeeded. Making art can feel so passionate; it felt like it tore my heart out on occasion to have to put my photos on the shelf because a piece of rope, or a piece of equipment in the corner of the photo revealed a potential safety violation. I survived childhood—a very tough home and my own fears that I might be a lesbian—by self-denial, public denial, deftly but barely escaping different institutions' attempts to censor/isolate/silence me. Many of us, when young and in a position of powerlessness, did what people do in that situation—beg, borrow and steal. To make art with communities, new rules have to be made, rules that require and rely on trust, integrity and honesty.

I returned to Natasha a few days later, opening night three days away. I had come to a painful decision. To say what I hadn't been willing to say until now. To offer to pull Natasha from CWT#3 if she asked me to. And to make the offer as relaxedly as possible. Natasha. Her character, for me as writer and performer, was the heart of the performance. "Natasha—who's not afraid to care." Not having her in the show...only one other person/character meant as much to me and the artistic construction of CWT#3.

What is too high a cost? Colleagues talked to me about decisions they've had to make. To fire this person. To not use this person's costumes, when they had worked their butt off to make them. Changing music, adding music, cutting music. We talked about "always making decisions in favor of the art." That the art had to come first. I asked them if they had ever decided differently. They had. And now in retrospect, did they think that they had made a mistake? What does it mean to "always make decisions in favor of the art"? Are people first? Is art first?

Natasha didn't answer me. I asked if I could show her the four-minute story. No answer. Was she giving me permission in her silence? Was she too polite, too kind, too timid to say "No"? Had she not made a final decision?

I stood there. Filled with wanting to believe that her silence was assent. We just looked at each other for a bit and then she started busying herself with the papers around her desk. I looked down and saw, back under her desk, the pile of high-heeled shoes that I had so wanted a photo of…she had begged me not to take it…sure that it would be documenting some unprofessional behavior on her part. I have no photo of the shoes, just a lovely short story about them that isn't in the performance. What gives me the right to cross these boundaries? What code, what policies do I set for myself? To whom am I accountable? Who repairs the rips and tears?

Natasha finally saw CWT#3, during the lunchtime performances at her workplace on the last day. I couldn't make myself look at her, sitting there slightly to the left in the first row of a conference room. The blinds drawn and covered with black cloth, the portable theater lights on a dimmer, Steve's solo cello music like a friend to me. She was within my physical reach for most of the performance. Later, my dear, wonderful tech crew said they had been, each of them, silently wishing me, directing me, sending me in her direction…each of us knowing what Natasha meant to me and to CWT#3. At the end, Natasha and me both crying, "Marty…you captured me. You got me. You got all of us, it's so beautiful…you framed us perfectly. Grace. Leah. It is so full of love. I love you…you…and I must hate you…look…what you do to me…you make me so emotional, I can't go work now…you ruined me! I love you, Marty. I love you."

Staying in touch when it's "over." Making sure there is enough time/going slow enough/planning time in throughout the project to allow yourself and those involved to assess, express, experience and address.

I owe Natasha a call.

Old guy down in tunnel 23b

Girls. Girls. Hi girls. You need masks. We got silicosis down here. Like asbestosis. From breathing the dust when we blast the rock. You don't want to breathe that. Oh no. My dad. That'd kill you. You need masks. I'll go get 'em. We got any masks?! We got any masks for these girls?! Any masks! I'll go get 'em, you girls stay right here. A couple of masks for your protection. From the dust. Could give you silicosis0 ell, not in such a short time, but most of us, the old timers, you're down here for most of your life. Me? My mask? Oh, I'm so old, but you're still young. I'm dead already.

Concrete Benefits: Thinking About How the Art Can "Move a Community Forward"

I knew from the beginning that one of my goals in *CWT#3* was to improve the safety consciousness and practice of the people working on the third water tunnel. During the research, I asked questions about safety, listening to people's issues and stories, as one way of offering resources. I made sure to have the first story in the body of the performance be about safety, and to address safety throughout the show.

Working in construction for 20 years, I have struggled with not wearing important safety equipment because of haste and the influence of male working-class culture—not believing you are important/valuable/worth enough to protect. One of my strategies was to make evident, through the performance and every aspect of *CWT#3*, the preciousness of all the people working; through making visible their love (usually unspoken) for each other, and through the quality of the materials/card/production/video/text/set of *CWT#3*.

Another opportunity existed, which was to use the announcement cards that accompany a performance/art event as a way of getting a powerful image(s) out to a community. Realizing that one image can be treasured forever, or thrown out in the two seconds it takes to look at it and walk to the wastebasket, I wanted to make that two seconds count and offer something that at least had the possibility of being used as "desk art" at work, or "refrigerator art" at home. Throughout *CWT#3*, I kept in mind the widest notion of audience, including the working people's families, neighbors and friends. In the end, those wider categories of people did indeed come to the performances and gallery exhibit. I wanted to open up the possibility of deepening ties between individuals' work lives, family lives and social lives, remembering the deep ignorance and silence in the communities I grew up in between what our fathers did and our daily lives.

There are two ends to a tunnel. A 100-year history of bullying and besting exists between NYC and the people who live where the water comes from—the Catskills and Delaware Reservoir System. NYC has had its way on almost every occasion. A current battle over water treatment vs. land use has been raging for the last 20 years. Traveling upstate to meet, interview, tape and video town supervisors, librarians, trout-fishing guides and grocers, I made sure to make a place in the performance for Upstaters to be heard, even to speak a bit of their minds to the NY'ers seeing the show. *CWT#3* has since been produced at two upstate arts centers to audiences filled with retired miners and their families, local politicians, NY'ers with second homes and members of the tightly knit community of mountain people.

Twenty-two people have been killed building the third water tunnel since 1970. Founding a memorial fund was an opportunity to use art to directly affect a community. It will finance the installation of a drinking fountain/sculpture in honor of the people who have died. We raised $20,000 at the Benefit Performance and will be fundraising the rest with an awards/in memoriam dinner in late 1997. Initial research accidentally led me to realize that it was unlikely that the various groups working on the tunnel—long, complex histories of competition, cooperation, co-optation—would be able to come together to fund such a memorial. I, as an artist, could act as the neutral, interested outsider and help this community realize a goal of their own: a public monument that makes their invisible, underground labor and sacrifice visible to the rest of us.

Pete—Safety man for general contractor

What are you doing here again? Cheez…you're like a bad penny! We can't get rid of you. Listen. I gotta explain something you clearly don't understand! We're trying to work here! Lemme give you an example. For instance, I'm sitting here holding [gesture] a $90 insurance claim, unpaid, which I submitted for some guy who stubbed his toe six months ago…on a $220-million-dollar job! Jeezch! And you come waltzing in here with your dancing or your drama…whatever it is you're doing—Cheezch! What did I ever do to you??

Are you girls Irish? You look like you could be Irish.

"Goddamn, I've Cut It Six Times and It's Still Too Short!"
(carpenter's joke)

Working on this community-art project was, on many days, a matter of: getting up, spending all day doing things that I could tell I was either bad or terrible at, going to bed; getting up the next day, spending all day doing things that I could tell I was either bad or terrible at, going to bed. Over the course of *CWT#3*, I got to make bad errors in judgment. I tried things that totally backfired. I lost, if not misplaced, a few people's friendships. I had more arguments than I've had with anyone in my life, outside of my parents and intimate partners. I also made more friends, learned more important things, sharpened my judgment on a thousand things, and reached farther for the full realization of my biggest artistic vision than ever before in my life. I will never be the same. If you're spending most of your time doing things that you already know how to do, why are you doing them? There were many days when I could barely stand to look at how many mistakes I'd made, how ineptly I'd handled something, how bossy I had been with someone, how unprepared I was for what needed to happen, how much that impacted on other people, how intimidated I was, how inarticulate. And then…new day…more art to be made. Being a carpenter for so many years helped me keep perspective. I already knew from years of mistakes, a good carpenter is someone who knows how to make their mistakes work for them.

John—Hoghouse man, Local 147, Shaft 26B

That's John, John O'Flaherty. A lot of people will tell you Flaherty, but no, that's not it. It's O—Flaherty. That's O.'. F.L.A.H.E.R.T.Y. O'Flaherty. I've been a miner for over 40-some years. Started up in Boston, working on their harbor tunnel. My brother was killed standing almost right next to me just about. Ye're asking me for a high point or a low point…I guess that'd be one or the other…depending on how you're speaking of it. That's when I came down to New York City, hooked up with Local 147. Been in this racket ever since. It's a good union. 147. It's been good to me. Tunnelworkers. We do all the work that's under 50 feet. All the construction work. Sandhogs, yeah, that's the nickname for us. Oh—if it was ever derogatory, we've lost track of that a long time ago. The Brooklyn

Bridge—she's our job. The caissons I mean. All the tunnels—Holland, Brooklyn Battery. The subways, most of the sewers. That's all our work. Anything below 50 feet, that's where we come in.

No it's not an easy job. If the "sili-" "sili-"—oh what do you call the breathing thing? If that don't get you—all the miners have it—your ears are shot from the noise. It's very noisy down there. Your joints are aching from the damp, it's very damp down there. If you make it to 60, that's all you can expect. No, no, she's not going to let you go easy.

"You Go Down with Ten Human Beings, You Come Up with Ten Human Beings." *(Dennis O'Neil, shift boss…only he said "men")*

It is not exactly unheard-of for there to be significant struggles for power and control in any situation, when a large amount of money is involved. *CWT#3*, in this respect, was no different. Once a substantial grant was awarded, relationships changed and I entered a period of education as an artist/producer working within a traditional arts-presenter culture. As battles for control became evident, I spent the next three months attempting to reach resolution with my key presenter via discussion and/or written proposals. Night after night I was up 'til 5 a.m., drafting new proposals, new letters of clarification, only to go to my job the next day living off the combination of fear and fury at what was happening. I finally decided that it was better to return the more than $175,000 to funders and start fund-raising from scratch rather than sacrifice my participation in decision-making about the budget, PR, planning, fund-raising as well as the artistic vision and realization of the project.

It was a devastatingly difficult decision to reach. But in the end, by just making the decision clear, and asking some colleagues to help, an agreement was reached that allowed me clear artistic control over the project, and responsible management of the specific funds critical to realizing the artistic vision. We went ahead with the project as original-ly planned, with two people agreeing to act as arbitrators/consultants when needed. Critical time on the project was lost forever, but if these issues of control, money, credit are not made clear in every project, a price will be paid either at the beginning, middle or end. Every artist needs to determine what is key to any particular project, what is worth fighting for, and then not succumb to notions of "anything is better than nothing" or fears that "you will never work again." It is very scary to be an artist. The structures of this particular version of the art world are well-stacked against us. We need each other.

These are the three big issues of contention in my experience in the field. I was used to the construction industry of small companies, where tangible problems and tangible results soak up much of the air-time that is spent on competition and battles for control and credit in art-related industries. In college, I had in fact left the theater department for good in an effort to not be a part of such destructive patterns. About ten years ago, I started performing and writing again, after a ten-year hiatus. Now, after doing *CWT#3* and then meeting this summer at Jacob's Pillow with a group of choreographers who work with communities, I want to make art so bad—I'm so excited by other people that make art, I'm so moved by the art they are making—that my desire to participate is greater than my upset at many of the nasty patterns still active in the artmaking community. Ironically, I assume this desire speaks to probably everyone who is in this community. I seriously doubt anyone wakes up in the morning and says, "Gee, I'd love to see some heads roll today." I assume that people wake up in the morning and hope that somehow today people will get along, that fair solutions will be reached, that money will come through.

Hope doesn't cut it. We have work to do. We don't have to live with these self-perpetuated obstructions. We are operating in a field poisoned with the patterns of classism—isolation and individualism not community; distrust not trust; an ideology of scarcity not abundance; greed not generosity; competition not cooperation. There is the magnetic pull of the culture in that direction and we consciously need to take it into account and resist it. We have enough tough challenges coming at us from the outside, which is where most of the patterns originated. But like our most intimate personal relationships, it takes hard, scary work to change, and, fortunately or unfortunately, we can't make it go away by hoping or by not talking about it. Pointing fingers isn't useful—we all struggle here, but honest assessment rather than ignoring or denial is a critical first step. Making art with communities requires new understandings of what we're doing, new relationships with presenters and producers and audiences, new rules for how we work together and new visions for both the art and the activities that result in the art. These are exciting challenges. Challenges that mirror what community organizers, unions, community groups, social-change organizations, schools and families are figuring out as well. Now is a splendid time to take this on. We are in excellent company.

Somewhere in the middle of the project, as I ran into my own and other's *mishegoss* (Yiddish for "craziness"), I realized I needed to make some long-range goals to help me keep perspective in the short-range confusions. The one that worked best all around was that I would be "on speaking terms with everyone connected to the project…within three years."

Scott —Geologist DEP 23B and 19B

My job is to reach an understanding of the rock we're going through. To build a picture of what has happened over the last several million years, and apply that knowledge to the work of construction. Once we know where we'd like to have the tunnel go, we drill core borings, test borings. To get these, we drive a truck along the route, and set a drill up which goes down six, seven, eight hundred feet and brings with it this piece of the puzzle. [holding up a small piece of rock/core boring.] This is vital information for the contractors to know when they are making their bids. If you think about it, this [holding up the test boring fragment] is the only concrete—pardon the expression—information the general contractor has to go on. They have to estimate how long it's going to take them to tunnel out, how they are going to do that, and how much it is all going to cost—without even seeing anything besides this. After the work begins, we geologists inspect all the rock as soon as it's revealed—looking for faults, cracks, loose shifting, settling, which could lead to a cave-in; trying to understand as much as we can about what has happened over the last millions of years. The patterns in the rock are beautiful, like rivers—for the matter, now solid, was once liquid. The rock we're going through now is from a time when the west coast of Africa, the Orkney Islands and New York City were all a part of the same land mass. It's very humbling. It's good to be humbled in your job every once in a while.

The Art-World Culture: The Circle Grows Smaller

Presenters/Artists/Funders—grave disparities exist in the relationships within this triangle. Some are becoming increasingly out of balance as the "censorship wars" have successfully removed direct funding for the artists (while raising millions and millions of dollars for reactionary causes—who says there's no money in art?). That in itself is a huge shift away from correct policy, leaving the artist and the art increasingly funded and selected only through presenters who are more and more vulnerable. Artists ourselves will have to take on these issues and find solutions, but the effects reverberate to the core of the triangle.

It appears that an increasing number of funders are currently in the midst of radically reconceptualizing their roles and relationships to the field. Funders are transforming presenters into "baby funders," offering them large block grants to serve as regranters—as a way of distancing themselves from the art being made? Now presenters are structuring the granting process, creating peer-review panels and choosing the artists to be on them—thus adding the role of granter to the already powerful role of presenter. Presenters are not publicly accountable in the way that government panels and organizations are. Critical questions and issues are raised and must be addressed. What strategies are being developed by each partner in the triangle to create structures that reflect the nature of the new relationships? Where are the discussions happening that address these challenges? What systems of accountability are being created that at least match those formerly in place?

Making art with communities often requires significant financial, administrative and spiritual resources. For me, the art was as much in the daily organizational activities—the contacts with people, the phone calls, the public relations, permissions—as it was in the final performances, the exhibits, the video installations. Imagine if every presenter/funder sat down and, for one hour, imagined that they were an artist figuring out how to realize a community-arts project; thinking it through every step of the way, the way a carpenter does before renovating someone's kitchen. Where do you go for money? What presenters do you want to work with? Where can you find information about the different presenters to make some choices about who would best fit your project? How many choices are there? What presenters are experienced in working closely with an artist, rather than the "artist as labor/talent" model? What role in decision-making do you need to have? Is the "art part" only what ends up in the final performance? What are the risks in "making demands"? How secure is your future? Can you afford a "bad reputation"? Who pays for your administrative time? Who pays for your lawyer as you responsibly negotiate with presenters, funders, community organizations, partners?

Another significant development to changes in the culture of arts funding is the elimination of smaller organizations from consideration of monies, simply on the basis of their size/budget. If "Think Globally, Act Locally" is a key direction for a future we can all live with, what are the effects of removing funding from many of the arts groups most intimately connected to local communities of difference and diversity?

Developing artmaking relationships with particular communities holds within it dynamic possibilities that can potentially transform the public's relationship to art. Art/performance can play an ongoing critical role in realizing a society where solutions the size of the problems come into being. Relationships can be built and understandings can come into being that have never existed between communities, peoples, nations. Art is that significant.

In Memoriam Story

As I speak the lines, I spill water out onto the floor—to the front and then to both sides.

For the 22 men who died building this third water tunnel.

For the men and women who love them, who miss them, who work jobs everyday to make ends meet. To making ends meet, which they seldom do, for women working for half the wage, it's not the men's fault, but something must be done. God bless a good wage. God bless all who will never make it.

For those of us who can't find jobs. For those of us who are laid off.

For those of us who are fired. For those of us who are unemployed. For those of us who are bought out, bought off. For those of us who are given early retirement. For those of us who have jobs that suck. For us with jobs we hate. For us who won't give up. For us who did.

I slowly start spinning in place as spilled water flies out onto the floor in a circle. The spinning gets faster and faster as the story goes on. I keep pouring water onto the floor, keep spinning—the desired effect is to have drops of water flying off in all directions as I spin and tell the story memorial.

To Mike. To Larry. To penknives sharp enough to cut a leg off, to hearts strong enough to do the job. To love that lets us care and remember we do. For Brian and the fucking scrubbers, for Tommy and his blue blue eyes. To me holding friends in my arms as they die…to saying goodbye when there's time, to saying it now when there wasn't. To Anthony Oddo—God bless you Anthony—I spill, drink, splash and cast water for you and for those who shared you. To Natasha who's not afraid to care. To Grace and moving up. To Leah who watches and waits. To Carlos and his coffee cans filled with pens and pencils. To Pete and his self-rescuing mask demonstrations. To Mike and his white oats with sugar on them.

It's not scary to go to work and know you or your friend may die. It's scary to not have work to go to. To not know how you will feed your family. It's scary to give up trying. To work a job that only gives a paycheck. No joy. Not love. Not challenge. Not the satisfaction of a job well done. A hard day over.

I'm dancing 'cause dancing is the story of winning.
And that's where we're going.

Spring 1997

The Citizen Artist

by Aida Mancillas

Aida Mancillas is a community artist working in San Diego, California. An artist who has received awards for her works on paper, she is a partner with Lynn Susholtz in the public-art firm Stone Paper Scissors. Here she talks about her entry into community art, motivated by the search for a good cup of coffee, a well-stocked bookstore and a pleasant place to eat within walking distance of her home.   —Eds.

We had known that sooner or later we must develop an explanation for what we were doing which would be short and convincing. It couldn't be the truth because that wouldn't be convincing at all. How can you say to a people who are preoccupied with getting enough food and enough children that you have come to pick up useless little animals so that perhaps your world picture will be enlarged? That didn't even convince us. But there had to be a story, for everyone asked us. One of us had once taken a long walking trip through the southern United States. At first he had tried to explain that he did it because he liked to walk and because he saw and felt the country better that way. When he gave this explanation there was unbelief and dislike for him. It sounded like a lie. Finally a man said to him, "You can't fool me, you're doing it on a bet." And after that, he used this explanation, and everyone liked and understood him from then on.

—From *The Log from the Sea of Cortez,*
by John Steinbeck

In the United States we presume that most of what we need to know about an individual, at least initially, can be generally inferred from what he or she does. We ask, "What do you do?" instead of the perhaps more useful "Who are you?" upon first meeting. When people in the community where I live ask me what I do (who I am), I tell them that I am an artist. Sometimes I am pressed for a bit more. My own

preference is the term "community artist," although recently the desig-
nation met with resistance from an art historian trying to define me
for an academic conference she was organizing. "Most of the artists
who'll be panelists do work about the community. Can't you just call
yourself an artist?" I thought about the countless community charettes,
redevelopment committee meetings, community association presentations, after-school arts programs, and planning, zoning and safety meetings I had attended or organized over the past several years. I was
quite certain that most of my fellow panelists did not work in communities at the micro-level at which I was now working. Still, like Steinbeck's friend, I wasn't about to argue the point that clearly seemed like
a lie to the art historian. "'Artist' will be fine," I said.

In 1991 my partner, the artist Lynn Susholtz, and I purchased a
home in the North Park neighborhood of San Diego. An older, inner-
city neighborhood and shopping district, it had fallen into a slump during the 1960s and '70s, the victim of the new malls and shiny suburbs
popping up north of the city center. In true artist fashion, we saw past
the tired facades of old buildings to see the splendid commercial and
residential architecture. North Park's appeal was its central location,
the diversity of its population, its architectural mix and a sort of Mid-
western small-town feel. Still, this was a district in trouble, with a
crumbling infrastructure, rising crime, a small but nagging gang problem, struggling retail and, as we would discover later, a general sense
of malaise.

I wish I could say that my initial venture into being an advocate
for my community was engendered by some lofty ideal of the artist's
place in society. An understanding of the relationship between the
artist and the community would come much later as a result of battles fought, won and sometimes lost in the struggle to revitalize the
neighborhood. In reality, my entry into community art was motivated
by the search for a good cup of coffee, a well-stocked bookstore and
a pleasant place to eat, all within an aesthetically vibrant, urban environment and a short walking distance. I was tired of driving to other
neighborhoods where the amenities I was seeking, as well as a vital
sense of public life, were present. In those neighborhoods, the hand of
the artist seemed present in everything from storefront displays and

facade colors, to landscape and gathering spaces.

Our neighbors, long-time North Park residents Don and Karon Covington, told stories about the heyday of the neighborhood, when you could easily walk to the commercial center and find every service you might want, from butchers and fishmongers, to locksmiths and violin makers. They described an interconnectedness among residents, business owners and the city itself that seemed as enviable as it was distant. The Covingtons were two of our initial guides into the complexities of community planning and politics. Both are historians, he an architectural historian and designer, she a genealogist. Their combined talents have been central to recovering and preserving the history of North Park, its people and its places. Their efforts are providing a wealth of primary resources to artists working in the community, architects, designers and city staff. Other key community members were also critical to the success of bringing Lynn and me into the neighborhood rebuilding process. These "community mentors" provided deep background on North Park, facilitating our entry into the often confusing and overlapping system of community and official planning groups. Without them we might have failed to place our energies and skills in the appropriate place at the necessary time. With every community project, we have benefited from the expertise of such guides, those who know how to work the political system: aides to councilmembers or state legislators, local businessmen, amateur gardeners, librarians, social-service workers, playground leaders, parents, journalists and clergy. They are, in effect, collaborators (co-authors) in community arts projects.

Despite a national climate that characterizes the arts as either superfluous or dangerous, on a local level, communities like North Park are using the arts as an important tool for everything from alternative recreation for youth, to the formation of neighborhood identity markers, economic development, cultural tourism, safe streets and much more. Community artists are viewed as creative problem-solvers, unfettered by a particular methodology, who can help communities resolve issues that seem intractable. Previous to our being hired as public artists for the Vermont Street Bridge project, a struggle over the proposed color of the bridge superstructure arose between residents of University Heights (a small section of North Park proper) and the consulting engineers. The struggle threatened to slow down the construction approval process. These color decisions were based on the notion of making the 500-foot-long bridge "blend" into the canyon it spanned. The uncertainty of the community over whether the bridge should be built—replacing, after 13 years, an old wooden span torn down for safety reasons—was reflected in their confusion over whether to celebrate or hide the new structure.

We presented ourselves and our ideas for the bridge at a community meeting where tension between the engineering professionals and the community was palpable. Since we did not perceive the audience members as our adversaries but as neighbors and fellow community activists, we were able to present the reasons for making the bridge an important community identity marker in an atmosphere of collegiality. A discussion about drawing attention to the bridge, rather than trying to minimize its visual impact, ensued. The community quickly came to the conclusion that a vibrant color statement was in order. It is a decision that the community has been happy with ever since, one in which the artists' participation helped focus the community on what they wanted all along—a strong statement of identity and neighborhood pride.

With artists and their organizations taking a public thrashing throughout the country, how does one account for the acceptance of artists on a local level? In San Diego, the hue and cry that arises when large public artworks are proposed (let alone installed) is disheartening predictable. Yet neighborhood efforts—tied to capital improvement projects in parks, on bridges and in alleys, on sidewalks and streets, on commercial facades, along neighborhood entry portals— are all met with general enthusiasm (with the exception of those citizens who consistently object to any type of spending that is not somehow tied to improved street lighting and more police). Community members recognize the value of these aesthetic improvements, both to their quality of life and to more concrete objectives such as economic development and public safety. Urban-planning critic Jane Jacobs' emphasis on the importance of "eyes on the street" and the diversity of a community's infrastructure finds its natural expression in the arts' role in the community-building process.

Small neighborhood arts programs, residencies, artists' work-shops and city-supported public art projects can act as catalysts for change. Artists who make a commitment to the neighborhoods in which they live are uniquely positioned to initiate community policy or programming that has far-reaching effects. A modest after-school arts program organized by Lynn and myself at the local recreation center has grown to accommodate additional community and staff requests. Murals are going up; the colors of the buildings themselves have been changed; a banner artist is hired to work with children to create symbolic flags for the gymnasium, flags that later become banners for the commercial district; a new playground is being designed. Because we are seen as community members with special design skills, as well as possessing a sensitivity to community needs and budget constraints, we were awarded a contract to design a master plan for the local park, which has suffered from years of neglect. This work is interconnected with other community revitalization efforts. A viable park raises property values (redevelopment), makes the neighborhood attractive to new homeowners (first-time homebuyers program), bolsters the adjoining commercial district (North Park Main Street Program) and provides a new elementary school with an expanded play area (city and school district joint use agreement). Clearly, our commitment to North Park makes it possible for our neighbors to see beyond the stereotype of the artist as intruder, and view us as partners working toward similar goals.

To effect community-wide changes, artists must immerse themselves in the most unglamorous media—community meetings, zoning boards, redevelopment reports, school-board task forces, planning groups and the occasional tree-planting party. For the most part, artists working at this level will not realize the "stardom" of the art-world mill. The heroic scale of Christo's work will be inappropriate, esoteric performances will only garner curious stares, monumental sculpture will set off alarms. The artist may wonder where and how his or her unique vision may be realized, without being subjected to the requirement of community consensus or issues of liability or public safety. In San Diego, artists and arts administrators are reconsidering the strategy of integrating public art into capital improvements, where it must walk a thin line between art and decoration. One questions whether art that disappears is better than no art at all. One also grows weary at being the point person for difficult projects that the city is trying to "sell" to the community. The artist as public relations person does not sit comfortably.

Perhaps community artists are, by definition, artists whose questions, proddings, concepts, schematics, master plans and working processes are the real artworks. The ability to integrate seemingly disparate points of view, to re-present the community to itself, to imagine solutions outside the usual, to forge alliances or act as bridges—these qualities of the community artist make possible a living, malleable artwork that will not fit easily into the gallery. Somehow this ephemeral, unseen work must sustain the artist. But personal satisfaction in the total expression of one's vision often runs up against long-term engagement with a process that does not necessarily end with a product. I confess, I have not resolved the conflict for myself. While I sometimes long for uninterrupted days working on my paintings or artist books, I cannot ignore the neighborhood around me. I continue to lend my skills to my neighbors, to advocate and educate. In return, I receive the fellowship and teachings of individuals of varying interests and backgrounds, united in their efforts to resuscitate a community they love. I suspect the work that binds us together will make of us more than good neighbors—good citizens as well.

Spring 1996

Bibliography

Adams, Don and Arlene Goldbard. *Crossroads: Reflections on the Politics of Culture.* Talmage, CA: DNA Press, 1990.

Augaitis, Daina, Lorne Falk, Sylvie Gilbert, Mary Anne Moser, ed. *Questions of Community: Artists Audiences Coalitions.* Banff, Alberta, Canada: Banff Centre Press, 1995.

Becker, Carol, ed. *The Subversive Imagination: Artists, Society, & Social Responsibility.* New York and London: Routledge, 1994.

Becker, Carol, ed. *The Artist in Society: Rights, Roles, and Responsibilities.* Chicago: New Art Examiner Press, 1995.

Boal, Augusto. *Theatre of the Oppressed.* Trans. C.A. and M.L. McBride. New York: Urizen Books, 1979.

Bolton, Richard, ed. *Culture Wars: Documents from the Recent Controversies in the Arts.* New York: New Press, 1992.

Broyles-Gonzalez, Yolanda. *El Teatro Campesino: Theater in the Chicano Movement.* Austin, TX: University of Texas Press, 1994.

Cleveland, William. *Art in Other Places: Artists at Work in America's Community and Social Institutions.* Westport, CT and London: Praeger, 1992.

Cocke, Dudley, Harry Newman, Janet Salmons-Rue, eds. *From the Ground Up: Grassroots Theater in Historical and Contemporary Perspective.* Whitesburg, KY and Ithaca, NY: Roadside Theater and Cornell University Press, 1993.

Cruikshank, Jeffery L., and Pam Korza. *Going Public: A field guide to development in art in public places.* Amherst, MA: Arts Extension Service, 1988.

Dickson, Malcolm, ed. *Art with People.* Sunderland, England: AN Publications, 1995.

Dreeszen, Craig. *Intersections: Community Arts and Education Collaborations.* Amherst, MA: Arts Extension Service, 1992.

Dubin, Steven C. *Arresting images: impolitic art and uncivil actions.* London and New York: Routledge, 1992.

Felshin, Nina, ed. *But is it Art?: The Spirit of Art as Activism.* Seattle, WA: Bay Press, 1995.

Freire, Paulo. *Pedagogy of the Opressed.* New York: Continuum, 1970.

Gómez-Peña, Guillermo. *Warrior for Gringostroika.* Saint Paul, MN: Graywolf Press, 1993.

Hendricks, Jon and Jean Toche. *GAAG: The Guerrilla Art Action Group.* New York: Printed Matter, 1978.

Jacob, Mary Jane, Michael Brenson, Eva M. Olson. *Culture in Action.* Seattle, WA: Bay Press, 1995.

Halprin, Anna. *Moving Toward Life: Five Decades of Transformational Dance.* Hanover, NH: Wesleyan/University Press of New England, 1995.

Kramer, Jane. *Whose Art Is It?* Durham and London: Duke University Press, 1994.

Kuoni, Carin. *Joseph Beuys in America: Energy Plan for the Western Man. Writings by and Interviews with the Artist.* New York: Four Walls Eight Windows, 1993.

Lacy, Suzanne, ed. *Mapping the Terrain: New Genre Public Art.* Seattle, WA: Bay Press, 1995.

Lerman, Liz. *Are Miracles Enough? Selected Writings on Art and Community.* Washington, D.C.: Liz Lerman Dance Exchange, 1995.

Lippard, Lucy R. *Mixed Blessings: New Art in a Multicultural America.* New York: Pantheon, 1990.

Lippard, Lucy R. *Get the Message? A Decade of Art for Social Change.* New York: E.P. Dutton, 1984.

Loeffler, Carl E., and Darlene Tong, ed. *Performance Anthology: Source Book for a Decade of California Performance Art.* San Francisco: Contemporary Arts Press, 1980.

Matarasso, François. *Use or Ornament? The Social Impact of Participation in the Arts.* Stroud, England: Comedia, 1997.

Miller, Celeste. *Dancing from the Heart: Life Stories.* Gloucester, MA: Celeste Miller & Co., 1994.

Montano, Linda. *Art in Everyday Life.* Los Angeles: Astro Artz, 1981.

O'Brien, Mark & Craig Little, ed. *Reimaging America: The Arts of Social Change.* Philadelphia, PA and Santa Cruz, CA: New Society Publishers, 1990.

Perlstein, Susan and Jeff Bliss. *Generating Community: Intergenerational Partnerships Through the Expressive Arts.* New York: Elders Share the Arts, 1994.

Raven, Arlene, ed. *Art in the Public Interest*. Ann Arbor, Mich.: UMI Research Press, 1989. (Reprint New York, NY: Da Capo Press, 1993).

Roth, Moira, ed. *The Amazing Decade: Women and Performance Art in America 1970-1980*. Los Angeles, CA: Astro Artz, 1983.

Schutzman, Mady and Jan Cohen-Cruz. *Playing Boal: Theatre, Therapy, Activism*. New York and London: Routledge, 1994.

Sakolsky, Ron and Fred Wei-han Ho, ed. *Sounding Off! Music as Subversion/Resistance/Revolution*. Brooklyn, NY: Autonomedia, 1995.

Tucker, Marcia. *Choices: Making an Art of Everyday Life*. New York, NY The New Museum of Contemporary Art, 1986.

Ugwu, Catherine. *Let's Get It On: The Politics of Black Performance*. Seattle: Bay Press, 1995.

Wallis, Brian. *Art After Modernism: Rethinking Representation*. New York: The New Museum, 1984.